SOCIETY FOR NEW TESTAMENT STUDIES

MONOGRAPH SERIES

General Editor: G. N. Stanton

60

THE PAULINE CHURCHES

The Pauline Churches

A Socio-historical Study of Institutionalization in the
Pauline and Deutero-Pauline Writings

MARGARET Y. MACDONALD

Department of Theology,
St Francis Xavier University,
Nova Scotia, Canada

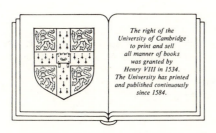

The right of the
University of Cambridge
to print and sell
all manner of books
was granted by
Henry VIII in 1534.
The University has printed
and published continuously
since 1584.

CAMBRIDGE UNIVERSITY PRESS

CAMBRIDGE
NEW YORK   NEW ROCHELLE
MELBOURNE   SYDNEY

Published by the Press Syndicate of the University of Cambridge
The Pitt Building, Trumpington Street, Cambridge CB2 1RP
32 East 57th Street, New York, NY 10022, USA
10 Stamford Road, Oakleigh, Melbourne 3166, Australia

© Cambridge University Press 1988

First published 1988

Printed in Great Britain at
the University Press, Cambridge

British Library cataloguing in publication data

MacDonald, Margaret Y.
The Pauline Churches : a socio-historical
study of institutionalization in the
Pauline and Deutero-Pauline writings. –
(Monograph series/Society for New Testament
Studies ; 60).
1. Bible. N.T. Epistles of Paul
2. Church – Biblical Teaching
I. Title
260 BS2655.C5

Library of Congress cataloguing in publication data

MacDonald, Margaret Y.
The Pauline Churches : a socio-historical study of
institutionalization in the Pauline and Deutero-Pauline writings /
Margaret Y. MacDonald.
    p.   cm. – (Monograph series / Society for New Testament
Studies : 60)
Bibliography.
Includes indexes.
ISBN 0 521 35337 8
1. Sociology. Biblical.   2. Bible. N.T. Epistles of Paul-
-Criticism, interpretation, etc.   3. Church history – Primitive and
early church. ca. 30–600.   I. Title.   II. Series: Monograph series
(Society for New Testament Studies) : 60.
BS2655.S6M33 1988
227'.067 – dc19   87-32561   CIP

For Hugh and Thérèse MacDonald, my parents

CONTENTS

PREFACE

This book is the culmination of my doctoral studies at Oxford University. I am especially grateful to the Revd R. Morgan, Linacre College, for introducing me to the use of the social sciences for New Testament interpretation and for suggesting many fruitful lines of enquiry. I also must express my appreciation to Professor E.P. Sanders, the Queen's College, for his bibliographical suggestions and for his careful reading of my work in its final stages.

I am indebted to Emero Stiegman, Lawrence Murphy, Paul Bowlby and Stan Armstrong of the Religious Studies Department and Helen Ralston of the Sociology Department at Saint Mary's University, Halifax, Nova Scotia. Without the encouragement of these fine teachers my time in Oxford would have been an impossibility.

During my studies, I have enjoyed and profited from many 'sociological' conversations with Harry Meier. In the course of his own studies, he discovered many useful works that he kindly shared with me.

The proof-reading efforts of Becky Gray deserve special mention. The attention given by Becky to this work far exceeded what could reasonably be expected from a friend. I am also grateful to Miriam Taylor and Bruce MacDougall for uncovering many errors in the text that would have otherwise gone undetected.

The unconditional support given to me by my husband, Duncan Macpherson, remains a constant inspiration. Duncan has endured lengthy separations, exorbitant phone-bills, and vacations spent proof-reading in England. Duncan's understanding and generosity have never faltered.

ABBREVIATIONS

CBQ	*Catholic Biblical Quarterly*
EvT	*Evangelische Theologie*
HR	*History of Religions*
HTR	*Harvard Theological Review*
IESS	*International Encyclopedia of the Social Sciences*
Int	*Interpretation*
JAAR	*Journal of the American Academy of Religion*
JBL	*Journal of Biblical Literature*
JR	*Journal of Religion*
JSOT	*Journal for the Study of the Old Testament*
NovT	*Novum Testamentum*
NTS	*New Testament Studies*
TDNT	*Theological Dictionary of the New Testament*
TZ	*Theologische Zeitschrift*
ZNW	*Zeitschrift für die neutestamentliche Wissenschaft*

INTRODUCTION

1

THE PROJECT

It is generally held that from the middle of the first century to the middle of the second century the church became more tightly organized. Most would put the kind of development evident in the years shortly following the resurrection of Jesus, as exhibited in 1 Thessalonians, at some distance from the more 'settled' church life reflected in the Pastoral Epistles. However, the nature of the historical circumstances related to the formation of a more established church continues to be a subject of debate. This socio-historical study traces the institutionalization of various aspects of community life: attitudes to the world/ethics, ministry structures, ritual forms and beliefs.

The Pauline and deutero-Pauline writings perhaps provide the most revealing material for a study of change in the early church; they have the advantage of manifesting continuity as works either written by Paul himself or by one of his disciples in his name. The Pauline corpus contains both the earliest church writings available to us (the authentic epistles) and writings dating from the early second century (the Pastoral Epistles). The documents probably bear witness to at least three church generations.

Demonstration of the thesis that the Pauline corpus reflects a movement that received its initial formation at the hands of Paul and his group of fellow workers but continued to develop after the death of the Apostle, depends on an illustration of continuity between Pauline and deutero-Pauline writings. Therefore, it will be necessary to begin with a brief study of Paul's communities. The general treatment of Pauline communities found in Part 1 of this book will rely substantially on past work on the social setting of Pauline Christianity and will focus especially on those aspects which are of direct relevance for understanding deutero-Pauline writings.

In investigating deutero-Pauline writings, one must be content to establish the probable and, often, only the possible. Important work has been accomplished by researchers using literary, linguistic and theological criteria to establish the authorship of documents. Commentaries on the disputed letters are often largely concerned with answering the question of whether or not 'the real Paul wrote this'. Unfortunately, heavy concentration on the problem of authenticity has led to the neglect of other important questions. This is not to deny the importance of attempting to arrive at conclusions about authorship, but to point out that commentators only infrequently consider the implications of their conclusions for the nature of early Christianity. If, for example, Paul did not write Colossians and Ephesians, what can this reveal about the social setting of Pauline Christianity? How might the death of Paul have affected his associates? What kind of leadership structures might be operative in communities which continue to appeal to the authority of the Apostle in his absence?

In this study, the question of authenticity is to a large extent left to one side in order to devote attention to some thus far unexplored questions. In an investigation of development, discussion of authorship and approximate dating is, however, a fundamental starting point for enquiry. The constant provided by the fact that all of the writings bear witness to a Pauline tradition makes determining the approximate period of a particular writing, and whether or not it should be considered pseudonymous, crucial for comparison. If the writings can be viewed as representative of different stages or generations of the movement's development, they may be compared in the hope of tracing the formation of a cultural system.

For the study of development in deutero-Pauline writings found in Part 2 and Part 3 of this book, the following working hypothesis based on the conclusions of past scholars is proposed:

1.   Colossians will be understood as written by a fellow worker or disciple of Paul either shortly after the Apostle's death or when imprisonment meant that direct communication with the Colossian community was impossible.

2.   Ephesians will be viewed as dependent on Colossians. The affinity of this epistle with the undisputed Pauline writings and Colossians leads one to conclude that it was most likely written by a close associate of Paul, probably fairly soon after Colossians.

3.   Because of the similar outlooks discovered in Colossians and Ephesians, they will be considered together as reflecting proximate stages of development.

4.   The Pastoral Epistles will be dated somewhere between

100–40 C.E. because of the apparent late stage of church development they exhibit, resembling the picture evident in the writings of the Apostolic Fathers.

5.   2 Thessalonians will only be given peripheral treatment here. The notoriously difficult problems of its dating and authorship make it virtually impossible for it to be employed in this analysis.

A study of development in the Pauline movement beyond the death of the Apostle requires a methodological framework that will allow for the most productive investigation. When New Testament scholars have compared the life of Paul's communities with the kinds of Christianity that came after Paul, they have focused particularly on the formation of church offices; they have often noted the disappearance of a Spirit-centred style of ministry and the gradual emergence of hierarchical organization. Bultmann, for example, in his *Theology of the New Testament*, envisions the Ecclesia as an eschatological congregation ruled by the Spirit's sway:

> The chief persons of authority are those endowed with gifts of the Spirit, beside whom those who act for the external order and welfare of the congregation's life play at first a subordinate role. The character of those having Spirit-gifts is determined by the fact that the eschatological congregation knows itself called into existence by the proclaimed word, and therefore gathers about the word, listening and also speaking   (1 Cor 14).[1]

According to Bultmann, the Spirit established what might be called a 'congregational democracy' in the Pauline communities:

> For the real question is just this: in what form will the rule of the Spirit, or of Christ, realize itself in history? At any rate, it is incontestable that the later order (in which congregational officials have superseded the Spirit-endowed, a monarchical episcopate has developed, and the distinction between priests and laymen has arisen) was preceded by an order that must be called democratic. For notwithstanding the authority of the Spirit-endowed – for this is not an authority of office – the congregation takes action as a totality.[2]

The starting point for Bultmann's investigation of the development of church offices is the question of whether or not incipient regulations were appropriate to the nature of the Ecclesia.[3] Implicit in his analysis is the idea that the Pauline correspondence provides standards for measuring all later development: '... did this budding ecclesiastical law have regulative character or constitutive, and did it retain its original character?'[4]

In works written within the first two decades of the publication of Bultmann's *Theology of the New Testament*, similar assumptions about the organization of Pauline communities are operative. H. von Campenhausen underlines the discontinuity between the kind of development he discovers in Paul's churches and what came later:

> Paul knows of no leading figures to whom is entrusted the safe keeping of the Gospel on behalf of everyone else, and *a fortiori* it never occurs to him to call upon facts of the natural order to supply the framework for the community. Paul bases everything on the Spirit. But however significant this may be for him and for his particular 'style', the distinctive approach which he exhibits at this point should not be pressed too far in interpreting his theological thinking. For Paul, too, knows and affirms the special Christian tradition which is no less a primary constituent of the Church than is the Spirit. It is simply that he drew no conclusions from it for the life and organisation of the community. The next generation was unable to maintain this position.[5]

In his investigation of church order in the New Testament, E. Schweizer states that historical investigation of the Church's development is subsidiary to his interest in how the New Testament church understood itself.[6] His interpretation of the situation in Paul's churches greatly resembles Bultmann's description of the eschatological congregation:

> As a Church that is still living in time, it consists of many members, none of whom is perfect, so that each depends on the other's service; and there is therefore an abundance of different gifts and tasks. At the same time, however, the Church is a new entity, established solely by God's action and not to be regarded as a historical development. The miracle of this newness is shown by there being no fundamental organization of superior or subordinate ranks,

because the gift of the Spirit is adapted to every Church member. Whenever such working of the Spirit actually takes place, superiority and subordination will always follow.[7]

An extreme view of the contrast between the concept of ministry and organization found in the Pastorals and that discovered in the authentic Pauline writings is held by E. Käsemann: a charismatic ministry involving all Christians stands before hierarchical structures upheld by church officials. According to Käsemann, hierarchy is an attribute of 'early catholicism' − a development which he connects with the disappearance of imminent expectation and the threat of gnostic take-over.[8] Writing on the relation between Paul and 'early catholicism', he states the crucial starting point for his thesis: 'To put it pointedly, but without exaggeration, the Pauline church is composed of nothing but laymen, who nevertheless are all, within their possibilities, at the same time priests and officeholders, that is, instruments of the Spirit for the enactment of the Gospel in the everyday world.'[9]

Work conducted during the past fifteen years with the explicit intention of relating Paul's letters to the realities of a human society, casts doubt on the depiction of the Pauline churches as purely Spirit-governed communities. Studies by J. H. Schütz (1975), B. Holmberg (1978), W. Meeks (1983) and N. Petersen (1985) stress the importance of investigating the nature of authority structures operating in the Pauline communities.[10] Work by Gerd Theissen (1974) on the leadership of Paul's communities leads one to question the validity of the statement that those who were in charge of the external order and welfare of the congregation played only a subordinate role.[11] These scholars illustrate the fruitfulness of attempting to discover what sorts of persons were able to issue demands in the early church and what kinds of social mechanisms were involved in the prevention of deviant behaviour. Moreover, their investigations cast doubt on approaches to the study of New Testament communities which presuppose that the straightforward action of ideas shapes development. The nature of community life cannot be explained simply by drawing a causal connection between a theological position and a style of organization.

Despite recent work on the nature of the social structures involved in the exercise of ministry in the Pauline communities, scholars have yet to resolve the issue of how one should understand the nature of the transformation of the church from its charismatic beginnings, evident in the authentic Pauline writings, to its more tightly organized form, evident in the Pastoral Epistles. A common understanding of the nature of the organization of Paul's communities formed through a comparison with what is known about later development is well represented in the conclusions of H. Conzelmann (1968):

> There is no organization of the whole church, but only minimal beginnings of organization in the individual communities. But no form of organization is capable as such of bringing salvation; there is no holy form of community life; only one which is appropriate to its end. There is no hierarchy of ministries, no priestly state with a position of mediating salvation, no separation of clergy and laity, no firm regulating of the cult, but only the occasional instruction when the 'management' threatens to get out of control (1 Cor 14). Even here, however, no definite liturgy is introduced – cultic enthusiasm is guarded against, but that is all. The Corinthians are not initiated into fixed forms of cult, but are called to 'οἰκοδομή'.[12]

This common understanding is also evident in H. Koester's study (1980) of the transformation of Pauline theology into ecclesiastical doctrine:

> The primary accomplishment of Paul is seen to be the organization of his congregations – which was indeed a task to which Paul had once devoted considerable time and effort, and which had occupied a central place in his missionary activities! But now the offices are fixed: one bishop or presiding presbyter (who should receive twice the salary of other officers, 1 Tim 4:17); under him presbyters, deacons, and widows (the latter are to be supported by the congregation, but should be thoroughly scrutinized so that they would not constitute an unnecessary burden to the community, 1 Tim 5:3–16); ordination by the laying on of hands (1 Tim 5:22; cf. 4:14), so that the charisma of the office can be passed on in an orderly fashion (2 Tim 1:6). The Pauline concept that all members of the church have special gifts as part of their possession of the spirit, thus qualifying them for service in the church, recedes into the background. Instead, moral qualifications are required for church officers, and the members of the congregation are reminded not of their Christian charismata, but of their general moral duties as good citizens.[13]

Although C. Rowland (1985) refers to the possibility of some kind of continuity between the patterns of ministry visible in Paul's writings and those visible in the Pastoral Epistles, he identifies a sharp contrast between the two:

> So the absence of specific details of ecclesiastical order should not lead us to suppose that Paul was indifferent to such things. He had a clear vision of the equal responsibility before God of all believers, to reflect the heart of discipleship, symbolically represented at baptism in their dying with Christ. How Paul maintained that aim, particularly when there was a possibility that he would be removed from the scene by death, we cannot now answer, unless that is, we consider that the Pastoral Epistles reflect at least in general terms the mind of Paul. If they do, we should have to say that the seeds of order already sown, grow into a pattern of ministry which, whatever its suitability for the peculiar needs of the period, inevitably did quench the prophetic spirit at work within the whole body of Christ.[14]

Rowland's remarks raise the question of how one should investigate the relationship between the community life discovered in the authentic Pauline writings and that found in the Pastorals. Conzelmann, Koester and Rowland's comments about the great disparity between the two find clear historical support. However, if sociological, as well as historical, methods are employed, one may arrive at a more complete understanding of how and why the transformation took place. A socio-historical investigation is not content with pointing to the existence of a contrast between stages of development, but seeks to discover relations between the stages in terms of the institution building process. With respect to the Pastoral Epistles, for example, it will be argued here that for those who recognize institutionalization as a process beginning in the earliest church and authority structures as being present in Pauline communities from the very beginning, the kind of leadership structures discovered in the Pastorals cannot be held up either as evidence of a sudden inculturalization into the ways of the world, nor as being completely opposite to the concept of ministry visible in Paul's writings. One of the major concerns of this work will be to investigate assumptions about the nature of Paul's communities upon which conclusions about development after Paul are based.

The following study is conducted with an eye for uncovering

aspects of the organization of Paul's communities which may be connected with the development that continued in the Pauline tradition after the Apostle's death. With the aid of sociological analysis, the process of institutionalization is traced from its earliest stages. Furthermore, this socio-historical investigation not only attempts to outline the effects of a particular theological position in the organizational realm, but also endeavours to explore the dialectical relationship existing between beliefs and social structures. Without denying the connection between the vision of salvation and church organization, nor the fact that decisions about the truth of doctrinal assertions are related to the establishment of mechanisms to protect truth, the investigation questions whether cerebral activities are the only, or even the primary, factors determining development within the early church. For example, a cursory glance at the Pastoral Epistles reveals the close association of household ethics with leadership structures. Although it is undoubtedly true that the establishment of offices is related to a perceived requirement to protect truth from false teaching, it is also clear that the Greco-Roman household – the foundational structure of Greco-Roman society – is a major factor in determining who is eligible for office. Indeed, the requirement to protect truth is not perceived in isolation from existing structures. This investigation illustrates that in the early church, not only do ideas shape social reality, but also, social reality affects the construction of ideas.

2

THE SOCIAL SCIENCES AND NEW TESTAMENT INTERPRETATION

In this investigation, insights from the social sciences will be drawn upon in addition to relying on historical methods with the aim of presenting a more complete description of development in the Pauline/deutero-Pauline circle. The following discussion sets out the social scientific theory that will be employed.

2.1 The symbolic universe

Peter L. Berger and Thomas Luckmann's *The Social Construction of Reality* is of primary significance for this investigation of institutionalization in the Pauline movement.[15] *The Social Construction of Reality* is a treatise on the sociology of knowledge − a branch of sociology devoted to the study of the relation between human thought and the social context in which it arises.[16] The fundamental thesis of Berger and Luckmann's study is that the relationship between the individual as producer, and the individual's social world, the product, is a dialectical one.[17] Berger and Luckmann consider society in terms of both subjective and objective reality; they explore how externalized products of human activity attain the character of objectivity. They assert that the objectivity of the institutional world is a humanly produced objectivity. However, the institutional world acts back on the producer. Internalization occurs when this world is retrojected into the consciousness of the individual in the course of socialization and becomes subjectively meaningful. In other words, the individual and the individual's social world interact with each other. Berger and Luckmann speak of three moments in social reality which must be considered in any study of the social world − externalization, objectivation and internalization. They stress the fact that these three moments characterize an ongoing dialectical process; they are not to be thought of as occurring in a temporal sequence. Society and the individual within society are simultaneously shaped by these three moments so that analysis of only one or two of them is insufficient.[18] Berger and Luckmann describe various levels of objectified meaning which develop during the dialectical process. The final level is represented by the symbolic universe: 'The symbolic universe is conceived of as the matrix of all socially objectivated and subjectively real meanings; the entire historic society and the entire biography of the individual are seen as events taking place within this universe.'[19]

If one were to employ the insights of Berger and Luckmann to analyse New Testament texts, one might understand the symbolic universe as the projection of the thought of a certain New Testament community. The symbolic universe gives order to the lives it embraces; it is continuously shaped by social experience and continuously shapes what is experienced. Moreover, the symbolic universe of the community constantly reinforces the social structures of the community and is constantly being reinforced by them. The advantage of drawing upon Berger and Luckmann's understanding of the social construction of reality for the analysis of New Testament texts is that it enables one to guard against the distortions that arise from presupposing that ideas shape social reality in a straightforward fashion. It provides a means of dealing with the difficult but central problem of the relation between ideas and their social setting.[20]

Berger and Luckmann's thesis about the dialectical relationship between the individual and the social world is the central construct or model employed in this study for understanding development. In addition to this broad understanding of the dialectical process which leads to the creation of a social world, an investigation of change in the early church requires more precise delineation of how change occurs in society. The work of Berger and Luckmann on 'institutionalization' and of Weber on the 'routinization of charisma' are especially relevant.

2.2 Institutionalization and the routinization of charisma

The dialectical social process through which a symbolic universe is both constructed and altered is broadly referred to by Berger and Luckmann as 'institutionalization'. Berger and Luckmann's definition of institutionalization will be employed throughout this investigation: 'Institutionalization occurs whenever there is a reciprocal typification of habitualized actions by types of actors. Put differently, any such typification is an institution.'[21] In their study of institutionalization, Berger and Luckmann point out that the process of habitualization precedes institutionalization. Habitualization occurs when action that is repeated frequently becomes cast into a pattern which can be reproduced with an economy of effort, and which is apprehended by the performer as being a pattern. Habitualization makes it unnecessary for each situation to be defined anew, step by step, and thereby frees the individual from the burden of much decision making. Habitualization refers to the individual's activity. But, when the individual moves into social interaction and patterns become shared, reciprocal typification occurs. In this process of typification, institutions with realities of their own are formed. The institution requires that actions of 'type x' will be performed by actors of 'type x'.[22]

According to Berger and Luckmann, institutionalization can be said to begin with the interaction of only two people, but the introduction of a third party changes the character of the relationship considerably. Before the introduction of the third party the institutions were easily changeable, but now they become crystallized. The institutions are now experienced by the individuals as possessing a reality of their own — a reality that confronts the individuals as an external and coercive force. 'There we go again' becomes 'This is how things are done'! Berger and Luckmann speak of the introduction of this third party in terms of the arrival of a new generation in a way that proves useful for understanding the mechanisms involved in the incorporation of a new generation within the church. Social formations can only be transmitted to a new generation as an objective world which confronts the individual in a manner similar to the reality of the natural world.[23]

If one follows Berger and Luckmann's definition of institutionalization, it must be admitted that institutionalization was a process that began among Jesus and his followers and continued with the construction of a church. It is precisely this line of reasoning that is adopted by Bengt Holmberg in his investigation of authority structures in Pauline communities.[24] He argues that the process of institutionalization is essentially 'open' (i.e. it may proceed in many directions). He believes that this partially explains the variety of institutional solutions to the needs of the churches in different regions. As time passes, however, the institutionalization of church life becomes progressively less free to develop in a variety of directions. As the social world gains stability, further institutionalization will be increasingly guided by a corporate tradition.[25]

Holmberg's insight that as time passes the institutionalization of church life becomes less free to develop in a variety of directions will be of great value as we trace the gradual solidification of the symbolic universe reflected in the Pauline and deutero-Pauline writings. His work on development in Pauline communities relies on Weber's description of 'charisma' and the 'routinization of charisma'. Weber emphasizes the importance of charisma as an innovating power in the institutional realm. However, Weber's notion of charisma stresses the duality of its nature – on the one hand, its tendency toward innovation, but on the other hand, the dependence of the permanence of the innovation on the routinization of charisma.[26]

Weber adopts the notion of 'charisma' from the vocabulary of early Christianity and defines it as a certain quality of an individual personality by virtue of which he or she is set apart from ordinary people and treated as a leader.[27] Weber describes an organized group subject to charismatic authority as a charismatic community. The administrative staff of the charismatic leader does not consist of 'officials' who are specially trained. There are no established administrative organs. The charismatic leader makes new obligations which are recognized by the members of the community as their duty or mission. According to Weber, pure charisma is foreign to economic considerations; it tends to repudiate involvement in the everyday routine world. Weber describes charisma as the greatest revolutionary force.[28]

As Holmberg points out, the transformation of the charismatic group around Jesus into a church with a doctrine, cult and organization, may be described in Weber's terminology as the routinization of charisma.[29] Weber asserts that in order for the innovation resulting from the outpouring of charisma to survive, routinization is necessary. The problems surrounding the death of the original charismatic leader give rise to the routinization process. Weber isolates the principal motives underlying this transformation as follows: (1) the ideal and material interests of the followers in the survival of the community; and (2) the even stronger ideal and material interests of the administrative staff or disciples in continuing their relationship.[30]

Both from an ideal and a material point of view, the members of the charismatic staff seek to ensure that their own status is put on a stable everyday basis; they strive to enjoy a secure social position in the place of the kind of discipleship which is cut off from ordinary worldly life involving family and economic relationships.[31] Thus, the routinization of charisma takes the form of the appropriation of powers of control and of economic advantage by the staff in order that they alone might exercise authority. In addition, the staff may set up norms for recruitment which often include training and tests of eligibility.[32] Weber points out that for charisma to be transformed into a permanent structure, it is essential that its anti-economic character be altered. The economic needs of the community must be met − a means of raising contributions must be derived.[33]

Weber insists, however, that even when charisma has been routinized and can no longer be said to be personal and anti-economic, one is still justified in speaking of charisma because there remains an extraordinary quality, which is not accessible to everyone, overshadowing the charismatic subjects.[34] After its routinization, charisma may serve as an important means of legitimating the authority of the successors of the charismatic hero.[35] For example, charisma may become routinized as the charisma of office. Charisma becomes disassociated from a particular individual and becomes an objective transferable reality. It may be transmitted from one bearer to another, for example, through the ritual of the laying on of hands.[36] Although when charisma changes into a permanent structure its essence and mode of operation are significantly transformed, it remains a very important element of the social structure.

Although Holmberg believes that Weber's analysis is extremely useful for understanding development in the early church, he makes some valuable criticisms of it. Holmberg censures Weber for not paying due attention to the possibility that the charismatic leader may play a role in the routinizing process and for placing too much emphasis on the private economic interests of the staff as the decisive factor in the process.[37] Holmberg insists that the message of the charismatic leader is of vital importance for the origin and existence of the movement. The charismatic leader demonstrates extraordinary qualities in leading a movement of change; leadership is inseparably linked to the needs and desires of those who follow. Holmberg argues that charisma is not merely the victim of routinization, but actively seeks institutional manifestation.[38]

Holmberg's corrections of Weber's analysis increase the possibilities of harmonizing Weber's insights with the Berger and Luckmann understanding of institutionalization as a process beginning in the earliest stages of interaction: there are institution building impulses inherent in the charisma itself. Weber's description of the routinization of charisma provides an additional tool for understanding how development in the early church proceeded. Weber describes how the innovation is given permanence as a social structure; his analysis is suggestive for investigating the formation and development of the

Christian movement. This is not to suggest that one reads Weber and concludes – this is the church! Weber's analysis operates by means of a description of ideal types which draw on numerous historical examples, but which are never perfectly represented by any one historical reality. Thus, in investigating the development of the church one may seek to identify parallels between the situation described by Weber and the realities of the early church. However, one may not conclude that what Weber lists as a component of a charismatic community is also true of the church unless there is independent evidence to support that conclusion.

Sociological analysis will not be employed here to provide ready-made explanations for historical phenomena in a manner that exceeds the constraints of the evidence. The ideal type provides examples of the kinds of things one should be careful to note. But, even where it is impossible to find a perfect fit between the ideal type and the historical reality, the ideal type remains useful as a means of under-lining the particularity of the development which stands out sharply against this constructed tool for investigation. For example, Paul's role does not fit perfectly within Weber's framework, but much of what Weber writes about the charismatic leader and the routinization of charisma is applicable to Paul's situation. On the one hand, Paul might be described as a charismatic leader, albeit one with apparently less independence and revolutionary significance than Jesus. On the other hand, by claiming authority as an apostle of Jesus Christ, Paul might be considered as part of the 'staff'. The evidence from Pauline and deutero-Pauline letters that Paul was surrounded by a circle of fellow workers suggests the possibility that the problem of succession and the interests of assistants were important factors determining development in the early church after Paul's death (as was probably the case after Jesus' death).

It is reasonable to draw upon social-scientific analysis of develop-ment in society in order to study development in a church so firmly grounded in the realities of society. In understanding institutionaliza-tion as a process beginning in the earliest days of the Pauline move-ment, one is prevented from claiming complete discontinuity between the situation in Paul's churches and the situation in the churches of those who wrote in the Apostle's name after his death; one must seek to describe as fully as possible the historical circumstance and ask, 'Why change?'. In drawing on Weber's insights on the routinization of charisma, one is better able to grasp the transformation from an apparently structureless church to one where bishops made their presence felt. Furthermore, one is reminded that such a transformation is not only governed by deliberate efforts from the actors, such as the need to continue while faced with the death of a great leader, but also unconscious needs and desires which are inherent in human interaction, such as the need to secure one's own leadership position.

2.3 Legitimation and cumulative institutionalization

In this investigation of development in the Pauline movement, an understanding of 'legitimation' and 'cumulative institutionalization' is particularly significant because these processes are concerned with the transformation of the symbolic universe.

According to Berger and Luckmann, with the appearance of a third party or new generation, the institutional world requires legitimation: '... ways by which it [the institutional world] can be explained and justified'.[39] The process of legitimation functions in the construction of the symbolic universe: 'It follows that the expanding institutional order develops a corresponding canopy of legitimations, stretching over it a protective cover of both cognitive and normative interpretation. These legitimations are learned by the new generation during the same process that socializes them into the institutional order.'[40]

Berger and Luckmann argue that as time passes and groups grow, there is a tendency for them to require greater organization. The multiplication of specific tasks involves a division of labour. A segmentation of the institutional order occurs with only certain types of individuals performing certain functions. The problem now arises, however, of integrating the increasing number of meanings within the common stock of knowledge. The danger of conflict increases. Legitimation now becomes even more crucial.[41] Legitimating formulas are incorporated within the symbolic universe which then expands and solidifies.

Berger and Luckmann believe that since socialization can never be perfect, and because all social phenomena are in fact human constructs, no symbolic universe can be completely taken for granted. When a problem arises, theorizing about the nature of the symbolic universe becomes necessary for universe maintenance.[42] The appearance of this kind of theoretical reflection may be described as the legitimation of the symbolic universe.

According to Berger and Luckmann, the problem of heresy has often given the first impetus to systematic theoretical conceptualization about the symbolic universe. The development of Christian theological thought is accelerated by heretical challenges to the tradition. In the process of theorizing, new implications within the tradition appear and the symbolic universe is pushed beyond its original form.[43] In this book, it will be argued that the apparently transformed nature of Pauline Christianity visible in the Pastorals, consisting of such things as established church offices and a desire to preserve sound doctrine, is inseparably linked to the need to defend the community against false teaching. It will be shown that the transformation is not simply the result of an intellectual conflict, but is related to a profoundly felt threat to the heart of the social order embraced by the symbolic universe.

The overall process through which legitimations operate in the formation, expansion, solidification and transformation of the symbolic universe is aptly described by Holmberg as 'cumulative institutionalization'. For his own purposes, Holmberg divides this cumulative institutionalization into primary and secondary institutionalization.[44] This enables him to point to where significant changes have occurred. He identifies primary institutionalization as the process that had already begun in the group around Jesus and notes the likeness between what is known about this group and Weber's charismatic community. Holmberg argues that an active part in the process of institutionalization was played after Jesus' death by the former 'staff', some of whom later became responsible for the leadership of the Jerusalem church. Within a few years, a system of doctrine, cult and organization evolved in a group that demonstrated a missionary zeal and a strong sense of uniqueness. It is in a church at the level of secondary institutionalization where Paul can be found.

Holmberg's notion of cumulative institutionalization will be employed in this investigation in order to underline where significant changes have occurred and to facilitate comparison of various stages of development. Holmberg's distinction between primary and secondary institutionalization will be maintained, although secondary institutionalization will be referred to as 'community-building institutionalization'. In Part 1, a brief investigation of Pauline communities will trace the formation and solidification of the symbolic universe embracing the social world. A further level of institutionalization reflecting the development in the deutero-Pauline letters of Colossians and Ephesians will be known as 'community-stabilizing institutionalization'. The problems experienced by the communities as a result of the disappearance of Paul, coupled with the increased dangers of deviation that come with growth and the passage of time, lead to the continued solidification and expansion of the symbolic universe. Investigation of the communities underlying Colossians and Ephesians in Part 2 will focus on the means through which these communities undertake the task of stabilizing community life. A final level of institutionalization as reflected in the Pastoral Epistles will be described as 'community-protecting institutionalization'. The severe threat posed by false teaching results in more radical transformation of the symbolic universe. The study of the communities underlying the Pastoral Epistles in Part 3 will be especially concerned with the nature of the problem threatening the existence of the symbolic universe and the structural machineries created by the community for the purpose of universe maintenance.

Although based on the information in the respective New Testament texts, there is no doubt that the levels of institutionalization differentiated above are of an artificially constructed nature. Stages of development are never perfectly distinguishable in the historical realm. However, it is only in making such divisions on the basis of general correctness that it is possible to study levels of development in the New Testament communities at all. Although these somewhat artificial divisions will be employed as a tool for categorization, the identification of the unique historical circumstances in particular communities that acted as catalysts to the institutionalization process in the early church will be a constant aim of this investigation.

3

METHODOLOGICAL LIMITS AND POSSIBILITIES

Having illustrated how sociological analysis might be employed to study development in Pauline communities, it is necessary to consider the potential hazards of such a methodology. The following investigation includes a discussion of where the social sciences stand in terms of an inter-disciplinary approach to New Testament studies and a response to the objections levelled against those employing social-scientific modes of interpretation.

3.1 Why employ social sciences?

The most powerful forerunner of present interests in socio-historical study of New Testament texts is found in one wing of the Chicago school where, between approximately 1894 and 1920, scholars exhibited a keen interest in the social history of early Christianity.[45] This short-lived movement was characterized especially by the work of Shailer Mathews and Shirley Jackson Case. For the most part, the insights of the members of the Chicago school were buried for decades under the pursuits of New Testament criticism that gave only peripheral treatment to the 'Sitz im Leben', drew occasional parallels with contemporary literature, or issued a seldom heeded cry for more attention to 'sociological realities'.[46] One such appeal was made by Oscar Cullmann in 1925 with respect to form-critical studies. He stressed the need for a special branch of sociology devoted to the study of the laws which govern the growth of popular traditions.[47]

Response to Cullmann's appeal has found its beginning in the work of Gerd Theissen who, in *The First Followers of Jesus* (1977), explores the relationship between the development of oral tradition and the role of the wandering charismatic disciples of the early Christian movement. Until very recently, however, the term 'sociology' was surrounded by a distrust shared by the majority of New Testament interpreters. Scholars with only a superficial knowledge of the social sciences were aware of Marx's description of religion as 'the opium of the people' or Durkheim's understanding of religion as the reflection of society, and concluded that sociological interpretation would inevitably be reductionist. However, over the past few decades social scientists have in general become much more cautious about 'explaining-away' religion; they have become sensitive to the problem of the investigator imposing his or her own belief system upon the evidence, have warned of the hazards surrounding cross-cultural translation and have become increasingly aware of the dialectic between beliefs and social structures. Similarly, New Testament scholars employing social-scientific analysis in the study of New Testament texts keep clear of bold explanations for development. In short, much of the hesitation which surrounds the use of insights from the social sciences for interpretation is outdated.[48]

The distortions caused by the virtual neglect of the social setting of early Christianity in New Testament interpretation for decades were noted in 1960 by the ancient historian E. A. Judge. He argued that ideas are never satisfactorily explained by investigating their philosophical connections. Rather, ideas must be pinned down in relation to the particular circumstances in which they were expressed.[49] Since Judge issued his critical remarks, many New Testament scholars have come to share his interests. They have reacted to what Robin Scroggs has referred to as 'methodological docetism' operating in the field of New Testament interpretation: the tendency to depict believers as if their minds and spirits were somehow disconnected from individual and corporate bodies.[50] Investigation of the social world of early Christianity can be broadly divided into two categories:

1. studies relying solely on the methods of social history; and
2. socio-historical studies incorporating (to varying degrees) theoretical insights from the social sciences.

On the whole, it may be said that studies falling under the first category are much less controversial from the perspective of methodology than studies falling under the second. Because this investigation falls under the second category, it is the methodological implications of that approach which are of primary concern.[51]

It is most often to sociology and cultural anthropology that New Testament scholars turn in the hope of gaining assistance in their description of the social world of the early Christians. The interpreter who perhaps has done the most intensive sociological work on New Testament texts, Gerd Theissen, has noted the major methodological problem surrounding the enterprise. He questions how one can hope to derive sociological statements from essentially non-sociological forms of expression. Theissen outlines three methods for the sociological interpretation of religious traditions: the 'constructive', the 'analytic' and the 'comparative'.[52]

The constructive approach depends on direct disclosures of the 'Sitz im Leben' – expressions which intentionally describe the social situation. The constructive approach draws on the evidence of these pre-scientific sociological statements, including biographical details and descriptions of groups, institutions and organizations. For example, 1 Tim 5 presupposes that the community of the Pastorals is being burdened by a problem with widows. In 1 Tim 5:16 believing women who have relatives who are widows are told to assist them so that the church will not be unnecessarily burdened. Can one infer from this statement that there were women who were well-to-do and in a position to render service to the community? In 1 Tim 5:5 real widows are described as those who are left alone. Is it legitimate to infer from this statement that there were women in the community of the Pastorals who were completely dependent on the church for financial support? Can these passages reveal anything about the social composition of the community of the Pastorals? Can they be harmonized with what is known more generally about the position of women in Greco-Roman society?

Much information about the composition of the early church can be gathered by means of the constructive approach, as Theissen's work on the social stratification of the Corinthian community illustrates well.[53] It is important to note that even if a statement that has the appearance of a historical fact can be shown to be unhistorical, it is still of great value since it either provides information about what a later generation thought possible about an earlier time or somehow reflects the ideals of a community's present experience.[54]

The analytic approach includes what can be inferred about the 'Sitz im Leben' from passages which do not directly refer to the social situation. It involves looking beneath statements to discover realities and motivations characteristic of community life and bringing questions to texts which are independent of the intention which originally shaped them. The analytic approach seeks to identify and investigate conflicts, draws information about operative norms from ethical exhortations and wisdom sayings, and endeavours to draw connections between symbolism and experienced reality. What kind of community norms underlie the heavy concentration of household ethics in the Pastoral Epistles, including the connections between appropriate household behaviour and leadership positions? What kind of norms underlie the wisdom saying in 1 Tim 6:10 that the love of money is the root of all evils? What is implied about the nature of community life in the symbolic depiction of the church as the household of God (1 Tim 3:15; cf. Eph 2:19; 1 Pet 5:17)?

The comparative approach involves the comparison of primitive Christian sources with texts that do not originate from, or describe, early Christian groups. It can be employed to gain understanding of the early Christian movement, either by contrasting it with various aspects of the surrounding culture or by looking for similarities between early Christianity and movements and groups of other times and places. In the first case, for example, in trying to identify the attitudes to the world characteristic of the Pauline movement, one might seek to draw comparisons with what can be known about the community at Qumran. Similarly, when attempting to understand the implications of the presence of the household code in Colossians, Ephesians and the Pastoral Epistles, one might investigate its relationship with contemporary philosophical thought. In the second case, in order to understand the tension experienced by members of the early church at the hands of outsiders, one might look for similarities with modern sects. Comparing the early church with cultural phenomena of the same era is neither a novel enterprise nor one which is very controversial. Most scholars today, for example, would recognize the importance of understanding the development of early Christianity against the background of contemporary Judaism. Comparing movements that differ radically in date and cultural setting is far more problematic for obvious reasons. One can hardly assume a common denominator when comparing a modern movement with a first-century movement. The advantage of making such comparisons lies in that so much more is known about the inner dynamics of modern movements. As Theissen points out, at the very least, this method provides a series of interesting hypotheses worthy of investigation.[55]

When drawing upon the social sciences during an investigation of the social world of early Christianity, the social historian is not undertaking the task of the modern sociologist of religion. Contemporary methods of empirical research – including participant observation, interview, questionnaire and statistical evaluation – are simply inapplicable.[56] Such methods presuppose the possibility of generating new data which is impossible under the confines of ancient texts. A sociological approach to New Testament interpretation must be content to call upon concepts which have proved successful in the sociology of religion. The notions of charismatic leader, routinization of charisma, institutionalization, and legitimation are some of the concepts employed in this investigation for the purpose of shedding new light on development in the early church. By generating new questions, these concepts play an instrumental role in the formulation of new insights and perspectives.[57]

To encourage the incorporation of insights from the social sciences in the field of New Testament interpretation is not to doubt the value of more time-honoured approaches.[58] It will be argued in the following section that in attempting to prevent reductionism, literary/historical criticism provides a fundamental means of control and correction. Gerd Theissen is surely correct when he observes that the sociological perspective itself is but one among others.[59]

3.2 History and the social sciences

This study contends that a cautious union between history and the social sciences in New Testament interpretation leads to well balanced investigation and fruitful results.[60] In tracing the formation of a symbolic universe in the Pauline movement, the interpreter must seek out the distinctive aspects of the historical situation in the hope of understanding the process of construction and make-up of the universe in all its particularity. However, because the interpreter with social-scientific vision understands New Testament texts as products of ongoing social interaction, he or she is directed beyond aspects of the particular to aspects of the typical, recurrent and general, which are essential for understanding the ordinary patterns of life within the social environment.[61] For example, in attempting to understand why false teaching with its household-upsetting potential (2 Tim 3:6; Tit 1:11) poses such a threat within the community of the Pastorals, one would ask what kind of unconscious social factors underlie relevant passages.[62] One might search the text and other contemporary sources for evidence of norms concerning appropriate household behaviour and the importance of social respectability; one might then make suggestions about the workings of existing social structures. Beyond the discovery of singular factors of a specific situation, the interpreter is concerned with the structure of social relationships characterizing many repeated situations.[63]

Historical and social scientific modes of interpretation can serve as a means of correction and control for one another. Too often historical investigation of New Testament texts has been dominated by the 'history of ideas'. The issues facing early Christians have been described in purely conceptual terms. New Testament documents have been composed, it is argued, mainly to combat heresies or to defend a particular notion of salvation. The influence of social needs, conflicts, and existing norms are for the most part left out of the picture. When the reciprocity between social realities and religious symbolism is ignored, distortion is inevitable. Furthermore, with its keen interest to understand the uniqueness of early Christianity, the history of ideas approach has often tended to account for similarities between the early church and its contemporary environment by giving somewhat 'ethnocentric' explanations. One might well argue that this is simply a case of 'doing bad history'; it is true that many historians today working on the New Testament do account for social realities and do not produce such distortive results. However, there is a certain advantage in employing both historical and sociological analyses with the recognition that each discipline has its specific and indispensable point of reference. The result is a more complete picture of early Christianity. As J. H. Elliott has said, our 'Religionsgeschichte' has all too often been a 'Theologiegeschichte' lacking a 'sozialgeschichtliche' component.[64]

With the case made for the importance of incorporating insights from the social sciences in New Testament interpretation, it is crucial to stress the fact that historical investigation provides the foundation for any such enterprise. The New Testament student who hopes to engage in sociological modes of interpretation of New Testament texts is completely dependent on the findings of the historian. Sociological conclusions must not contradict or exceed the historical data. In addition, the text itself must provide the primary starting point and focus for sociological investigation of New Testament texts. Exegetical study involving linguistic and literary analysis remains fundamental.[65]

Despite the caution that characterizes the work of virtually all interpreters employing insights from the social sciences, many scholars remain suspicious of the validity of the enterprise. They are worried about the possibility of sociological interpreters filling in gaps in the evidence on the basis of assumptions about patterns in human behaviour. As Wayne Meeks has observed, these scholars are concerned about the historical distortion that comes from modernization – people from the past are depicted in the interpreter's own image, and the vast differences between contemporary culture and the world of antiquity are ignored. Critics insist that the interpreter pay heed to what the text says; the interpreter must report the facts and be wary of broad theories and unproven laws.[66] E. A. Judge is suspicious of the use of all social-scientific models for investigating the social world of the New Testament and argues for the exclusive use of models from the environment.[67] For example, the structure of the Greco-Roman household might be compared to the organization of the early church. There is undoubtedly a great deal to be learned from such an investigation as subsequent work on ministry structures in the Pauline movement will illustrate. However, more 'modern' models are not to be completely ruled out as tools for investigating the social world of the early Christians. One might, for instance, employ a model based on the investigation of modern sects. In this investigation, Bryan Wilson's description of a 'conversionist sect' will be referred to as a means of gaining greater understanding of the tensions characterizing the relationship between the Pauline communities and the outside society. It will be necessary to remember that a modern notion of 'conversion' is far removed from the process through which first-century persons entered the community, but the description remains useful as a heuristic device for understanding the inner dynamics of community life.

There is a tendency among critics of the use of models from the social sciences for New Testament investigation to imply that theory-less or presupposition-less research is possible. Judge, for example, makes the following criticism of Holmberg's work:

> It couples with New Testament studies a strong admixture of modern sociology, as though social theories can be safely transposed across the centuries without verification. The basic question remains unasked: What are the social facts of life characteristic of the world to which the New Testament belongs? Until the painstaking field work is better done, the importation of social models that have been defined in terms of other cultures is methodologically no improvement on the 'idealistic fallacy'. We may fairly call it the 'sociological fallacy'.[68]

Although Judge's plea for careful historical work is fair, he completely overlooks the value of Holmberg's insight into the institutionalization of the early church. He stresses the uniqueness of early Christianity to the neglect of the process of pattern-making that was integral to its development. Ironically, in his eagerness to connect early Christianity to the realities of Greco-Roman society, he virtually disconnects it from its societal base:

There may well be no comparable phenomenon known to history, and it could therefore prove a fundamental error to attempt to explain primitive Christianity by sociological methods which work through analogy and presuppose the repetitiveness of human behaviour. Until the work of mapping out their social identity and behaviour has been developed much further in juxtaposition with the conventions and practices of contemporary society, we are in no position to say who or what the first Christians were.[69]

Judge appears to be arguing in favour of a search for the 'social facts' of early Christianity free from theoretical presuppositions. What he fails to realize is that his belief in the possibility of carrying out historical 'field-work' prior to the use of models is itself a fallacy.[70] It is a mistake to think that an approach that relies on even the most disciplined common sense and not explicit theory completely avoids the dangers of 'modernizing' the early Christians. Common sense itself is, after all, a cultural phenomenon.[71] In his book entitled *The Shape of the Past: Models and Antiquity*, T.F. Carney describes a model as '... a framework of reference, consciously used as such, to enable us to cope with complex data'.[72] Carney notes that we have no choice in whether or not we employ models. Even if we are not unconscious of the fact that we are using models, mind-sets dominate our thinking. The concepts, arguments, assumptions and theories which are tied to the model-building process are constantly employed by everyone because they are the only conceptual tools available. The greatest benefit of the conscious use of models is that they can bring hitherto unconscious levels of thought into awareness; they enlarge our control over data. Models can also facilitate understanding for the reader by clearly identifying the writer's frame of reference and by making it more readily available for criticism. The use of models can lead to greater comprehensiveness when doing interpretations by providing categories and suggesting relations between categories.[73]

All of this discussion of the inevitability of the influence of 'mind-sets' in the process of investigating the early church is not to deny the importance of keeping as close as possible to the 'observed facts'. The historians of early Christianity have done much to remind us of the distortions inevitable when such facts are ignored. The foregoing constitutes a response to some of the objections levelled at New Testament interpreters employing insights from the social sciences within their studies. The purpose has been to illustrate that such an enterprise is not inevitably historically reductionist. Social scientific models can be used for the purpose of comparison and can assist in the task of explanation. They cannot, however, be employed to furnish new data. The use of social scientific models complements historical investigation when models are employed as suggestive, rather than generative, tools for analysis.

3.3 Theology and the social sciences

For one interested in investigating the social world of early Christianity, it is essential to explore the relationship between beliefs and social realities. The sceptic might retort, however, that the sociology of knowledge model of the dialectical process leading to the formation of a symbolic universe employed in this book, is theologically reductionist; the solidifying overarching canopy, humanly constructed, keeps God firmly out.

The notion of a symbolic universe calls to mind an invisible canopy of symbols stretching over a society. In his essay 'Religion as a Cultural System', the cultural anthropologist, Clifford Geertz, defines symbols as '... tangible formulations of notions, abstractions from experience fixed in perceptible forms, concrete embodiments of ideas, attitudes, judgements, longings, or beliefs'.[74] Although Geertz sometimes speaks generally about symbols and the process of symbolization, he is particularly interested in sacred symbols: '... sacred symbols function to synthesize a people's ethos − the tone, character, and quality of their life, its moral and aesthetic style and mood − and their world view − the picture they have of the way things in sheer actuality are, their most comprehensive ideas of order'.[75] Sacred symbols arise from an apprehension of an all-pervading reality; they allow for the formulation of conceptions referring to the order of existence.[76]

Sacred symbols are always human constructs, but they nevertheless arise from an apprehension of something which is understood as transcending the purely human − an apprehension of the sacred. However, the symbolism resulting from this apprehension of the sacred is a social product; it is shaped by the language shared by the members of the symbolic universe. To understand early Christianity as a socially-constructed religion might imply a kind of 'methodological atheism', but this is not to be interpreted as atheism 'tout court'. The point is made elegantly by Peter Berger:

... to say that religion is a human projection does not logically preclude the possibility that the projected meanings may have an ultimate status independent of man. Indeed, if a religious view of the world is posited, the anthropological ground of these projections may itself be the reflection of a reality that includes both world and man, so that man's ejaculations of meaning into the universe ultimately point to an all-embracing meaning in which he himself is grounded.[77]

In this study of the formation of a symbolic universe in Pauline movement, connections will be drawn between communal realities (social needs, conflicts, norms, etc.) and the beliefs embodied in sacred symbols. However, the relationship between beliefs and social realities will be understood as dialectical; no simple causal connections will be posited.[78] Discussion of sacred symbols will focus on their order-giving potential, but the nature of the symbol itself, as embodying an apprehension of the sacred, will also be remembered. Understanding the early church as encompassed by a symbolic universe will not deny the possibility of actual apprehensions of the sacred at the heart of the symbolization process.

4

WHERE FROM HERE?

The preceding introductory remarks have highlighted problems with past approaches employed in the investigation of development in the early church. They have also suggested alternative methods and considered both the hazards and potentials of such methods. In the following investigation, the proposed theoretical framework for interpretation will be applied to the New Testament texts. Development in Pauline communities will be studied in terms of the three levels of institutionalization:

1. Paul's letters (community-building institutionalization);
2. Colossians and Ephesians (community-stabilizing institutionalization); and
3. The Pastoral Epistles (community-protecting institutionalization).

These three stages will be compared in terms of four aspects of community life:

1. Attitudes to the world/ethics;
2. Ministry;
3. Ritual; and
4. Belief.

PART 1

PAUL: COMMUNITY-BUILDING INSTITUTIONALIZATION

The following study constitutes a general treatment of the nature of Pauline communities. The connection of these communities with the structures and values of Greco-Roman society will be considered. It will be necessary to explore early Christian attitudes to the outside world as well as the ethical stance adopted by communities at once separated from, and rooted in, the realities of that world. Ministry will be studied not only in terms of visible traces of leadership organization, but also with a view to discovering the often hidden social structures functioning in the exercise of authority in community life. Ritual forms will be investigated in the hope of gaining insight into the assertion and reaffirmation of communal identity. Beliefs, the key elements of the developing Christian identity, will be considered with an awareness of the ongoing dialectic between ideas and their social setting. The interrelationships between the various aspects of community life will be sought throughout the enquiry. The ambiguities and tensions experienced by a movement in its initial stages of community building will be highlighted.

This work is by no means intended to be a comprehensive investigation of Pauline Christianity. Many interesting and crucial questions having to do with the complexities of Paul's thought are here left to one side. Our field of vision is limited to what can be gleaned from the text about the life of members of Paul's communities – what they believed and what they did. This will mean looking beneath Paul's statements for evidence of communal norms, traces of ritual forms and latent authority structures. The investigation of Pauline Christianity will be conducted with a view to the major subject of this book: development in communities grounded in the Pauline tradition after the Apostle's death. Of particular importance will be the consideration of assumptions about the nature of Paul's communities which have provided the foundation for conclusions about development after Paul.

1

ATTITUDES TO THE WORLD/ETHICS

This section explores the place of the Pauline movement within the urban world of antiquity. It presents evidence of tensions experienced by the Pauline group in their attempt to preserve the boundaries of their community. The investigation also clarifies some of the patterns of life designed by the early Christians as a means of ensuring their survival in the face of precarious social situations.

1.1 Sectarian boundaries

In reading the Pauline correspondence, one finds evidence that the Pauline communities are involved in a process of self-definition. There are patterns for entry, prescriptions for life-style and even criteria for determining when expulsion is required. In a manner that recalls the efforts of the Qumran community to maintain a separate existence from other Jews, the Pauline communities engaged in the process of separating themselves from those who did not accept their views of the saving events that occurred in Christ.[1]

In 1 Cor 10:32 Paul refers to Jews, Greeks and the Church of God. This tripartite terminology suggests the existence of the Christian movement as a third entity. As E.P. Sanders has pointed out, however, Paul would probably have been horrified to read that, in claiming the necessity of faith in Christ for both Jew and Gentile, he had made the Christian movement into a 'third race'. The communities he was building were the reflection of a re-created humanity (Gal 3:28; 6:15; 1 Cor 12:13; 2 Cor 5:17) and not merely the representatives of one group among others.[2]

There is ambiguity in Paul's thought with respect to the existence of the church as a third entity. Although conceptually it seems that those who are in Christ are the 'true Israel' (Rom 9:6; cf. Gal 3:16, 29; 2 Cor 3:16), the fact that the term 'Israel' (with the possible exception of Gal 6:16) is not used by Paul to describe the third group implies that he knew that there were real Israelites, real Jews, who were not in Christ.[3] Moreover, Paul would surely have rejected the conclusion that his thought was moving in the direction of a third entity since he believed that all Israel would be included in the 'true Israel' (cf. Rom 11).[4]

Despite the ambiguity in Paul's thought, it is evident that in terms of concrete social reality, the Pauline movement exists as a third entity. Gentile converts could not participate in the life of the church as if it was one of many religions (1 Cor 10:21). Moreover, although it is conceivable that some members could have attended both church and synagogue, it seems that they were distinct social realities (cf. 1 Cor 5:1–5; 6:1–11; 11:17–22; 14:23–36). Gentile converts who entered into a Pauline community did not simply join Israel. They were not required to undergo circumcision and accept other legal observances that distinguished Jew from Gentile. Entry into a distinct social entity was based on a separate entrance requirement (faith in Christ) and a separate entrance rite (baptism).[5]

The notion of entry into a Pauline community raises the question of whether or not it is appropriate to describe the process as a 'conversion'. Some scholars have argued that it is inappropriate to think of conversion with respect to the entry of Jews.[6] Unlike the Gentiles, the Jews are not required to turn to another God (cf. 1 Thess 1:9; 1 Cor 6:9–11; 12:2). Paul does not instruct the Jews to cease obeying the law (cf. Gal 6:15; 1 Cor 7:19; Rom 14:1–6). Paul can even describe himself as living as a Jew (1 Cor 9:20).[7]

As Sanders indicates, however, in 2 Cor 3:16, those who 'turn' to the Lord and have the veil removed which obscures the meaning of the law must include Jewish Christians. In 1 Thess 1:9 Paul can speak of Gentiles 'turning' to God from idols. In addition, in 1 Cor 9:19–23, Paul uses 'to win' with respect to both Jews and Gentiles. There is at least a sense in which both groups need to be converted.[8]

One of the things to which members have had to die is the law (Rom 6:1–7:6). Paul did not insist that Jews who entered the church begin disobeying the law (Rom 14:1–6). But, as Sanders points out, the language of dying to the old self, which is symbolized by the law and epitomized as sin, is language of 'conversion'. Something is given up in order to accept something else.[9] That Paul could indeed require Jews to give something up is implied by his reaction to Peter's behaviour at Antioch (Gal 2:11–14). It seems that if Jewish and Gentile Christians were present together, Jews were to give up those aspects of the law which Paul believed would act as a social barrier to unity.[10]

In addition to the existence of characteristic practices and requirements, the social distinctiveness of the Pauline movement is suggested by evidence of certain 'attitudes to the world' – indications of how the Pauline communities viewed themselves and their relationship to the outside world. That the Pauline communities possessed an identity by which they distinguished themselves from the outside society has long been recognized.[11] If one wishes to move beyond the fact that the Pauline communities set themselves apart from the outside world to a consideration of the possible social consequences of a separation, an obvious tool for analysis would be the notion of 'sect' as defined by sociologists. While one must be cautious about employing descriptions based on observations of modern sects in a manner that leads to a reduction of first-century complexities, descriptions can be useful as heuristic devices for investigating the nature of the tensions between the Pauline movement and the outside society.[12]

In his study of 1 Peter, John H. Elliott has successfully illustrated how sociological investigation of sects can be employed in New Testament interpretation.[13] As in Elliott's work, Bryan Wilson's definition of a sect will be employed here:

> The sect is a clearly defined community; it is of a size which permits only a minimal range of diversity of conduct; it seeks itself to rigidify a pattern of behaviour and to make coherent its structure of values; it contends actively against every other organisation of values and ideals, and against every other social context possible for its adherents, offering itself as an all-embracing, divinely prescribed society. The sect is not only an ideological unit, it is, to greater or lesser degree, a social unit, seeking to enforce behaviour on those who accept belief, and seeking every occasion to draw the faithful apart from the rest of society and into the company of each other ... the sect, as a protest group, has always developed its own distinctive ethic, belief and practices, against the background of the wider society; its own protest is conditioned by the economic, social, ideological and religious circumstances prevailing at the time of its emergence and development.[14]

The more specific subtype of sect to which the Pauline communities might belong is best defined by the conversionist response to the world described by Wilson:

The world is corrupt because men are corrupt: if men can be changed then the world will be changed. Salvation is seen not as available through objective agencies but only by a profoundly felt, supernaturally wrought transformation of the self. The objective world will not change but the acquisition of a new subjective orientation to it will itself be salvation.

Clearly this subjective conversion will be possible only on the promise of a change in external reality at some future time, or the prospect of the individual's transfer to another sphere. This is the ideological or doctrinal aspect of the matter, but the essential sociological fact is that what men must do to be saved is to undergo emotional transformation – a conversion experience. This is the proof of having transcended the evil of the world. Since it is a permanent and timelessly valid transcendence, some future condition of salvation is often posited in which objective circumstances come to correspond to the subjective sense of salvation, but the believer also knows, from the subjective change, that he is saved *now*. Thus he can face the evil of the world, the processes of change that threaten men with decay and death, because he is assured of an unchanging condition *and feels this*. This response is the *conversionist* response to the world. It is not concerned simply with recruitment to a movement, but with the acquisition of a change of heart.[15]

When one reads the Pauline texts with the above descriptions in mind, the correlations are remarkable. What follows is a basic outline of the conversionist response exhibited by the Pauline sect.

The most obvious examples of connections between Wilson's descriptions and the Pauline text are those where the 'supernaturally wrought transformation of the self' (a characteristic of the conversionist response) enables the believer to apprehend the future change of all things, giving meaning to present life in the world. While one cannot assume that the Pauline Christians have undergone a 'conversion' in the modern sense, they have clearly undergone some kind of powerful change; they have transferred into a community gathered around Christ.[16] They have been justified by faith in Christ. They have been set apart from the evil world and now possess new life in the Spirit (Rom 5:6–11; 6:1–11, 20–3; 7:1–6; 8:1–8; 1 Cor 6:9–11; 2 Cor 5:17; Gal 1:3–5; 2:20–1; 1 Thess 1:9–10).

God has acted in a new way; the one God of the Fathers has raised Jesus from the dead (Rom 4:24; 8:11; 2 Cor 4:14; Gal 1:1; 1 Thess 1:10). The Gentiles who do not know of God (1 Thess 4:5; Gal 4:8) and are therefore enslaved to non-gods (Gal 4:8) are contrasted with the Pauline Christians who know God and are known by him (Gal 4:9). The Gentiles have many gods and many lords, but the Christians have only one God and one Lord, Jesus Christ (1 Cor 8:4−6).

It is the one God of Jews and Gentiles together that unites believers into one community (Rom 3:22−4, 29−30; 10:12−13; Gal 3:28). When the sect is threatened by division, an appeal is made to the unity of the Lord (1 Cor 12). Salvation is to be experienced now in the Pauline communities, for Jesus has given himself to deliver them from the present evil age (Gal 1:4; 2 Cor 6:1−2). Jesus' crucifixion and resurrection have already set in motion a certain shift in the order of the world. Salvation is, however, also something that will be fulfilled in the future. The sect members expect that the present age will soon come to an end; the Lord will return and a final judgement will take place (1 Thess 1:10; 4:13−5:11; 1 Cor 3:13−15; 4:5; 5:5; 6:2−3, 9−10, 13; 7:26−31; 11:26, 32; 15:24; 15:51; Phil 3:20−1). The unity of Gentiles and Jews now in the sect is the foretaste of a more complete union in the future (Rom 11:25−32). All of this is part of a secret revelation made to Christians alone (1 Cor 2:6−10; 4:1; cf. Rom 16:25−7).

It is the sharing of certain beliefs which is the major factor leading to the development of the sect and contributing to its continued cohesion. A sect might be described, in the language of E. Shils, as one type of 'ideological primary group'. The bond that unites the members of the group is related to the fact that they perceive one another to be in possession of, or possessed by, the sacredness inherent in the acceptance of the ideology. A comrade is a comrade in light of his or her beliefs.[17] The ideological system of beliefs, as described by Shils, functions to motivate the members of the sect by assuring their continued contact with the sacred. Furthermore, the ideology seeks to explain to members and non-members alike why an elect status is claimed.[18] In short, ideology serves to legitimate the sect's existence.

Bryan Wilson has written: 'No sect arises without ideological justification.'[19] In the introductory discussion of 'legitimation', it was observed that the process begins as soon as a third party (or new generation) is introduced and patterns, once simply shared by two, now have to be explained and justified to the other. After the death of Jesus, those who had been followers of him were faced with the problem of explaining his life, death and resurrection to those who had never known him. It is to this earliest period, when beliefs about Jesus were being concretized, that Paul's communities belong. The existence of Paul's letters is proof of this very need for legitimation. The ideology expressed in Paul's letters acts to motivate a certain kind of behaviour in believers by assuring them that salvation is in Christ, that they have been removed from the evil of the world, and that the Lord will soon return. The letters serve to explain the content of the revelation to the members of the sect with a view to accounting for their behaviour to the outside world. Underlying Paul's instructions concerning marriage to non-believers in 1 Cor 7:12—16, for example, one discovers a probable attempt to respond to the problems surrounding marriage to an unbeliever. What are the consequences of being joined to an unbeliever? Should one remain married to an adamant unbelieving spouse? Underlying the problem of food sacrificed to idols in 1 Cor 8:1ff and 1 Cor 10:14ff is perhaps the need to explain why separation from past associations might be necessary — a difficult problem when such associations were once considered venerable and necessary in one's workaday world.[20]

It is clear from Paul's writings that he is bound to give ideological justification for the existence of his communities *vis-à-vis* Judaism. This need for legitimation is probably less related to the everyday needs of community members than are the marriage and food questions discussed above. But, for a Jewish leader of a new movement that proclaimed the resurrection of the Messiah and included Gentiles on the basis of faith in Christ, the question of the group's position with respect to the law required attention. Moreover, Galatians and Romans give an indication that the Apostle to the Gentiles was bound to do some explaining to Jewish colleagues based in Jerusalem (cf. Gal 2; Rom 15). Paul's struggle over what to make of the law in light of the new revelation is evident in the confusing passages of Rom 7. However, in Rom 9—11 the problem of the sect's relationship to Israel is especially visible. Paul must, in fact, redefine Israel so that having descended from Israel does not guarantee belonging to Israel (Rom 9:6—13). Furthermore, he must explain that although it may appear that the Jews have rejected the salvation that comes through Christ, they will eventually become jealous of the Gentiles and unification will take place (Rom 11:11—36). Yet despite his belief in the full inclusion of Gentiles and Jews in the promises of salvation, Paul can also unhesitatingly state that this new covenant far exceeds the old (2 Cor 3:6–18). Much of the apparent contradiction and confusion in Paul's thought is due to the fact that, with the aid of time-honoured traditions, he was compelled to articulate the boundaries of a new situation. Throughout the passages, Paul legitimates the existence of a newly formed sect.

The Pauline sect's identity is reinforced by what Wayne Meeks has called 'language of belonging'.[21] Paul often calls the members of his communities 'saints' (1 Cor 1:2; 16:1; 2 Cor 1:1; 8:4; 9:12; 13:13; Rom 1:7; 15:25; 16:15; Phil 1:1; 4:21; Philem 5; 7). The members of the sect consider themselves to be the elected or called ones (Rom 8:30, 33; 9:24–6; 1 Cor 1:9, 27; 7:15, 17–24; Gal 1:6, 15; 5:8, 13; 1 Thess 1:4; 2:12; 4:7; 5:24). The Pauline letters are rich in emotionally charged language. The concluding directives of the letters often include the phrase, 'Greet one another with a holy kiss' (Rom 16:16; 1 Cor 16:20; 2 Cor 13:12; 1 Thess 5:26). Particularly frequent is the language which speaks of the members of the Pauline groups as if they were members of a family, as brothers and sisters, or as the beloved (e.g. 1 Thess 1:4; 2:8; 4:10; 2 Cor 11:2–10).[22] Paul can also speak of the members of the churches founded by him as his children (Gal 4:19; 1 Cor 4:14; 2 Cor 6:13; 12:14; 1 Thess 2:7, 11). The members of the Pauline group can even be spoken of as the children of God (Rom 8:16, 21; 9:8; Phil 2:15; Gal 3:26). Gal 3:26–4:7 and Rom 8:15–17 bring forth the idea that the experience of being initiated into the community through the ritual of baptism is related to the image of being God's child and receiving a new family of brothers and sisters.[23] The members of the sect feel that they are loved by God (Rom 1:7; 5:5, 8; 8:35, 39; 15:30; 2 Cor 5:14; 13:11, 14; 1 Thess 1:4). The language of belonging in the Pauline community reflects a feeling of intimacy that contributes to the cohesion of the group. The practice of hospitality allows this feeling to permeate throughout the whole network of Pauline churches, reinforcing the unity between them (cf. Rom 16:1–2; Philem 22).[24]

The language of belonging evident in Paul's letters may be sharply contrasted with the 'language of separation'.[25] As noted previously, Bryan Wilson describes a sect as a protest group. In the case of the Pauline sect, however, it is impossible to determine against what, if anything, members were protesting with respect to society at large. It is impossible, for example, to arrive at definite conclusions about whether or not the members of the Pauline sect felt that they had been estranged by political powers, or whether they were burdened by problems involving economic security or social mobility. The sect, however, did perceive its common ideas and values to be at variance with society at large. Paul often distinguishes the Christians from the wicked of the world (Rom 1:18–32; 12:1–2; 1 Cor 5:9–13; 2 Cor 6:14–18; Gal 1:3–5; Phil 3:18–19; 1 Thess 4:4). This is particularly well brought out by the discussion in 1 Cor 5:9–13; it is not the judgement of outsiders which is the concern of the sect, but the judgement of insiders according to the standards of the sect. The Christians are instructed not to go to outside law courts (1 Cor 6:1–6). They are simply not to act as ordinary people (1 Cor 3:3). Ordinary people are perishable, but the members of the Pauline sect are imperishable (1 Cor 9:24–7).

1.2 Sectarian tensions

Although the Pauline Christians consider their citizenship to be in heaven (Phil 3:20), it is clearly impossible for them physically to leave the world (1 Cor 5:10). Paul's communities do not appear to resemble the 'introversionist' type sect (perhaps useful for study of the Johannine community or the community at Qumran) described by Wilson, for the Apostle expects that the members will have to deal with the evil of the world (1 Cor 5:10).[26] Indeed, Paul understands his mission as preaching to the world (Rom 1:8–15; 15:15–21; 1 Cor 9:19–23; 10:31–3). The tension visible in the early church's understanding of itself as being somehow outside the world, while at the same time remaining in the world, is often given the theological explanation of an eschatological congregation which is bound within the limits and structures of the world.[27] However, there may be important social aspects (as well as often noted theological ones) of the tensions experienced by the members of the early church with respect to outside society. Indeed, one might argue that the theological significance of the tensions gains a greater depth of meaning when understood in terms of the real conflicts encountered by community members as they strove to maintain their identity amidst the complexities of the Greco-Roman world.

Bryan Wilson has argued that the preservation of the identity of sects requires a continued separation from the outside society. The sect must remain unspotted from the world; its distinctiveness must be evident to both its own members and outsiders.[28] However, if a conversionist sect is to be successful in the missionary enterprise, it must be willing to enter into dialogue with others and, indeed, present itself as a distinctive and attractive alternative to the other groups vying for allegiance:

> ... for the proselytising sect ... the social status of its members may radically affect its prospect of winning recruits. Even the sect of the very poor is usually pleased when a prominent personage is converted, and often accords him a place of honour because of his status in the wider society.[29]

This may help explain why, according to Theissen's analysis, the leaders of the Pauline churches exhibited the highest social status among members.[30] Faced with practical problems, such as finding a large house to hold gatherings, it would be reasonable for Paul actively to seek the conversion of a relatively well-to-do householder. Yet, implicit in this campaign lies the danger of compromising sectarian values. The manner in which the tension between world rejection and mission is maintained is directly related to the nature of sect development:

> The sect's desire to be separate from the world and its concerns – and the values which express that separateness – results in certain distinct tensions for the organisation and for its members. For each sect there must be a position of optimal tension, where any greater degree of hostility against the world portends direct conflict, and any less suggests accommodation to wordly values.[31]

It is in the conversionist sect, with its strong interest in the evangelization of others, that conditions are likely to arise which lead to the transformation of a sect into a more church-like organization or 'denomination' (a new level of institutionalization). It is with the conversionist sect that accommodation to the world is most likely:

> Evangelism means exposure to the world and the risk of alienation of the evangelising agents. It means also the willingness to accept into the sect new members. This throws a particular weight on the standards of admission if, through the impact of recruitment, the sect itself is not to feel the effect of members who are incompletely socialised from the sect's point of view.[32]

The principal tension visible in the conversionist sect resulting from a simultaneous interest in avoiding and evangelizing outsiders, is clearly visible in Paul's writings. We have already noted various passages where Paul encourages members of the sect to avoid outsiders, but have also seen that the notion of evangelization is absolutely fundamental to his thought. Paul hesitates to suggest that believers become completely cut off from non-believers because of the possibility that they too might be gained for Christ. Paul can encourage the believer who is married to a non-believer to remain married. Perhaps the believer will be able to save the non-believer (1 Cor 7:12–16). Furthermore, Paul believes that an outsider who enters into the worship of the community may be converted (1 Cor 14:23–5).

Related to the tension visible in the conversionist sect resulting from a simultaneous interest in both evangelizing and avoiding outsiders, is the discrepancy in the way in which addressees are encouraged to relate to outsiders. This discrepancy is particularly visible in the passages which deal with the problem of food sacrificed to idols. In 1 Cor 8 (cf. Rom 14:20–3), Paul approves of the opinion of liberal community members while at the same time cautioning that the consciences of the weaker members must guide their actions. It seems as though public participation in a cultic meal which might be construed as actual idol worship is especially dangerous (1 Cor 8:10). If it will end in a brother falling, one must not eat meat (1 Cor 8:13). Priority must be given to fellow members of the sect.

If one turns from 1 Cor 8 to 1 Cor 10, Paul's position on food sacrificed to idols seems more complicated. After a passage describing the idolatry of the Jews (1 Cor 10:1–13), Paul instructs the Corinthians to shun the worship of idols (1 Cor 10:14). He reminds them that pagan sacrifices are offered to demons and not to God. It is impossible for community members to drink of the cup of the Lord and of the cup of demons, to partake in the table of the Lord and the table of demons (1 Cor 10:20–1). In 1 Cor 10:23–33, however, Paul seems almost to contradict what he has previously said. One should eat whatever is sold at the meat market without asking questions. Unless the conscience of another is offended, one should accept invitations to dinner from non-believers and eat all foods.

With respect to meat sacrificed to idols, Paul may be prohibiting believers from public participation in a cultic meal (and activity that might be construed as such), but allowing the consumption of all foods in a private setting.[33] Beyond this general distinction, however, Paul seems to be allowing believers to face considerable ambiguity in their relations with outsiders. In 1 Cor 10:31–3, Paul gives a theological explanation for his actions which may help clarify the discrepancies in this thought. Once again we discover the tension arising from a simultaneous interest in both avoiding and evangelizing outsiders. The conscience of the brother or sister must be protected, but possibilities for the evangelization of outsiders must not be overlooked. Paul seeks to please all in order to save all.

According to Bryan Wilson, the tension between mission and world rejection found in conversionist sects often takes the form of a tension between the desire for separation from the outside and the desire for social respectability.[34] Endeavouring to please all is connected with a wish to be respected by all. Paul does not hesitate to state in 1 Cor 14:22−5 that the opinions of outsiders are important. He is worried about the over-enthusiastic use of the gift of tongues in the Corinthian community. Instead of becoming a believer, the unbeliever who hears them speaking in tongues may conclude that Christians are mad (1 Cor 14:23)! The same desire for social respectability probably underlines Paul's instructions to the community about how worship should be conducted (1 Cor 14:27−40), including the statements about women keeping silent in church (1 Cor 14:33−6).[35] Paul states that all things should be done decently and in order (1 Cor 14:40).

The desire for social respectability may also not be far removed from Paul's statements on the importance of head-covering for women (1 Cor 11:2−16). Although the statements made by Paul about marriage (1 Cor 7:1ff) are largely tied to the desire to free Christians from any anxiety in a world passing away (1 Cor 7:31−2), could not Paul also have been speaking cautiously about such an important household-linked institution in the Greco-Roman world? A cautious attitude may also characterize his ambiguous responses to the question of slavery (1 Cor 7:21−3). Similarly, underlying Paul's statements in Rom 13:1−7 about subjection to governing authorities and the payment of taxes, there may be a concern for the appearance of the sect with respect to the outside world. Hostility between the sect and the outside society could make preaching the gospel to the world a very difficult task indeed. The apparent concern visible in Paul's writings as to how outsiders might interpret the behaviour of sect members is inseparably linked to his identity as an apostle within the Greco-Roman world and his mission to preach within that world (Rom 1:1−15; 15:15−21).

1.3 Patterns for life: love-patriarchalism

In considering the conflict over food sacrificed by idols, the teaching on marriage, the role of women, the question of slavery, and the attitudes to governmental authorities with respect to the tensions experienced by the Pauline sect, we have been dealing, even if somewhat indirectly, with what is usually understood as the ethics of the Pauline communities. When Paul addresses believers, he knows that they are already baptized and belong to Christ, but they are faced with resolving specific moral issues that their new membership has brought about. Paul expects that the members of the sect will have a different vision of morality from those outside (e.g. 2 Cor 6:14–18). Participating in Christ through an identification with his death and resurrection means becoming part of a community gathered around him – a community characterized by a distinctive way of life. Specific values, beliefs and patterns of behaviour separate sect members from the outside society. According to Paul, it should be obvious that the wicked person of 1 Cor 5 belongs on the outside (1 Cor 5:2, 13). The communal context of the life of the Pauline Christians is a guiding influence for their activity as well as for the style of leadership demonstrated by Paul.[36]

To provide an overall description of the life patterns characteristic of the Pauline sect, Theissen's definition of 'love-patriarchalism' is very useful:

> This love-patriarchalism takes social differences for granted but ameliorates them through an obligation of respect and love, an obligation imposed upon those who are socially stronger. From the weaker are required subordination, fidelity, and esteem. Whatever the intellectual sources feeding into this ethos, with it the great part of Hellenistic primitive Christianity mastered the task of shaping social relations within a community which, on the one hand, demanded of its members a high degree of solidarity and brotherliness and, on the other, encompassed various social strata.[37]

It is perhaps only in Paul's teaching on the union of Gentiles and Jews in one church that we find evidence of revolutionizing consequences in the social realm. Despite the theological exposition of equality in Gal 3:28, it seems that with respect to the position of slaves and women, Paul felt it wiser to advise that the existing order of society be maintained, although interpreting these states according to new life in Christ (1 Cor 7:21ff; 11:2–16; 14:33–6). The love-patriarchal attitude with respect to community affairs is evident, for example, in Paul's recommendations to Philemon with regard to his runaway slave Onesimus. In writing to the householder, Paul recognizes a certain obligation to inform him of his slave's whereabouts and to return him to his master (Philem 14). Paul's comments disclose a certain respect for the structures of the master/slave relationship. At the same time, he recommends that Philemon receive the runaway Onesimus as a brother (Philem 16). Paul takes the social position and power of Philemon for granted, but pleads that he treat his believing slave with respect and with love – in fact, that he be treated as Paul himself (Philem 17). Onesimus may in the end have been granted manumission, but this is not assumed or demanded by Paul. It is likely, however, that at least the nature of the relationship between Philemon and Onesimus was somehow transformed according to new life in Christ and by means of the designs of love-patriarchalism.[38]

Theissen argues that 'love-patriarchalism', which allows social differences to continue but demands that all relationships be marked with a spirit of concern and respect, played a major role in the development of early Christianity. He argues that its organizational effectiveness was rooted in its ability to integrate members of different strata.[39] The connection between 'love-patriarchalism', described by Theissen, and the tension between world rejection and the evangelization of the world exhibited by the conversionist sect, as identified by Wilson, is clearly visible in Paul's writings. If the salvation of all is a central goal of the Pauline sect, then an ethos will be required that allows for the accommodation of all. In this study it will be argued that the ethos of love-patriarchalism became even more sharply pronounced in communities that continued to appeal to the authority of the Apostle after his death. Work on Colossians, Ephesians, and the Pastoral Epistles will illustrate that as Pauline communities grew and greater organization became necessary, the ethos of love-patriarchalism played a major part in stabilizing community life.

1.4 Conclusion

The preceding study of the attitudes to the world/ethics visible in the Pauline text investigated how community members perceived their relationship to Greco-Roman society. The appropriateness of understanding the Pauline communities as a sect exhibiting a con-versionist response to the world was illustrated. Discussion of the patterns of life designed by the Pauline sect, marked by a tension between a desire to remain separate from the world and a desire to evangelize the world, revealed the emerging ethos of love-patriarchalism.

2

MINISTRY

The following study traces the development of ministry structures in Pauline communities. The relation between Paul's leadership style and emerging patterns of organization is analysed. Ministry roles are considered in terms of the realities experienced by a sect in the early stages of institutionalization. Of particular significance is the examination of common assumptions about the organization of Pauline communities which often provide the starting point for discussion of development after Paul.

2.1 Authority structures

As groups grow, they require greater organization. The multiplication of tasks invovles a division of labour. A segmentation of the institutional order occurs with only certain individuals performing certain roles. In the Pauline sect, the multiplication of tasks and differentiation of roles is clearly present. There are apostles, fellow workers, local leaders and members of the communities. There are also powerful figures in Jerusalem to whom Paul and his churches are somehow connected. The roles of the Apostle and the others we hear about in the Pauline correspondence are shaped by authority structures outlining what may reasonably be expected and demanded by actors. Paul's letters abound with his claims of authority with respect to the Jerusalem church and his own communities. In addition, by means of his recommendations, Paul reinforces the authority of the local leadership. They, in turn, would undoubtedly appeal to their connection with the Apostle to legitimate their demands. How is authority distributed in the Pauline sect?

In his book entitled *Paul and the Anatomy of Apostolic Authority*, John Schütz defines authority as '... the interpretation of power, i.e. the focus of power, its disposition and allocation, the opening of accessibility to power for members of social groups'.[40] As an interpreter of power, the person in authority must respond to a particular social situation. Even when demonstrations of power take on apparently irrational forms, the exercise of authority is dependent on an acknowledgement of the appropriateness of the communication of the power holder.[41] Despite Paul's frequent claims of weakness, it is evident that he was a powerful leader with a team of assistants and numerous contacts in the churches he himself founded. Although Paul's authority was sometimes seriously questioned, he passionately defended his rights as the Apostle to the Gentiles. His letters stand as proof that his authority was recognized by many others as well.

Paul's authority may be described in the language of Weber as 'charismatic authority'; his powers and qualities are not regarded as accessible to everyone, but are viewed as stemming from divine orgins.[42] Paul's understanding of his own authority centres around the fact that he is an apostle (1 Thess 2:6; Gal 1:1; 1 Cor 1:1; 9:1–2; Rom 1:1; 11:13).[43] By calling himself an apostle, he places himself on the level with the highest authorities in the church (1 Cor 12:28; 15:9–11; 2 Cor 11:5). For Paul, apostleship involves a commission received from the risen Lord (1 Cor 15:8–9); his mission as the apostle to the Gentiles is authorized by revelation (Gal 1:15f). Having been set apart by God (Gal 1:15; Rom 1:1), Paul has been given responsibility and authority with respect to the Gentiles (Rom 1:5, 11–15; 11:13; 15:14–24). In fact, when Paul preaches, it is as if God were the speaker (1 Thess 2:2–4, 13; 4:15; 1 Cor 14:37; 2 Cor 5:18–20). Anyone denying Paul's gospel rejects God (1 Thess 4:8; Gal 1:8).

Related to Paul's self-understanding as a divinely appointed apostle, is the evidence he gives for his own Spirit-endowment. Paul speaks of miracles as being a definitive sign of the apostle (Rom 15:19; 2 Cor 12:12). He transmits his gospel not only verbally, but also through pneumatic acts (cf. 1 Thess 1:5; 1 Cor 2:4). Paul possesses the gifts of tongues (1 Cor 14:18; cf. 1 Cor 2:13), prophecy (1 Thess 3:4; 1 Cor 15:51; Rom 11:25ff; Gal 5:21) and healing (2 Cor 12:12; Gal 3:5; Rom 15:19). He is a spiritual man (1 Cor 2:15) who sows spiritual things (1 Cor 9:11; cf. 1 Cor 2:13). Paul's authority is such that it even allows him to add his own directives to the command of the Lord about the permanency of marriage on the basis that he has the Spirit of God (1 Cor 7:40; cf. 1 Cor 7:12ff). Similarly, because the situation encountered on his mission route demands it, he continues to earn his own living, disregarding the Lord's command that the ones preaching the gospel should live by the gospel (1 Cor 9:14ff).[44]

When Paul appeals to revelation as a means of reinforcing his authority, one perceives the innovatory tendencies of his charismatic leadership. This is clearly evident in Galatians. As Rowland points out, in Galatians, Paul does not choose to begin with the questions about circumcision and the law, but with his claim to be an apostle and his account of his visits to Jerusalem. Paul must underline his apostolic authority in order to legitimate his radical teaching. Without a convincing demonstration of his credentials, his arguments from scripture in Gal 3−4, that his interpretation of the gospel is in accord with God's plan of salvation, may be of no consequence.[45]

From Gal 1−2, it is clear that the charismatic basis for Paul's leadership is being seriously questioned in certain sectors. Even at this early stage of development, speculation is taking place (at least in Paul's own mind) about the relationships of the various church leaders to one another. Such factors recall Weber's insights on the routinization of charisma. Weber points to the necessity of the routinization of charisma in order to ensure the survival of innovation. He focuses especially on the interests of the charismatic staff in ensuring its existence and stabilizing its place in the world while faced with the disappearance of the charismatic leader.[46] These interests may underlie the voice of the Jerusalem pillars echoed in Gal 1−2. The question of who possesses authority and how it should be distributed is forcefully expressed here.

Concern to secure a leadership position is also disclosed by Paul himself. As one who did not know the earthly Jesus, as a past persecutor of the church, as the last to whom the resurrected Christ appeared, Paul's authority is particularly precarious. By his own admission, he is the least of the apostles who is not worthy to be called an apostle (1 Cor 15:9).[47] Lacking the personal connection with the earthly Jesus characteristic of the Jerusalem pillars, Paul must appeal directly to heaven to legitimate his mission (Gal 1:1, 11ff).

The confusing passages of Gal 1−2, where Paul makes references to his relationship with the Jerusalem church, provide evidence of the existence of emerging authority structures defining who is eligible for the highest leadership positions. Paul's independent apostolic authority is being questioned. Paul's journeys to Jerusalem are clearly a source of embarrassment for him; he feels pressure to explain the nature of his dealings with the Jerusalem leadership. Despite his strong desire to illustrate the lack of human directives underlying his commission and actions (Gal 1:1, 11ff; 2:2), one gains the impression that he is more reliant on the support of those that were apostles before him than he will admit.[48]

Dependence may also be inferred from the passage dealing with the collection (Gal 2:10; 1 Cor 16:1–4; 2 Cor 8–9; Rom 15:25–9). Paul endeavours to make the communities recognize their continuity with Jerusalem and acknowledge their gratitude.[49] In Gal 2:10 Paul indicates that the collection was part of an agreement made by him with the Jerusalem church which he was eager to fulfil.[50] Rom 15:16 implies that the financial offering was understood by Paul and the pillars as having a place in the eschatological scheme in which the Gentiles would make a pilgrimage to Zion to worship the God of Israel in the last days. Although 'the offering of the Gentiles' refers to the Gentiles themselves, the similar language employed by Paul to speak of both Gentiles and financial offering in Rom 15 illustrates the close connection between the two in Paul's understanding of his mission.[51] As Holmberg suggests, the collection for the Jerusalem saints may have been understood by the authorities there as a duty or even as an acknowledgement of their spiritual supremacy.[52] This is supported especially by Paul's appeal to the church in Rome to pray that the collection will be acceptable to the saints (Rom 15:30ff).

In Paul's dealings with the Jerusalem pillars, we find evidence of competing understandings of how authority should be distributed. This phenomenon may be symptomatic of the situation of a movement in the earliest days of institutionalization. Who is worthy of the title 'apostle'? This question may underlie Paul's response in 2 Cor 10–13. There are apparently other apostles who have been active in the Corinthian church.[53] These intruders do not recognize the principle of non-intervention which Paul values highly (2 Cor 10:14; cf. Rom 15:20). Community members are willing to acknowledge the status of others in a way which angers Paul. From Paul's remarks, we catch glimpses of some of the characteristics of these 'super-apostles'. They are of Jewish extraction (2 Cor 11:22), have impressive physical presence, perhaps bear letters of recommendation (2 Cor 3:1–3) and, above all, demonstrate exceptional rhetorical skill (2 Cor 10:10, 12–18; 11:6) for which they receive financial support from their admirers (2 Cor 11:7ff; 12:14ff).[54] In addition, it is most likely that the Corinthian intruders tell of mystical revelations and perform miracles (2 Cor 12:1ff).[55] In an effort to denigrate the talents of his opponents, Paul ironically demonstrates his own rhetorical skill and reminds the Corinthians that he too possesses many of the same skills and qualities they admire in these others. But by forcing him to respond to such comparisons, the community members have led him to make statements he labels as 'foolishness'. At the heart of his defence is a vision of authority which he perceives as different from his opponents and tragically unrecognizable to the community he fathers. Paul's authority as an apostle is rooted in the fact that his personal strength/weakness echoes the strength/weakness of the crucified/resurrected Christ (1 Cor 13:3ff).

Noting the importance of the appeal to tradition in Jewish teaching, Rowland has rightly pointed to a tension visible in the early church between charismatic authority and tradition.[56] This tension is evident in Paul's conflict with the 'super-apostles'. In 2 Corinthians, Paul must respond to norms institutionalized in the community about an apostle's identity by means of an argument based on his inner conviction concerning his connection with the reality of the crucified and resurrected Messiah. Furthermore, it is plausible that these opponents base their authority on a special connection with Jerusalem (2 Cor 11:22), where a group of leaders claim unique authority to expound the Christian message and to make decisions about the organization of the evangelizing mission in a way that is disapproved of by Paul.[57] The tension between charismatic authority and tradition is also visible in Paul's response to the conflicts recorded in Galatians. In favour of a reliance on tradition, it is readily understandable why some leaders want to ensure that the tested, and indeed biblically sanctioned, means through which the Jews reinforce their identity in a pagan environment are preserved in a community gathered around the crucified and resurrected Messiah.[58]

Although Paul stresses that his claim to apostleship is based on a direct revelation from God in order to legitimate his innovative teaching, he relies substantially on traditions from the Jewish scriptures and on certain elements of Christian teaching (e.g. 1 Cor 11:23ff; 15:3ff) to support his arguments. In fact, Paul's ambivalent relationship with the Jerusalem church may be related to the fact that he has more respect for a claim to possess authoritative traditions than he will admit. In Paul's writings we find the earliest and the most personal struggle in the New Testament concerning the question of how authority should be distributed. The tension between charisma and tradition which one discovers in the text became more acute as time passed, as numbers grew and as the problems of how to organize communities in the absence of the earliest witnesses heightened.

The passages exhibiting an obvious conflict over authority in Paul's writings are a strong indicator of the interplay of emerging beliefs and social structures in the early church. Paul's struggle over independent apostolic authority with respect to Jerusalem shapes, and is shaped by, the nature of his understanding of the one Gospel (Gal 1:1–6). Beliefs about one God over Jews and Gentiles united in one community are articulated in the midst of human tensions: Does Paul run in vain (Gal 2:2; Phil 2:16)? Will the collection be acceptable to the saints (Rom 15:30)? The success of Paul's mission of universal salvation is apparently dependent upon acknowledgement by the saints in Jerusalem. Truth and authority are interrelated.[59] The connection between theological reflection and social setting is also visible in Paul's struggle against his opponents in 2 Cor 10–13. The accusations levelled at Paul concerning his weakness as an apostle trigger the response that the death and resurrection of Jesus are reflected in his own stature. Paul's presence itself is a vehicle of power. Confronting his own weakness and revealing the injury of a betrayed lover (e.g. 2 Cor 11:2; 12:15), Paul makes perhaps his firmest assertion of authority over the Corinthians (2 Cor 13:2ff).

2.2 The freedom of the congregation

It is impossible to study the leadership of the Pauline communities without considering the nature of Paul's relationship with them. The freedom of interpretation and flexibility of decision-making which Paul gives to his audiences is one of the most striking features of the relationship.[60] This phenomenon has been of particular interest to von Campenhausen.[61] He points out that Paul reacts strongly when authority is seen as belonging only to certain individuals within the community (1 Cor 3:5). Congregations are not to be subject to apostles or teachers, but only to Christ. Paul was not crucified for the Corinthians, and the Corinthians are not baptized in the name of Paul (1 Cor 1:13). It may be Paul who plants, Apollos who waters, but it is God who gives growth (1 Cor 3:5–9). The freedom of the congregation is implied by Paul's plea in 1 Cor 11:1, 'Be imitators of me as I am of Christ.' Paul does not give orders. He is even concerned about whether the collection might prove burdensome on the members of his communities (2 Cor 8:8–15; cf. 1 Cor 7:35).[62]

Von Campenhausen notes that Paul appeals to the congregation's own sense of judgement and responsibility, taking their freedom very seriously (e.g. 1 Cor 4:14; 5:1–5; 9:12, 18; 2 Cor 12:13; 1 Thess 2:7). When it becomes necessary to warn, threaten or convict, he does so only with reluctance.[63] Paul is an apostle who attaches little importance to a tidy definition of apostolic authority; he constantly brackets himself with Barnabas, Apollos and various other church members.[64] Von Campenhausen notes:

> Such an attitude fits in with his conception of the apostolate as entirely a matter of proclamation, not of organisation. The Church lives by her awareness of the Christ-message, the Gospel; it is on this, and not on the privileged position of certain individuals whom God has called to his service for this purpose, that all depends. The emphasis on the special character and unique importance of the original apostolic office and testimony for its own sake is completely post-Pauline.[65]

Von Campenhausen relates the freedom of the congregation to the lack of 'fixed offices' in the Pauline communities:

> There is no need for any fixed system with its rules and regulations and prohibitions. Paul's writings do as little as provide such things for the individual congregation as for the Church at large. The community is not viewed or understood as a sociological entity, and the Spirit which governs it does not act within the framework of a particular church order or constitution. 'If you are led by the Spirit, you are not under the Law.' In the Church 'freedom' is a basic controlling principle; for the Spirit of Christ, which is the giver of freedom, urges men on not to independence and self-assertion but to loving service. It is love which is the true organising and unifying force within the Church, and which creates in her a paradoxical form of order diametrically opposed to all natural systems of organisation.[66]

Von Campenhausen's observations about the freedom of the Pauline congregation are valuable. It is true that Paul's perception of the coming Messiah, marking the end of the time when the law shaped the limits of God's people, may be connected with his desire not to burden his congregation with rules.[67] As Rowland indicates, the transference of the allegiance of Paul from pharisaic Judaism to the early Christian group inevitably led to the questioning of patterns of authority which sought to base themselves on tradition and continuity, rather than prophetic inspiration.[68] However, if we connect the apparent freedom which Paul gives to his communities with the realities experienced by a sect in its earliest stage of institutionalization, we will gain a more complete understanding of the social world of these early Christians. Such an enterprise is especially useful when attempting to make sense of the disappearance of this freedom in the development after Paul.

In response to von Campenhausen, it seems unlikely that Paul's concern in 1 Cor 1–3 is first and foremost the prevention of leader-centred authority. Is not Paul's main worry the simple fact that the Corinthians have broken into factions? It is true that the Corinthians appear to have their priorities wrong, but is not the real issue here, and throughout the letter, the problem of unity? Von Campenhausen appears to imply that Paul applies a kind of well-thought-out concept of the relationship of church leaders to their congregations to the divisions in Corinth, when it is more likely that the practical realities of the situation have triggered a response aimed at reducing tension. Theological thought is articulated in relation to a particular social setting.

As von Campenhausen indicates, the independence of the members of his communities was of utmost importance for Paul. In the light of the social setting of his communities, why might this independence have been so crucial? If Paul's mission was essentially to found churches, to become a father to Gentile converts (Rom 15:19–24), would not the limited time available for Paul to spend with individual congregations and the growth of the Gentile mission make independence crucial? In 1 Cor 5–6, Paul is angered because the Corinthians have not acted appropriately in his absence. If Paul is the father of the Corinthian community, he certainly wishes they would begin to act like mature adults! In his dealings with the Corinthians, could Paul have been experiencing the beginnings of the problems of management that would necessitate changes in church order after his death (the routinization of charisma)? This leads us to the question of the nature of the leadership roles in Paul's communities which will be discussed in detail below. However, at this point, we must question the direct link made by von Campenhausen between the principle of freedom in Paul's thought and the lack of established offices in his communities. His comments reflect a common tendency in New Testament interpretation to describe social realities as being the direct result of the application of ideas. How accurate is von Campenhausen's statement that Paul was concerned with proclamation and not organization? Does not the establishment of churches imply a good deal of organization?

If Paul was essentially a 'community organizer' as Gerd Theissen has described him — one whose mission was to travel throughout a district in order to found churches — it is plausible that the ways in which established communities were governing themselves only interested him if conflicts were taking place, as was the case in Corinth.[69] This does not mean that there was no intimate connection between Paul and his churches, but rather that his heart lay first and foremost on the mission route and not in any one community. Paul may have had a hand in the establishment of local leaders, but his involvement in the actual development of leadership structures was probably limited. In any event, leadership roles may have taken different shapes in different communities (compare 1 Cor 12 and Phil 1:1). At this stage of development, institutionalization was an essentially 'open' process — it could proceed in many different directions. The patterns dictating how things should be done were merely beginning to take shape, although Paul played an important role in determining their direction.

Contacts can be seen between the nature of Paul's leadership of communities in these early days of community-building institutionalization and the general lack of system in Paul's thought. This lack of system has been illustrated by E. P. Sanders with respect to Paul's understanding of the relation between the law and new life in Christ.[70] Sanders argues that Paul's detailed and confusing explanations suggest that he is struggling to sort out how the 'new' revelation is related to the 'old' tradition. Paul is faced with a dilemma: he knows that God gave the law, but he also knows that salvation is through faith in Christ and is for all.[71] In general, Paul moves beyond the dilemma by connecting the law with sin and assigning it a place in God's plan of salvation (e.g. Gal 3:22–4; Rom 5:20–1).[72] Despite the fact that the solutions given to the dilemma always turn on the centrality of Christ, contradictory statements remain. Sanders writes:

> ... I have come to the conclusion that there is no single unity which adequately accounts for every statement about the law. Against those who argue in favor of mere inconsistency, however, I would urge that Paul held a limited number of basic convictions which, when applied to different problems, led him to say different things about the law.[73]

Sanders' study underlines the fact that Paul's theological exposition on the role of the law cannot be separated from a struggle for definition in the midst of the realities of a Jewish/Gentile world. Similarly, the freedom which he gives to his congregations cannot be removed from the limits and possibilities faced by a leader who must engage in the process of founding communities throughout Greco-Roman cities. In order to identify connections between exhortations and the social experience of the Apostle, one must exercise a 'socio-logical imagination'.[74] One must imagine what it was like to be a leader in an emerging Greco-Roman sect − what might reasonably be achieved − and make cautious suggestions about the relationship between the recommendations found in the text and social realities. A denial of the theological profundity of such notions as the distri-bution of the variety of gifts in one Spirit and the necessity of all gifts for the welfare of the body (1 Cor 12) is not implied here. Rather, the connection of such teaching with the experience of a movement engaged in the process of community-building institutionalization is being stressed.

2.3 Structural differentiation

Structural differentiation occurs with the passage of time and the growth of a social group. With the multiplication of perspectives comes the problem of maintaining a stable canopy for the entire group. Plurality and conflict call for the continued legitimation of the symbolic universe.[75]

The structural differentiation of the Pauline sect is implied by the impression gained from the text of a fluid and complex network of leaders linking the communities together. Silvanus, Sosthenes and Timothy are each listed at least once as co-authors of a letter with Paul (1 Cor 1:1; 2 Cor 1:1; Phil 1:1; 1 Thess 1:1). Timothy was sent to the Thessalonians on behalf of Paul to give them support (1 Thess 3:2). Both Timothy and Silvanus played a role in the establishment of the Pauline sect in Corinth (2 Cor 1:19). Titus was somehow in-volved in the relations between Paul and the Corinthians, including the arrangements for the collection (2 Cor 2:13; 7:6−16; 8:6, 16−24). Apollos evidently worked independently of Paul, but nevertheless was intimately connected with him as a 'fellow-worker' and brother with a different task within God's work (1 Cor 3:5, 8; 4:6; 16:12). Barnabas shared in Paul's mission to the Gentiles. The events described in Gal 2 underline the independence of Barnabas, but Gal 2 and 1 Cor 9 indi-cate that Paul understood himself as connected to him in relation to the Jerusalem leadership (1 Cor 9:6).[76]

The lack of hard division between local leadership, leadership for the maintenance of connections between the various cells of the whole movement, and leadership for evangelization is related to the social situation in the days of community-building institutionalization: structural differentiation is in its initial stages. For example, Stephanas is clearly involved with the leadership of the Corinthian community at the local level (1 Cor 16:15ff), but he also can travel with Fortunatus and Achaicus to bring news of the community to Paul and perhaps perform some service for him (1 Cor 16:17). The connection between ministry in an individual community and involvement in a broader enterprise is especially visible in Paul's comments about Epaphroditus, Paul's fellow worker and the Philippians' apostle (Phil 2:25–9; 4:18).[77] After serving Paul in prison, this leader is sent back to the community for which he longs. Paul recommends that such people he held in honour (Phil 2:29). The role of Adronicus and his wife Junia, whom Paul greets in Romans, is ambiguous (Rom 16:7).[78] These leaders were converted before Paul and are described by him as notable among the apostles (οἵτινές εἰσιν ἐπίσημοι ἐν τοῖς ἀποστόλοις – although this phrase does not necessarily mean that they themselves were apostles). Adronicus and Junia were possibly a husband/wife missionary team, as perhaps also were Prisca and Aquila. The latter couple provided their household for community gatherings (Rom 16:5; 1 Cor 16:19), and were of service to Paul and to all the churches of the Gentiles (Rom 16:4).

While 1 Cor 16:15ff and Phil 2:25ff explicitly connect individuals with the leadership of specific communities, evidence of the role of leaders in the missionary enterprise or in the service of the whole sect far exceeds the references to ministry devoted specifically to the interests of particular communities. This may be related to Paul's own interest in founding churches and joining them together according to his vision of universal salvation.[79] The inner workings of communities may only have interested him if problems arose, as in the case of the Corinthians. Furthermore, in this period of community-building institutionalization, no clear definitions as yet existed for how communities should be organized.

1 Cor 12:8–10, 28–30 underlines the freedom of charismatic leadership. Yet, although there is no mention of the existence of formal offices in Paul's letters, it is clear that roles have begun to be delineated and their relative importance debated. This process of definition has clearly caused problems in Corinth; the status associated with particular functions has become too important for

community members. Throughout his correspondence, Paul stresses the mutual responsibility of believers baptized by one Spirit into one body (1 Cor 12:13). The emphasis on the unity and equality of those who drink of the same Spirit stands out sharply in a socially stratified society. However, societal realities do impinge on the sect of the Spirit-filled. Certain leadership roles (and probably also certain leaders) have come to be held in higher esteem than others. This is perhaps related to the station of members in the outside society as well as to their demonstration of gifts of the Spirit inside the group. The strength of Paul's theological exposition in 1 Cor 12 is that he is able to give meaning to even the most insignificant task performed in the ekklesia. In a congregation of newly converted people – people who have likely been uprooted by change – Paul's response functions to ease tensions and to secure a meaningful pattern of relationships among members.[80]

Paul's ranking of apostles, prophets, and teachers suggests that some formalization is taking place in his communities (1 Cor 12:28).[81] The importance of the apostles is stressed frequently throughout the text, but particularly in Paul's defence of his own leadership position. It is clear from 1 Cor 14 that Paul holds prophecy in high regard because of its edifying possibilities. The centrality of teaching in the sect is evident from the recommendation made in Gal 6:6 (cf. 1 Thess 5:12). Local leaders are to receive (financial?) support from the congregation.

On the basis of Paul's lists of gifts and functions, it is impossible to make clear distinctions between groups of leaders (1 Cor 12:8–10, 28–30; Rom 12:6–8). Nevertheless, it does appear that there existed a group that was less directly involved with teaching and transmitting divine revelation than with such practical matters as caring for the sick, practising hospitality, taking on administration, and providing their houses for group gatherings. There is no reason to doubt, however, that some individuals performed many different tasks. For example, the ability to provide hospitality for travellers or for the gathering of the community may be related to the estimation of a community member as an important teacher.

1 Cor 12:28 mentions helpers and administrators (ἀντιλήμψεις, κυβερνήσεις). Rom 12:8 tells of the one governing (ὁ προϊστάμενος), while the plural of this expression appears in 1 Thess 5:12. 1 Thess 5:12 also refers to 'the ones labouring among you' (τοὺς κοπιῶντας ἐν ὑμῖν) and 'admonishing you' (νουθετοῦντας ὑμᾶς). 1 Cor 16: 15–16 calls for the subordination of the Corinthians under the

auspices of Stephanas and his household. Rom 16:1 describes Phoebe as a minister of the church (διάκονον τῆς ἐκκλησίας) in Cenchrae (cf. Rom 12:7). Finally, Phil 1:1 includes an address to the saints with the overseers and ministers (σὺν ἐπισκόποις καὶ διακόνοις).[82] Is it possible to discern any connections between these various governing and nurturing services performed and the nature of the organization in Paul's communities?

Gerd Theissen's study of the social stratification of the Corinthian community concludes with the proposition that the interior life of the church was dominated by a minority of comparatively high social status. In light of biographical information found in the text of 1 Corinthians, Theissen sites four criteria characterizing the most influential church members:

1. to be active in a civil or religious office in Corinth;
2. to possess a house;
3. to have served Paul or the church or both; and
4. to be able to make a journey (the last two categories are not sufficient in themselves to point to high social status).[83]

It is reasonable to conclude that Paul may have actively sought to convert the head of a family who was relatively well-to-do and who, most importantly, could provide a house large enough to act as a base for church meetings. That the household served as an important model for the formation of the ekklesia is suggested by the references to communities gathering in individual households (Rom 16:5; 1 Cor 16:19; Philem 2).[84] In 1 Cor 1:14–16, Paul speaks of those he baptized, and among them were Crispus (who is described in Acts 18:8 as the ruler of the synagogue) and his house, the respected Stephanas (1 Cor 16:15) and his house, as well as Gaius who could act as 'host' to Paul and the whole church (Rom 16:23) – he evidently had a large enough house.[85] If Theissen's findings are related to the list of gifts and functions described above, the result is enlightening.[86] Both in 1 Cor 12:28 and in Rom 12:8, a leading function is mentioned after a 'helping' function (1 Cor 12:28 – ἀντιλήμψεις, κυβερνήσεις; Rom 12:8 – ὁ μεταδιδούς, ὁ προϊστάμενος). In addition, the in-direct references to Phoebe's ministerial role in Rom 16:1–2 are not incompatible with the suggestion that she was an independent, relatively well-to-do woman who rendered service to poorer members of the community and travellers in need.

Perhaps the most enlightening passage with regard to the relation-ship between status and leadership in the Pauline communities is

1 Cor 16:15–18. Stephanas and his household are described as being of service to the saints. Paul urges the Corinthians both to be subject to, and to give recognition to, such people (ὑποτάσσησθε τοῖς τοιούτοις – v.16; ἐπιγινώσκετε οὖν τοὺς τοιούτους – v.18). It is obviously impossible to draw conclusions about the establishment of offices in Corinth from this ambiguous passage. However, Paul definitely seems to be granting Stephanas some governing authority and this may be related to his status in the community as a house owner.[87] By the very fact that Paul makes such a statement, he is creating, or at least solidifying, a leadership structure.[88] Furthermore, it is suggestive that Paul links Stephanas with 'every fellow worker and labourer' (παντὶ τῷ συνεργοῦντι καὶ κοπιῶντι – v.16). In 1 Thess 5:12, the notion of 'labouring' (τοὺς κοπιῶντας) appears again with a word suggesting authority to govern (προϊσταμένους). Leadership in the Pauline communities is connected with the performance of certain services.

The phrase 'καὶ παντὶ τῷ συνεργοῦντι καὶ κοπιῶντι' in 1 Cor 16:16 prevents one from arriving too hastily at any conclusions about Paul placing one householder over the whole Corinthian community. However, Paul does appear to be instructing the Corinthians to be subject to, and to recognize, their leaders. Could the Corinthian congregation have exasperated Paul so much, and the problems of management have become so real, that Paul found it necessary to take some measures? His comments in 1 Cor 16:15–18 may simply have acted to legitimate an existing leadership pattern; they may have reinforced the correctness of a pattern in a community prone to conflict. Once again the Corinthian community's dependence on Paul's direction comes to the fore – a dependence which Paul himself recognizes while at the same time calling for independence.

The variety of patterns of leadership disclosed by references in the other letters (Rom 12:6–8; 16:1–2; Phil 1:1; 1 Thess 5:12), points to the fluidity of roles in the Pauline churches and suggests that, in other communities, leadership roles may have developed more smoothly than in Corinth. Paul may have been content to allow leadership to develop in different ways in different communities as long as stability was maintained. It is impossible to determine the function of the overseers and ministers in Phil 1:1. However, the seeming existence of fixed titles implies that the institutionalization of roles is taking place (cf. Rom 16:1–2).

Furthermore, the fact that the same terms could be applied to the formal church offices of bishop (ἐπίοκοπος) and deacon (διάκονος) in later generations indicates a certain continuity between earlier and later stages of development in terms of an ongoing process of institutionalization. Nevertheless, the fluidity of roles and the possibility that leadership developed in varying ways in different communities suggest that, in Paul's communities, institutionalization was open to proceed in many directions.

2.4 Conclusion

The picture of the organization of the Pauline communities as being purely pneumatic, which represents the starting point for much writing on the development of the church, is deficient because it does not fully take into account the relationship between beliefs, social structures and social setting. The leadership structures of Paul's communities are not shaped in a straightforward manner by his theology; the relationship between the structures and the ideas is dialectical. Similarly, Paul is at home in a particular social setting; once again, the relationship between the individual and the social world is dialectical. A purely charismatic ministry and concept of authority based exclusively on Spirit-endowment presents an unrealistic picture of the human society of the Apostle.

Although it is impossible to speak of fixed offices in the Pauline communities, the formalization or institutionalization of roles is progressing rapidly. The fluidity of these roles is related to the 'open' level of institutionalization in the church; leadership patterns are free to develop in different ways in different communities. The existence of authority structures can be detected in Paul's dealings with the Jerusalem church, his fellow workers and his communities. Moreover, leadership in Paul's communities may be related not only to Spirit possession, but also to social status. A dependence/independence relationship between Paul and his congregations is visible in Paul's father-type leadership; he allows for his childen to remain dependent on him while at the same time calling for self-sufficiency. With the death of Paul, it can be expected that the Pauline communities' need for independence will become more crucial and further institutionalization will be required to deal with the problems of leadership. Already, however, Paul's legitimation of leadership patterns contributes to the stabilizing of roles by guiding their development in a certain direction.

3

RITUAL

The following study examines the worship of the Pauline communities. The function of ritual forms in the articulation and the preservation of the sect's identity is considered. The investigation analyses the connection between baptism and the assertion of communal identity. The role of the Lord's supper in the maintenance of boundaries separating the Pauline Christians from outsiders is investigated. The relationship between what is experienced in ritual and the process of symbolization is discussed.

3.1 A ritual context

As in the case of ministry structures, there has been a tendency in New Testament scholarship to contrast Paul's attitude to the 'sacraments' with the later developments of a more highly structured church. For example, both Bultmann and Käsemann have argued that Paul consciously disavowed himself of the idea that the Lord's supper had the magical effects of the 'medicine of immortality' – quoting the well known Ignatian phrase.[89] Similar, though less extreme, comparisons are found in Conzelmann's work:

> Paul shows particularly clearly in 1 Cor 10f that the sacrament does not change a man in a mysterious way, but brings him into the historical fellowship of the faithful in the church; it is not a magical protection, but leads to life in community. Of course, it must be granted that ideas from the mysteries appear in the Hellenistic milieu. In Ignatius, the sacramental food has become the 'φάρμακον ἀθανασίας' (medicine of immortality). In that case, the cult no longer serves to establish 'everyday' faith in the world, but to mark out a holy realm from the world.[90]

In the interest of differentiating Paul's attitude to 'sacraments' from later catholic concepts, these interpreters have played down or ignored the more 'mystical' attributes of ritual forms in the early communities. They have not paid enough attention to the relation between the mysterious experiences of worship and the formation of communities, including the development of beliefs and norms. In this investigation, connections are made between what is experienced by the Pauline Christians through participation in ritual forms and the entry and continued membership within the sect. Moreover, instead of simply drawing a contrast between the earliest and later understandings, Paul's attitude to rituals is related to the social situation of a sect engaged in community-building institutionalization.[91]

The choice of the word 'ritual' rather than 'sacrament' is deliberate; it enables one to include more in the definition than what the later church identified as sacraments. The term 'ritual' is part of the vocabulary of the social scientist; when applied to Pauline communities, it implies comparison with the rites of other social groups. The discipline of cultural anthropology is particularly useful for an investigation of ritual in the ancient world. However, in order for an approach to the study of New Testament texts which incorporates insights from cultural anthropology to be fruitful, one must be open to the discovery of contacts between aspects of the early Christian experience and those from other cultural milieus.[92] The uniqueness of the early Christian movement is not being denied here, nor is religious experience being reduced to the purely magical (with all its negative modern connotations).[93] Rather, what is being advocated is the willingness to locate Pauline communities within a societal context. If, for example, ritual can repeatedly be shown to reinforce the identity of a variety of social groups, one must ask if ritual functions to reinforce the identity of the Pauline sect.

In this study, Clifford Geertz's definition of ritual as 'consecrated behaviour' will be employed.[94] According to Geertz, it is in acting out the roles involved in ritual that the conviction of religious conceptions as truthful, and religious directives as sound, is somehow generated. Religious belief, Geertz argues, involves a prior acceptance of an authority which transforms human experience — experience marked by the problem of meaning.[95] This authority is discovered at some point in the world where one worships — in the midst of ritual — where one accepts the lordship of something other than oneself.[96]

Ritual action is distinctive in that it involves behaviour which is set apart for contact with the sacred. Unlike the detached observer, the participant experiences a simultaneous transformation and ordering of his or her sense of reality. For the participant in a religious performance, the ritual becomes the realization of a particular religious perspective – a model of what is believed and a model for believing it. In these dramas, individuals attain their faith as they portray it.[97]

We come to the Pauline communities, by necessity, as 'detached observers'. We are aware of the incompleteness of our dissection of Pauline statements removed from their ritual context. We cannot share exactly in the experience of these early Christians. Yet, in the text we find evidence suggesting what ritual forms may have looked like. We read statements of belief obviously connected to the enactment of rituals. We know enough to make suggestions about the significance of ritual for the members of the Pauline sect. Speaking of a ritual context enables us to include more than baptism and the Lord's supper. The community gathering, the act of prophecy, the reading of scripture, the singing of a hymn, the gestures of intimacy, the preaching of the gospel and even the reading of a letter are all part of a ritual context. The Pauline correspondence itself grows out of, and is rooted in, what is experienced in the midst of ritual.

Noting both the communicative and performative functions of ritual, Wayne Meeks argues that an appropriate question with which to undertake a study of ritual in the early church is: 'What do they do?'[98] In this investigation, a more motive-oriented question will be added to Meeks' functionalist one: 'Where do the members of the Pauline sect believe the sacred may be encountered?' The most obvious answer to this latter question is in the gathering of the ekklesia. Although it is not certain how often the group met, whether there was a central meeting place for all members in one region or whether a variety of meetings took place for various reasons, it is clear that the Pauline Christians did come together (1 Cor 11:17, 18, 20, 33, 34; 14:23, 26; 1 Cor 5:4).[99] It is in these ritual contexts that individuals discovered for the first time, or renewed their acceptance of, the authority that transformed their experience. The Pauline Christians discovered the Lordship of Christ. 1 Cor 14:23–5 indicates that when the whole church came together, there was a possibility that outsiders witnessing the ritual might become 'converted'. They would acknowledge the presence of authority, proclaiming the lordship of something other than themselves. They would declare that God is truly present among the gathering of the ekklesia (v. 25).

There is not much information in the Pauline correspondence about what actually occurred during the gathering of the ekklesia. In 1 Cor 14:26, Paul writes that when the Corinthians come together each has a hymn, a teaching, a revelation, a tongue, an interpretation. This statement, coupled with the fact that Paul's letters contain citations from scripture, elements of Christian tradition and numerous exhortations, leads to the following suggestions about what was going on. If one were to enter the crowded meeting held in the room of a generous Corinthian householder, one would expect to hear the exposition of scripture and preaching, including statements explaining the significance of the Christ event. One might be reminded of the old life before baptism and be told about the shape one's new life should have now. Difficulties associated with a new life in the Lord might be discussed: Should one remain married to a non-believer? How should one relate to non-believers with whom one was forced to mingle during daily tasks? Revelations of 'words of the Lord' might break the sombre atmosphere. Prophecies about things to come would bring encouragement in the face of difficulties. The cruel treatment of the unbelieving master can be endured in the face of the promise of universal salvation. The jubilant sound of tongues might fill the room with the most elevated prayer.[100]

In 1 Cor 14:13–15, Paul states that one can pray either by 'tongue' or 'rationally'. Tongues suggests, at least to the modern reader, the most novel and spontaneous type of consecrated behaviour in the early church. However, it is important to remember that tongues and other manifestations of the Spirit, such as spontaneous prayer or prophecy, are not completely formless; there exists a framework where the individual carries out actions.[101] In order for ritual either to communicate an experience of the sacred, or to bring the participant in contact with the sacred, a pattern must exist. Evidence of a framework for even the most spontaneous of rituals is found in 1 Cor 14:26–33 where Paul gives explicit instructions concerning the number of glossolalists allowed and the time when they should be permitted to speak.[102] Paul calls for order and control; there is a time for tongues, a time for revelation, a time for interpretation, a time for prophecy. All things should be done for edification, in an orderly fashion, not with confusion, but with peace.

As a modern onlooker at the gathering in the crowded room of the generous Corinthian, one might understand the ritual behaviour to be a mixture of the familiar and the novel – a blend of the spontaneous and the customary.[103] The patterns which determine the structure of ritual have not as yet become very solidified; the institutionalization of ritual behaviour is free to develop in various directions. However, even at this early stage, Paul's concern for decency and order is beginning to guide institutionalization in one particular direction. As time passes and patterns become more and more established, we can expect that there will be less room for the more spontaneous rituals. At any rate, from the time of the earliest church, the novel must be interpreted in terms of the familiar, the spontaneous in terms of the customary.

The ritual of the Pauline Christians is at the heart of the process of community-building; it acts to stimulate group solidarity.[104] Members of the Pauline sect become members and remain members by sharing patterns of symbolic action. In Geertz's language, rituals both induce an ethos and define a world view.[105] This is perhaps related to what Paul points to as the most important function of consecrated behaviour, upbuilding (οἰκοδομή). Paul evidently prefers the clear speech of prophecy to glossolalia; the test is whether words build up the assembly (1 Cor 14:1ff). Hymns, teachings, revelations, interpretations and even tongues are for upbuilding; they are vehicles for teaching and admonition (1 Cor 14:26). Faced with newly formed communities, Paul must deal with the problem of education. By participating in upbuilding rituals, the sect's knowledge will grow. This knowledge includes attitudes and beliefs which are appropriate for those who are now in Christ. When Paul appeals to members of the sect to admonish or exhort each other, he is calling for the participation in certain ritual actions. Instruction and consolation appear to be especially expected of those who prophesy (1 Cor 14:3, 19). 1 Thess 5:12 suggests that local leadership is linked to the practice of admonishing. Whether one is giving this special instruction or receiving it, one is participating in ritual. Ritual involves learning, and learning shapes the way one will behave in the furture. Geertz writes: 'Even within the same society, what one ''learns'' about the essential pattern of life from a sorcery rite and from a commensual meal will have rather diverse effects on social and psychological functioning.'[106]

3.2 Baptism: purification and sect formation

The 'learning' function of ritual is especially visible in the Pauline sect's practice of baptism. Baptism was probably only possible after one had acknowledged a specific authority (the Lordship of Christ) and had acquired a certain knowledge; it might be described as a celebration of learning. Because baptism was connected with entrance into the sect, it provides a good example of how ritual functioned in sect formation.

Gal 4:6 and Rom 8:15 are most likely rooted in a baptismal setting. The newly baptized person may have come out of the water crying 'Abba!' (Father!). The Spirit was understood as speaking through the individual. He or she was being adopted as God's child.[107] Baptism appears to be recalled in the Pauline communities as a fundamental experience of transformation. Moreover, Paul's instructions indicate that this experience is understood as having implications for community life. In Rom 8:16−18 Paul provides encouragement in the face of suffering by arguing that being children of God means being heirs of God. The members of the community are joint heirs with Christ. They suffer with him in order that they may be glorified with him (cf. Gal 4:6−7). In Rom 6:2ff Paul articulates the implications of having been buried with Christ by baptism into his death. Community members have died to sin (v. 2); they should not yield their members to sin as instruments of unrighteousness (v. 13). In Gal 3:26−8 baptism is recalled by Paul in relation to his argument that circumcision should not be a requirement for the entry of Gentile converts into the community. Baptism into Christ is described as putting on Christ (v. 27). Unity in Christ is associated with transformation of relations between groups (v. 28). With respect to the relations between Gentiles and Jews in Christ, the primary concern underlying the argument of Galatians, Paul views this unity in Christ to have revolutionizing consequences in the social realm.

The close connection between the Christ event and the experience of baptism implied in the language about being buried with Christ and adopted as a joint-heir underlines the significance of the 'mystical' baptismal experience in the Pauline sect. The language about the abolition of differences of Gal 3:28 may provide some insight into the breaking down of barriers that was experienced during the rite. It is important, however, to realize that ambiguity surrounds the transition from participation in a formative entrance rite to life in a group of people whose lives have been shaped by a similar experience of the sacred. To come out of the water crying 'Jesus is Lord!' (cf. Rom 10:9; Phil 2:11) and to experience a divine adoption and unity with one's fellow initiates in Christ is a transforming experience which must come to an end, but which demands articulation with respect to everyday reality.[108] Individuals who partake in the ritual of baptism form community with fellow children of God. There is need for group cohesion.

Adoption as a child of God necessarily means separation from those who are not the same kind of children. Baptism functions as a cleansing rite; a water bath symbolizes a transition from a 'dirty' world into a 'clean' sect. The members of the Pauline sect can be distinguished from those in the outside world because they have been cleansed and sanctified; they have been justified in the name of Jesus Christ and in the Spirit of God (1 Cor 6:11). This washing is connected with the image of dying and rising with Christ (Rom 6:3–11). The participation in a symbolic death and resurrection even has a purifying effect on the dark world of the dead, as the peculiar practice of being baptized on behalf of the dead implies (1 Cor 15:29).[109] The drama is heightened by the taking off and putting on of clothes, as is suggested by the description of putting on Christ (Gal 3:26–7).[110] Having undergone baptism, the participant leaves a world inhabited by demonic powers and enters the domain of a new universe.

In his book *The New Testament World*, Bruce Malina employs insights from cultural anthropology in his discussion on Christian purity arrangements. He defines purity in terms of the boundaries separating inside from outside that are necessary in order to perceive 'set-apartness'.[111] Malina describes the sacred as that which is set apart. The Pauline Christians might be seen as drawing a line around where they expect the sacred to be found. The sect — sometimes perceived as the body of Christ — becomes sacred space. This space must be kept pure, which means that categorization is necessary. The construction of a classification system implies that certain things will be kept on the outside.[112]

The centrality of interaction in Christ for determining purity in the Pauline communities is suggested by the use of temple language to describe the sacred space of the sect.[113] The group itself is called the 'temple of God' (1 Cor 3:16–17; 2 Cor 6:16) or the 'temple of the Holy Spirit' (1 Cor 6:19). Sacrifice also takes on a new meaning in the sect; it refers specifically to Christ and the actions of individuals in Christ (e.g. 1 Thess 5:19–24; Rom 12:1; 15:16; 1 Cor 5:7).[114]

The zone of interaction between existence in Christ and the world of Jews and Gentiles is somewhat problematic for group members; the means of preserving the purity of the group is uncertain. This ambiguity is especially visible in Galatians where the issue of how to deal with the entrance of Gentiles into the community comes to the fore. How much heed should be given to previous biblical injunctions?

With respect to food, Paul is persuaded that nothing is unclean of itself (Rom 14:14; cf. Gal 2:11ff). Yet, leaving room for much uncertainty, Paul instructs members that they should weigh individual situations accordingly. In his instructions to the Corinthians, Paul reveals his concern for the unity of the community and for relations with outsiders (perhaps reflecting his hope that they too might be won for Christ, cf. 1 Cor 10:32ff). Paul states that food, which may or may not have been offered to idols, is intrinsically harmless (1 Cor 10:25f). This statement, however, receives important qualifications. On the one hand, no unnecessary offence should be given to outsiders (1 Cor 10:24–7, 32). On the other hand, perceptions of members who believe in divisions between clean and unclean must be given primary consideration (1 Cor 8:7–13; 1 Cor 10:28–30). Paul's concern for harmony in the community that comes from respecting individual opinions is even more strongly expressed in Romans (Rom 14:1–6, 13–15, 19–21). His desire to promote unity is especially visible in his statement that eating, abstaining, observing days and esteeming all days the same, are all good when they are done for the honour of the Lord (Rom 14:5–9; cf. Gal 4:10).

A concern for purity is also visible in 1 Cor 5–6 where the question of how to deal with transgression within the group arises. Paul instructs the Corinthians to cleanse out the old leaven so that they might be a new lump (1 Cor 5:7). The wicked person whose immorality corrupts the purity of the sect should be driven away (1 Cor 5:13). It is not the immorality of the outside world that is in danger of polluting the body, but the immorality that has somehow been allowed to penetrate the sacred space (1 Cor 5:9–13). Paul forbids the community members to eat with the believer who is guilty of immorality (1 Cor 5:11), while apparently legitimating eating with unbelievers, irrespective of their life-styles (1 Cor 10:27). The believer who is guilty of immorality can corrupt the group in a way that is impossible for the non-believer, for the believer alone is subject to the requirements that membership in the church entails.[115] The importance of the disputes being settled within the boundaries of the pure sect and according to the judgements of those on the inside is evident in Paul's angry response to the fact that members have gone to the courts of unbelievers (1 Cor 6:1–11). Once again, one gains the impression that ambiguity surrounds the dealings of the Pauline sect with the outside world.

A discussion of Christian purity arrangements sheds light on the connections between ritual experience and the separation of the

Pauline sect from the outside world. The individual who is initiated into the community through the ritual of baptism has entered sacred space. This entry, however, leads to new questions: How are the members of the Pauline sect to interpret what they have experienced in ritual in relation to life in the everyday world? How are the boundaries surrounding the community to be maintained?

Perhaps the most obvious aspect of the language used to denote baptism by Paul is that it involves some kind of change. Geertz observes:

> Having ritually 'lept' (the image is perhaps a bit too athletic for the actual facts — 'slipped' might be more accurate) into the framework of meaning which religious conceptions define and, the ritual ended, returned again to the common-sense world, a man is — unless, as sometimes happens, the experience fails to register — changed.[116]

Having ritually 'lept' from baptism to the everyday world, the Pauline sectarian sees the everyday world as part of a wider order-giving reality — the symbolic universe. However, in order for the new convert to maintain the boundaries between the new universe and everything outside, it will be necessary for the individual to renew his or her own experience of the sacred. Baptism marks the beginning — but only the beginning — of an experience that must be nurtured and rekindled if membership in the sect is to continue.

3.3 The Lord's supper: conviviality and continuance

While baptism enables the individual to be initiated within the community, the ritual of the Lord's supper integrates the member into the community time and time again. Like the initiatory rite, the memorial rite retells the story of the death and resurrection of Jesus and enables the believer to become personally identified with the events by participating in consecrated behaviour.[117] In Paul's letters there are only two explicit references to the Lord's supper: 1 Cor 11:17–34; 10:14–22. It is clear from these passages that the Lord's supper is a locus for the articulation of beliefs. The traditional language surrounding the events of Jesus, the mention of a new covenant, the commemorative phrase 'this is my body which is for you', and the eschatological phrase 'until he comes' underline the connection between the participation in this common meal and the process of self-definition (1 Cor 11:23–6).[118] Traditional forms and language act as a means of reinforcing the central beliefs of community members, but also as a means of regenerating the experience of the sacred that called the community into being.

Related to the fact that the Lord's supper enhances the internal coherence of the Pauline sect, is its function in the maintenance of purity boundaries. This is especially visible in the contrast drawn by Paul between the Lord's supper and idolatrous pagan sacrifices (1 Cor 10.14–22). The activity of the Pauline sect is distinguished from that of other cultic associations. One cannot partake of the table of the Lord and of the table of demons.[119]

Although the Lord's supper generates unity in the sect, it can also become a subject of controversy. Paul cites the eucharistic traditions of 1 Cor 11:23–6 in order to address the conflicts that have arisen in the Corinthian congregation. In his analysis of 1 Cor 11:17–34, Gerd Theissen has argued that the divisions in the group (11:18) are primarily between the rich and the poor.[120] He suggests that the relatively well-to-do host of the gathering, in keeping with the practices of the day, provided greater quantities of food and better quality food for those of higher status.[121] The behaviour of the wealthier Christians during the group gathering elicited criticism. According to Theissen, Paul suggests a compromise where the wealthier are to have their private meals at home, while at the Lord's supper everyone should begin to eat together, sharing bread and wine equally (1 Cor 11:33–4).[122]

In the conflict over the Lord's supper more evidence is discovered for the lack of clarity surrounding the relationship between the community and the outside world. Social stratification is a real characteristic of the social world in which the Corinthians live. But how is this situation to be reconciled with the unity that is experienced in Christ? Paul believes that the divisions that have occurred in Corinth contradict the deepest meaning of the ritual of the Lord's supper. In 1 Cor 10:16–17 Paul speaks of the bread and wine in terms of the community's identification with the body and blood of Christ and its unity as a group gathered around Christ.[123] Such an association recalls the unifying baptismal experience where the divisions of role and status are replaced by a communion in Christ (Gal 3:26–8).[124] Like baptism, the Lord's supper involves activity which is set apart for contact with the sacred. Behaviour during the rite can act as a basis for future judgement.[125] Corruption can be dangerous. Sickness and death can be blamed on such violations (1 Cor 11:27–32).

There is a peculiar tension between what appears to have been experienced in ritual in the Pauline communities and the position of the sect within its Greco-Roman environment. The social realities of the everyday world could be transcended and given new interpretation in sacred dramas. At the same time, however, what was experienced could not be disconnected from the realities of the society of the day: 'There is neither slave nor free' is a more cogent statement in first-century Galatia than in the advanced societies of today. Moreover, the social consequences of what was experienced during ritual performances had to be interpreted in terms of existing values and beliefs. Having 'ritually slipped' from the gathering for the Lord's supper to the crowded streets lined with households, how should one relate to the fellow sectarian of a different sex and/or social status?

3.4 Conclusion

It is useful to envision the worship of Pauline communities in terms of a ritual context encompassing many different forms of consecrated behaviour. As a means of bringing individuals in contact with the sacred for the first time or of renewing crucial experiences, as a means of reinforcing existing beliefs and as a powerful educational medium, ritual plays a central role in building up the ekklesia. Ritual in the Pauline sect is a combination of the spontaneous and the customary. However, even the most spontaneous sacred acts are given a framework within the ritual context. Moreover, as institutionalization progresses and the body of tradition increases, we can expect that there will be less room for spontaneous acts in the Pauline communities.

Baptism and the Lord's supper play an important role in the consolidation and continued existence of the Pauline sect. The definition of a world view and ethos is clearly related to what is experienced in these rituals. In addition, both baptism and the Lord's supper function in the drawing and maintaining of boundaries separating the Pauline sect from the outside world, hence enabling it to remain 'pure'. The ritual experiences of the Pauline sect cannot be disconnected from the realities of Greco-Roman society. Moreover, the social consequences of the experience, which must be articulated with a view to existing social structures, are often ambiguous.

4

BELIEF

The social life of the Pauline sect cannot adequately be explained by describing a simple shaping of societal development by doctrines. Although it is true that doctrines influence social reality, it is also clear that social experience affects the construction of doctrines. The tensions between the group and those on the outside, the conflict between leaders over the distribution of authority, and the mystical experiences in ritual are all connected to the process of symbolization. In this section specific attention will be given to the nature of beliefs in the Pauline sect. Correlations will be drawn between beliefs and the social contexts where they are articulated.

4.1 Sect, society and symbolic universe

Whether one speaks of a religious system, a symbolic universe or an ideology, it is evident that the Pauline communities are in possession of such a body of sacred symbols.[126] Shils argues that in contrast to other patterns of beliefs, ideologies are usually integrated around one or a few pre-eminent symbols.[127] In the case of the Pauline communities, it is the symbol of the crucified and resurrected Messiah that stands out most sharply. This symbol is an example of what Mary Douglas has described as a 'condensed symbol'; it encompasses a wide range of references.[128] The symbol of the crucified and resurrected Messiah encompasses a story and calls for a certain life-style; it stands at the centre of the effort to build communities.

The importance of the symbol of the crucified and resurrected Messiah for the Pauline sect can be seen in the fact that it is the belief that salvation is now in Christ which determines entrance into the communities.[129] In drawing a contrast between faith in Christ and works of the law, Paul distinguishes between the group where salvation is to be found now and the group where it is not to be found.[130] Implicit in Paul's language is the notion of the movement from a condemned state to the body of those who will be saved (Rom 5:8–10, 18, 19; 6:4, 7; 7:4–6; 8:1f; 1 Cor 6:9–11; Gal 2:16; 3:2, 7, 14, 21, 26; Phil 3:6–11).[131] Paul is interested in showing that this transfer does not depend on works of the law. He argues that all were under sin (Gentiles and Jews), but thanks to God's action in Christ, all can be saved. To get into the group of those who will be saved requires faith in Christ; to stay in the group requires behaviour appropriate for one who is found in Christ.[132]

It is evident that social experience shapes doctrine in the Pauline sect. Paul's faith/works contrast cannot be understood apart from the actual situation faced by him in his Jewish/Gentile world. However, the influence of doctrine on social reality is also apparent throughout the Pauline correspondence. Paul's understanding of how God has acted in Christ shapes the kind of missionary enterprise he undertakes, the arguments he has with those who do not share his particular views, and the means through which he organizes his communities. His discussion concerning the law must be understood in terms of the situation faced by the Jewish leader of a sect unsure of its relation to Judaism. Paul must attempt to illustrate why faith is only in Christ in terms of the symbols that are available to him. With numerous references to Jewish scripture, Paul illustrates that both Gentiles and Jews have a place in God's plan of salvation; Abraham is the father of all who believe (Rom 4:16–25). A novel understanding is interpreted in terms of existing beliefs within a specific cultural context.[133]

The symbolic universe of the Pauline sect is constructed in relation to the beliefs and norms of Greco-Roman society. The activity of the group in setting itself apart is of crucial significance for the formation of the universe, as the connection between faith in Christ and entrance into a community suggests. As it develops, however, the symbolic universe also acts back on its producers to reinforce the identity of the social group and to encourage its cohesion. Nowhere is this more clearly visible than in the language of incorporation found in the Pauline writings.[134] The language of incorporation articulates the 'mystical' experience of salvation at the centre of the effort to build communities, while also functioning to integrate members in the body of those who are being saved.

The expression 'ἐν Χριστῷ' is somewhat ambiguous in the text. The use of the preposition 'ἐν' usually indicates the locative sense: Where is salvation to be found 'ἐν Χριστῷ'? However, the dative case (although usually not accompanied by 'ἐν') can also indicate an instrumental use: How is salvation to be attained 'ἐν Χριστῷ'? In this sense the expression is best translated as 'through Christ' or 'by Christ'. If one looks at the passages where the expression 'ἐν Χριστῷ' occurs (e.g. Phil 3:3, 9; Rom 6:23; 8:1, 2; 12:5; 16:3; 1 Cor 1:4; 3:1; 2 Cor 5:17; ἐν κυρίῳ – Rom 16:2; 1 Cor 1:31), it seems that at some points it is best to interpret the expression in terms of the locative use of 'ἐν' (e.g. Phil 3:9), while at others the dative of instrument is more appropriate (e.g. 1 Cor 1:4). Most often, however, both interpretations seem to fit. If salvation is gained through attachment to the Messiah, is it not to be found in a community which is centred around the Messiah? It seems that when Paul uses 'ἐν Χριστῷ' he means both that salvation is attained through attachment to the Messiah – participation in his death and resurrection – and that salvation is to be found in the community of believers which is centred around Christ. The participation in the Christ event is central for Paul, but the individual must become part of a community of others rooted in the same experience. The expression 'ἐν Χριστῷ' reinforces the boundaries separating the body of those who will be saved from those on the outside; it connects the revelation of Christ with the existence of a community of believers.

The link between the Christ event and the life of the community is also evident in Paul's use of the symbol of the body of Christ. Discussion concerning the significance of this expression has often surrounded the question of whether it is mainly a metaphor for the community, or whether it somehow refers to the actual body of Christ.[135] In 1 Cor 6:15–20 (cf. Rom 7:4), Paul speaks of individuals' bodies being joined to Christ in the most intimate manner possible – as members of his body. 1 Cor 12:12–27 and Rom 12:5, however, depict the body of Christ as the community of believers that is centred around Christ. In the few passages where 'σῶμα' is linked with the Lord's supper it is particularly difficult to determine whether Paul is emphasizing the community of believers or attachment to the Messiah, a fact which underlines the connection of both these aspects with the ritual context of the Pauline correspondence (1 Cor 10:16–17; 1 Cor 11:27–9). Contact with the sacred is experienced in imitation of, in identification with, and in incorporation into, Christ. This Christocentric experience carries implications for the community of believers. Membership in the body requires harmonious relations among members (1 Cor 12; Rom 12:4ff). When Paul employs the symbol of the body of Christ, he does more than use a metaphor for community; his language is rooted in an identification with the death and resurrection of Christ and a mission to build a community gathered around Christ. Once again, attachment to the Messiah and incorporation into a community where members share that attachment go hand in hand.

The phrase 'ἐν Χριστῷ' and the concept of the body of Christ functioned both to encourage unity in the Pauline communities and to delimit firmly the boundaries separating them from the outside society. Adopting the Jewish position on the oneness of God completely, the Pauline sect distinguished itself from the pagan world of many gods (1 Thess 1:9; 4:5; 1 Cor 8:4–6; 2 Cor 4:4; Gal 4:8, 9). However, the Pauline sect appears to have adopted a distinctive means of separating itself from its pagan environment. The method of incorporation of Gentiles advocated by Paul may be distinguished from the means by which proselytes became attached to Judaism and even from the way other early church leaders felt it should be done. For Paul, faith in Christ determined entry; Gentiles and Jews were to come into one body gathered around Christ. Rituals commemorating the death and resurrection of Jesus and incorporating believers into his body were perhaps replacing circumcision and other legal observances as boundary markers.[136] Within the process of separation from those on the outside undertaken by the Pauline sect, however, stands a vision of unity. Rom 9–11 makes it clear that the separation from Jews is a present necessity, but does not truly represent the way things should be or, in fact, will be. God's purpose for the world includes a final unification of Gentiles and Jews. Paul's 'all-language' brings one to the centre of the vision of universal salvation of the Pauline sect. Paul and his fellow workers endeavoured to plant tiny cells throughout the Greco-Roman cities – communal representatives of a unified and restored humanity.[137] Yet, ironically, the Pauline movement was marked by a tension between separation from the world and mission to save the world; it exhibited a sectarian response to the world which is aptly described as 'conversionist'.

4.2 The symbol of the crucified and resurrected Messiah

Paul appeals to the significance of the Christ event to support his understanding of the union of Gentiles and Jews in one community. It is indeed a considerable 'theological leap' from redemption in Christ Jesus to Paul's position on the matter. The opposition to which Paul responds in Galatians prevents one from concluding that his views were uniformly held.[138] Nevertheless, the fact that Paul wrote letters to communities making his ideas clear implies that his authority was respected in some sectors. Furthermore, the impression of a team of fellow workers gained from his letters suggests a certain common understanding of how communities should be organized and who should be allowed to come in. It seems safe to assume that Paul's understanding of the unity of Gentiles and Jews was shared by at least some of the members of his communities.[139]

It is likely that members of Paul's communities shared much of his understanding of the implications of the Christ event. They sought to live as members of a group where there was no distinction between Jews and Gentiles. If one were to ask where such beliefs were promulgated and reinforced, an obvious place to look would be the ritual context of communal life. The belief that there is neither Gentile nor Jew may be closely related to what is experienced in baptism (Gal 3:26–9; 1 Cor 12:13). It is not inconceivable that revelations of unity took place during the communal gatherings. When Paul addresses the problem of division in Corinth by speaking in terms of a body characterized by various gifts, he apparently believes that his stressing that the gifts are the manifestations of the same spirit will be of special significance for the Corinthians. Perhaps he is reminding them of something he is sure will convey the need for harmony (1 Cor 12). For Paul, the Lord's supper also appears to have had a unifying significance (1 Cor 10:17). The ritual context would provide an opportunity for the vision of unity to grow and solidify.

Throughout his correspondence, Paul stresses the identification of believers with Christ. The promise that lies at the end of life in imitation of Christ − life characterized by suffering − is that God who raised the Lord Jesus will also raise the Pauline Christians (2 Cor 1:3–7; 4:14; Rom 6:5; 8:1–11). Considering the few details of the life of Jesus in the text, it is somewhat surprising that the Christians are called to model their behaviour after him. It is here that Geertz's remarks about the confrontation and mutual reinforcement of ethos and world view in ritual are especially enlightening.[140] Participation in baptism, the Lord's supper and the various activities characteristic of the gathering of the community results in the articulation of meaning of the Christ event. Even if few details of the actual life of Jesus are known, the story of the death and resurrection is repeated, re-enacted and applied to lives of community members. The world view condensed in the symbol of the crucified and resurrected Messiah is attached to an ethos which determines life-style in the community. As Meeks points out, in the Pauline paraenesis, Christ's voluntary submission to death becomes a model for other-regarding actions and attitudes (Rom 15:1–3, 7; Gal 6:2; 2 Cor 8:9).[141] In Phil 2:1–11, Paul appeals for unity and love, and warns against selfishness by describing the whole mythic pattern of the Christ event.

The members of the Pauline sect are persuaded that God, having raised Jesus, will also raise them (2 Cor 4:14). However, the conciliatory tone of 1 Thess 4:13–18 shows that the resurrection of those who have already died is by no means self-evident.[142] The Thessalonian community, found in the early days of institutionalization, has not as yet worked out the problem of those who have died before the parousia. That ambiguity surrounds the symbol of the crucified and resurrected Christ is also suggested by 1 Cor 15. The Corinthians appear to have understood their own resurrection as some kind of transcendence of the ordinary world which they already experience. In the early stages of development, emerging symbols are open to various interpretations.[143] In Thessalonica and in Corinth, the fluidity of the symbolic universe appears to have caused problems for Paul. His comments serve to guide the institutionalization of beliefs in a particular direction.

4.3 Christian existence: social existence in a universe of meaning

Despite the overall pattern of weakness to glory in Paul's letters (e.g. Rom 8:18; Phil 1:28–9), existence in the sect appears to have a paradoxical quality.[144] Rom 5–8 provides valuable insights into Paul's understanding of the character of Christian existence. In this section, Paul contrasts new life in the Spirit with old life based on Torah (which is characterized by sin and death) in such a way that it provides valuable examples of how symbols function in the Pauline sect.

If one analyses the verbs found in Rom 5:1–11, one is struck by the balance of present and future tenses (cf. Rom 5:9, 10). Paul speaks of the present life of the believer as being rooted in a salvation occurrence that has already happened and one that is yet to come. The paradox of Christian existence is expressed in Rom 5:3–4. Here a chain of words associated with suffering culminates in the word 'hope' ($\dot{\epsilon}\lambda\pi\dot{\iota}\delta\alpha$). In Rom 5:2 Paul speaks of a rejoicing in the hope of the glory of God. It is because of this hope that rejoicing can take place in afflictions. What the promise of the glory of God is all about is made clear by Rom 8. The salvation of community members is guaranteed by the fact that they have the Spirit (e.g. Rom 8:9, 11, 23; cf. 5:5). The believers have received a spirit of adoption by which they cry, 'Abba!' (Rom 8:15). As children of God and joint heirs with Christ, believers may suffer with him in order that they may be glorified with him (Rom 8:16–17). But, the future holds more. The suffering of the present is not worth considering in light of what is to come (Rom 8:18). All of creation will some day be freed from its 'fleshly' bondage and be brought in union with God as his children (Rom 8:21). The members of the Pauline sect eagerly, but painfully, await their adoption and the redemption of their bodies (Rom 8:22–3).

The examples from Rom 5, 8 illustrate the connection between hope and suffering in the Pauline sect. Paul makes a remarkable identification between the suffering and resurrection of Christ and the situation of the Pauline sect who share in that reality (e.g. Rom 8:17). His comments bring to mind his conception of apostleship. Weakness becomes an authentic sign of an apostle who withstands suffering in imitation of Christ (2 Cor 12:9–10). However, weakness by worldly standards does not preclude the power that comes from identification with Christ. In his dealings with the Corinthians, the resurrected Christ speaks through him by the power of God (2 Cor 13:3–4).

The Pauline Christians are not told to avoid suffering. Rather, suffering becomes an expression of the imitation of Christ (e.g. Phil 1:29).[145] The symbol of the crucified and resurrected Messiah continuously reminds them of the realities of suffering, while at the same time giving meaning to their suffering – hope. The members of the sect are encouraged to have patience – to endure (Rom 5:3; 8:25). But what were they suffering from? There is no evidence for 'pre-conversion' suffering in the Pauline text. Rom 7 should not be considered as an autobiographical account of the frustration experienced by Paul as a practising Jew, but rather as a description of the pre-Christian or non-Christian life as seen from the perspective of faith.[146] Paul hardly seems to have been troubled by 'existential anxiety' during his life as a Pharisee (Phil 3:4–7). It was during his life as a Christian that suffering appears to have become problematic for Paul. Physical illness, loss of status, persecutions, whipping, imprisonments, hunger, the hazards of travel and the trickery of false brethren are all endured (e.g. 2 Cor 4:16–18; 5:1ff; 6:4–5; 7:5; 11:23–33; 12:10; Phil 1:7, 12–18; 3:7–8). But why would a Pharisee who was blameless in the law be willing to suffer such loss? Paul's reply is consistently the same – for the sake of Christ (Phil 3: 7–9).

As to the nature of the suffering undergone by the Pauline communities, there are no precise details. Although some persecution is suggested by 1 Thess 2:14–16, no ongoing systematic persecution of members is supported by the text. The suffering may have had to do largely with travelling lonely trade routes, having unjust masters, experiencing sickness or witnessing death. All suffering in the Pauline sect is given meaning by the symbol of the crucified and resurrected Messiah. If the Pauline Christians can share in Christ's sufferings and become like him in death, they will be joined with him in resurrection.

The connection between suffering and hope leads to a brief consideration of another central aspect of the Pauline symbols system. The notion of a swiftly coming day of judgement, manifesting both God's anger against sin and salvation brought to earth plays a prominent role in Paul's letters (e.g. 1 Thess 1:9).[147] The members of the Pauline communities believe that God acted to raise Christ from the dead and that Christ will soon come again in order to vindicate the elect (e.g. 1 Thess 4:15; Phil 3:20–1). The eschatological world view is connected to a certain ethos in the Pauline sect. The list of admonitions in 1 Cor 10:7ff terminates with the identification of the Corinthians as those 'upon whom the end of the age has come' (1 Cor 10:11). Life in the Spirit is characteristic of this eschatological time (Rom 8:23; 2 Cor 1:22). Having been delivered from 'the present evil age' (Gal 1:4; cf. 1 Cor 2:6ff), the members of the sect are to live in a manner appropriate to their transference (Rom 12:2).

Meeks' discussion of the eschatological language in the Pauline correspondence illustrates both the many dimensions of such language and the variety of applications in the text to the practical concerns of community life. In 1 Thessalonians, the problem of suffering (2:14– 16; 3:2–4), coupled with the Thessalonians' fear that those who have died prematurely will not share in the glory promised to those who await God's son from heaven (4:13ff), leads Paul to give a vivid depiction of the coming of the Lord (4:13–5:11).[148] In Galatians the emphasis falls on the present fulfilment of eschatological hopes. Paul must justify his innovative teaching; he legitimates his position by appealing to a revelation of Jesus Christ 'δι' ἀποκαλύψεως 'Ιησοῦ Χριστοῦ' (Gal 1:12, 16).[149] In contrast, Meeks points out that in 1 Corinthians future eschatological language is used by Paul in connection with his attempt to restrain innovation and counsel stability and order (e.g. 1 Cor 4:5; 5:5; 6:2, 3, 9; 7:26–31; 15:24;

15:51ff). Despite his own defence of the radical change in the relation between Gentiles and Jews in the light of the new age of the Messiah, Paul disapproves of innovation which he understands as threatening to the stability of community life.[150]

Without turning the Pauline Christians into modern introspective beings, it is at least possible that before their 'conversions', their social experience was leading them to question their ability to understand the world.[151] For example, if one were a travelling merchant or artisan, having been deprived of a tightly-knit household community, one might well call into question the general order of society.[152] Bryan Wilson has described the social circumstances where conversionist sects appear to arise most readily in a manner that is suggestive for understanding the development of the Pauline movement:

> ... individuals may find need of spiritual and social accommodation in an alien social context. Likeness of circumstance – as with slaves, displaced people, foreigners – may be sufficient to overcome differences of cultural background and ethnicity in the welding of new religiously-based communities. Such may have been the conditions of the early spread of Christianity. This, then, is a socially enforced process of individuation of social circumstance: it may not go deep into human consciousness, but it is a situation in which the individual is separated from his home culture and must make some new accommodation for himself. The obvious accommodation is to reunite himself with a group – a group which cannot be a natural grouping, but must be one which capitalizes the commonality of circumstance of detached individuals and which draws them into a new synthetic community of love.[153]

It is not difficult to understand why a merchant or artisan, whose life was characterized by travel from city to city, would welcome membership into the small groups of people of like circumstances which offered the possibility of being integrated into a world-wide community of love. Moreover, such an individual may have been particularly receptive to symbols of a world on the verge of transformation, while at the same time playing a role in the articulation of such symbols. This is, however, at best, reasonable conjecture. It is impossible to draw a simple correlation between social experience and symbolization. However, some relation is suggested by the apparent reversal of standards of power and success in the sect.[154] God's action in raising Jesus from the dead has apparently had the effect of turning existing structures upside down. The proclamation of the Gospel contradicts expectation based either on Jewish tradition or Gentile reason (1 Cor 1:18–2:12). The cross might be folly to those who are perishing, but to those who are being saved, it is the power of God (1 Cor 1:18). God has made foolish the wisdom of the world (1 Cor 1:20). The rulers of this age have not understood the secret wisdom of God (1 Cor 2:6–7).

In Rom 5:12–21; 6; 7, Paul discusses the human plight without Christ. The purpose of the law and its relation to flesh, sin and death are considered. At first glance, these passages might appear to be the most revealing for drawing connections between social experience and beliefs. However, for Paul, it seems that the conviction of a universal solution preceded the conviction of a universal plight.[155] Paul did not begin with an analysis of the nature of the individual's sinful state.[156] Rather, he made a connection between the law and evil in the light of his vision that salvation was now to be found in Christ.[157] Paul was not apparently troubled by a subjective sense of guilt; he speaks of his former life with pride (Gal 1:13ff; Phil 3:4–6). In his comments about a pre-Christian plight, Paul may have been creating needs in order to justify his innovative stance. It would not be unreasonable for one who had experienced a sharp change in his associations and life orientation to explain the shift to himself and to others in terms of a contrast between the present/future salvation and past evils.[158]

Despite the clear 'in faith' perspective in Paul's writings, it is difficult to imagine such a transfer into a sect without some prior dissatisfaction.[159] If Paul's letters reveal anything about the nature of his missionary preaching, it is that he devoted most of his energy to proclaiming that salvation was now in Christ and that his listeners must now enter into the body of those who will be saved. But, did he also try to impress on his hearers that the world was wicked – that they had to set themselves apart from an evil society?[160] Describing the pagan world as one full of vices probably would come naturally to a Jew such as Paul (e.g. 1 Cor 6:9ff; Gal 5:19ff). Yet his radical determination to build communities centred around Christ leads one to conclude that he thought the only possible response to the world was to come into the body of those who will be saved.[161] In a world on the brink of transformation – a world that awaits God's judgement – a rejection of evil is of the utmost importance (Rom 12:9ff; 13:12ff). Paul sought to ensure that, in the sect, life was lived as it ought to be. By encouraging an attitude of love-patriarchal-ism, he re-interpreted existing power relations in order that individuals might be treated as they deserved.

In discussing the relation between the sectarian response of the Pauline communities and an apprehension of evil, it is, however, crucial to remember that evil in Paul's world was probably conceived of in quite different terms than in the modern world. The evil one sought to escape was probably not the modern kind which creeps into the individual conscience to haunt the offender, but rather the first-century kind which makes its way into the sect and causes members to become sick and even to die (1 Cor 11:30). In a society where demons could cause considerable havoc (1 Cor 10:20−1) and where Satan was an agent to contend with (2 Cor 2:11), the body where life was lived in Spirit offered protection from the destructive forces in the universe.

4.4 Conclusion

In this investigation of beliefs in the Pauline communities, correlations were drawn between social experience and the process of symbol-ization. However, no simple causal relationship between doctrine and social setting were discovered. In the Pauline sect, sacred symbols affect social reality and social reality affects symbolization. This dialectical process of development should not be reduced to a uni-directional phenomenon. Often, doctrine has been envisioned as acting in a straightforward fashion to shape development in Pauline communities. This has had important repercussions for understanding development after Paul. If Pauline beliefs are analysed in a vacuum, the changes that occur after the death of the Apostle cannot help but appear as unintelligible and perhaps even regrettable. To bear in mind the dialectical relationship between individuals and their symbolic universe is to envisage a church where change is part of the fabric of existence. This is of course not to suggest that one should not be critical of change, but rather to underline the importance of consider-ing the particular historical circumstances connected with change from the perspective of the dialectic existing between social setting and belief.

The Pauline communities are characterized by an intricate but flexible system of symbols which might be described as a symbolic universe or an ideology. The ambiguity that surrounds the meaning of symbols and the freedom with which they are employed is connected with the early stage of institutionalization in the sect. The symbol of the crucified and resurrected Messiah stands at the centre of the Pauline symbol system. Its articulation is related to the process of sect formation, including the determination of the group's stance toward Judaism. The process of symbolization is also rooted in a ritual context; both the world view and the ethos of the Pauline sect are connected to what is experienced in the midst of ritual.

Paul's writings must be related to their Jewish/Gentile world. It is crucial to connect Paul's doctrinal statements, especially his statements about the law, to the experience of having been transferred into the body of those who will be saved. It is useful to consider how the members of the Pauline sect deal with problems of meaning, such as suffering, bafflement and evil. The connection between suffering and hope leads one to consider the function of eschatological language in the Pauline sect. Paul speaks of present and future salvation with flexibility, depending on the particular situation faced by his communities. There may be some connection between the appeal of the Pauline symbol system and the social situation of members of the sect as travelling artisans and traders. Furthermore, the desire to separate from the outside world may be related to an apprehension that things are not as they should be on the outside. It is clear that the ideology of the Pauline sect contributes to its cohesion. This is not only due to the sharing of beliefs, but also to its vision of unity. The belief that salvation is now only to be found in Christ is accompanied by a universalist vision where evangelization strives to gather all — Gentiles and Jews, slaves and free, men and women — into the body of those who will be saved. Ironically, this vision of unity is bracketed within a sectarian response to the world. The Pauline communities may be described as a conversionist sect which is characterized by a tension between remaining separate from the world and saving the world.

5

GENERAL CONCLUSION

The preceding study of the Pauline communities has been conducted to illustrate that norms, ministry structures, ritual forms and beliefs are shaped by the realities experienced by a sect in the early stages of institutionalization. It is through the process of institutionalization that the symbolic universe is constructed. The symbolic universe may be envisioned as interacting across a dialectic with the lives it embraces. Throughout community-building institutionalization, the universe is in the process of solidifying. At this stage, much ambiguity surrounds the question of how members of the community should act and how beliefs should be interpreted. Institutionalization is relatively free to proceed in different directions. We can expect that as the body of tradition grows larger, institutionalization will become set along a more definite course. As problems of management increase, more firmly established guidelines for living will be required. When deviance becomes a problem, the universe must be maintained and further legitimation is required. In the following study of Colossians and Ephesians, we will investigate how problems of management affect development. We will trace the continued solidification and alteration of the symbolic universe in communities that appealed to the authority of the Apostle in his absence.

PART 2

COLOSSIANS AND EPHESIANS: COMMUNITY-STABILIZING INSTITUTIONALIZATION

Colossians and Ephesians reflect the continued existence of Pauline churches in the absence of the Apostle. The following study explores the nature of the community life underlying these writings. It does not constitute a defence of the pseudonymity of Colossians and Ephesians. Rather, it considers the implications of pseudonymity for understanding the social mechanisms at work in the early church. The investigation traces the development of a Pauline movement that stretched beyond the boundaries of the Apostle's own lifetime.

Throughout this section, comparisons will be made between the authentic epistles, and Colossians and Ephesians. The relationship between the writings will be analysed in terms of the ongoing process of institutionalization. When differences appear, suggestions will be made as to the historical factors acting as catalysts for change. Similarities will be discussed with a view to comprehending the continued relevance of certain aspects of the Pauline symbol system for communities faced with new social situations.

The means employed by the communities of Colossians and Ephesians to deal with the absence or death of Paul will be of primary significance for this study. As the Pauline movement incorporated new generations, it was faced with different problems from those of the early days of community formation. However, the existence of Pauline traditions provided some guidelines to cope with new situations. The following study of attitudes to the world/ethics, ministry, ritual, and belief in Colossians and Ephesians relates these aspects of community life to the activity of Pauline Christians engaged in the process of community-stabilizing institutionalization.

1

ATTITUDES TO THE WORLD/ETHICS

The following study describes the identity of communities that continued to appeal to Paul as a leading authority despite the fact that communication with him was no longer possible. It is concerned with how the communities underlying Colossians and Ephesians perceived themselves and their relations with the outside world. The significance of the Haustafel is of primary interest. The function of this type of ethical exhortation in the communities underlying Colossians and Ephesians is considered.

1.1 Institutionalization in the absence of Paul

The authenticity of the letter to the Colossians has long been disputed. On the basis of language, thought and style, many scholars have argued convincingly that the letter was not written by Paul himself.[1] However, the similarities between the authentic epistles and Colossians weigh in favour of a fairly close connection between the author and the Apostle. In fact, it is not impossible that the epistle was written by an associate during Paul's imprisonment.[2]

The linguistic, stylistic and theological features of Ephesians make its pseudonymity overwhelmingly probable.[3] The abundant literary parallels between Ephesians and other letters in the Pauline corpus suggest that beneath the writing lies the effort of an author to repeat Pauline traditions for the exhortation of community members.[4] C. L. Mitton understands Ephesians to be a presentation of Pauline theology made relevant for the author's own day.[5] He notes, for example, that Eph 2:8−9 provides a comprehensive description of Paul's teaching, but also represents an example of how interpretative modifications are introduced to make Pauline affirmations more intelligible to the later situation addressed by Ephesians.[6]

The absence of the words 'ἐν 'Εφέσῳ' (Eph 1:1) from some manuscripts has led some to conclude that Ephesians is an encyclical designed with an audience of several churches in mind.[7] This theory gains support from the apparent lack of close relationship between the author and the addressees and of specific reference to the concrete problems of an individual community. Moreover, the 'ekklesia' refers exclusively to the universal church in Ephesians, whereas in Paul's letters and in Colossians, it is employed both in a local and trans-local sense.[8]

The probable dependence of Ephesians on Colossians implies that Ephesians was written after Colossians by an author who was familiar with the letter.[9] The close connection between the two writings has resulted in their being considered together in this book. The fact that the author of Ephesians could adopt so many ideas from Colossians suggests affinities between the communities underlying the writings. The communities may reflect similar stages of development.

There has been a general neglect of the social implications of the pseudonymity of Colossians and Ephesians.[10] The question, 'What does the fact that associates wrote in Paul's name to address new situations tell us about the development of the Pauline movement?' has received inadequate attention. This is perhaps due to the heavy concentration on the theological disparity existing between the true Pauline writings and those that wrongly bear his name. Käsemann, for example, compares the use of tradition by the author of Ephesians with Paul's usage. The author of Ephesians is a skilled craftsman who selects and orders the elements of tradition available to him in accordance with deeply pondered thematic considerations.[11] Nevertheless, the methodology of this worthy disciple is sharply contrasted with the creative approach of the Apostle:

> Paul also, as form criticism shows, frequently relied on extant tradition. Yet he did not do it in order to help express his own ideas but to strengthen their validity, just as he did with scriptural proof. For Paul, the tradition is not the basis and limit of his assertions. On the contrary, time and again he breaks away from the beaten path toward new conceptual horizons, and it is not uncommon for him to use critically and dialectically the very ideas and slogans of his environment against those who advance them.[12]

Käsemann's analysis is unrealistic. His arguments imply that the reliance of the author of Ephesians on tradition falls short of Paul's ability to break through the boundaries of tradition. If, however, the author of Ephesians was primarily interested in making an authoritative teacher speak, Pauline tradition was integral to his purpose. It is surely to make too much of this pseudonymous effort to say that it represents an 'early catholic' tendency to make a particular message normative.[13]

Furthermore, the picture painted by Käsemann of Paul as the creative theologian does not take into account the social situation of a leader of a newly formed sect. Paul's methodology is that of a leader who must legitimate a novel proclamation and the gathering of those who share that proclamation. This same need for creativity is not part of the social setting of one who tries to bring Paul's teaching to a new situation. An abundance of Pauline traditions exist in a sect with a fairly clearly defined identity. In fact, the correlations of Ephesians with Colossians and Paul's own letters, as well as with Acts and 1 Peter, point to the fact that the first generation of the early Christian movement left behind an initial body of tradition as a guide for life-style.[14] Moreover, the kind of creativity attributed to Paul by Käsemann was not only no longer necessary, but probably no longer possible, for those in possession of the time-honoured teachings of the earliest witnesses. Käsemann's analysis does not take into account the ongoing process of institutionalization in the early church.

Understanding the development of the Pauline movement in terms of a process of institutionalization that results in the construction of a symbolic universe makes the heavy reliance on traditional material in both Colossians and Ephesians more readily understandable; it enables one to grasp better the relation between these writings and the authentic letters, as well as the social implications of pseudonymity. Failure to recognize the existence of a symbolic universe which expands to include new understandings, while at the same time providing categories against which to interpret these new under-standings, can lead to distortion. Consider, for example, Mitton's reconstruction of the situation that led to the composition of Ephesians:

> The message of Christ, as proclaimed in the generation after Paul's death, had tended to become but a diluted version of the full, life-transforming Gospel which he had so fearlessly proclaimed. To this disciple, looking back with regretful longing to the days of the first missionary enthusiasm of the Church, Paul seemed to be the apostle who beyond all others had grasped 'the truth as it is in Jesus'. To him it seemed that the Church of his day needed nothing so much as to hear

afresh this truth, in the fullness and with the clarity and vigour with which Paul had declared it.[15]

Like Käsemann, Mitton does not acknowledge the ongoing process of institutionalization in the early church. The image of the author of Ephesians taking Paul 'off the shelf' so that members of the early church could hear afresh his truth is also unrealistic. It is unlikely that the author would write a piece so obviously intended to promote unity with language that was for the most part unfamiliar to the audience. It is much more likely that the writing is firmly rooted in the worship of a community or communities where the authority of Paul and the Pauline symbol system are of great significance. This is supported by the existence of other deutero-Pauline writings. The important point is not so much whether the author of Ephesians was actually in possession of Paul's letters, but rather that a system of symbols associated with the life of the Apostle remained relevant after his death, undergoing changes as it stood in a dialectical relationship to communities in new times and circumstances.

The appeal to Paul's authority in his absence points to a changed situation in the communities underlying the deutero-Pauline writings. The level of development reflected in Paul's own letters has been described as 'community-building institutionalization'. For the sake of clarity, the stage of development evident in Colossians and Ephesians will be called 'community-stabilizing institutionalization'. This level of institutionalization is associated with the disappearance of the earliest witnesses, authorities and propagators of the early Christian movement (e.g. James the brother of the Lord, Peter, Paul). Although the Apostle to the Gentiles was faced with explaining the meaning of the Christ event to those who had not witnessed the appearance of the risen Lord (cf. Gal 1:16; 1 Cor 15:8), it now became necessary for the associates or disciples of Paul to explain its significance to those who were even farther removed from the happenings that brought the sect into being. It was impossible for these authors of the deutero-Pauline writings to base their authority on the kind of revelation to which Paul appealed. Therefore, they turned to Paul in order to legitimate their authority. With the passage of time and the expansion of the Pauline mission in the absence of the Apostle, new social concerns needed to be addressed. The changed situation was reflected in theological statements.[16]

During the first few decades after the death of Jesus, when Paul wrote his letters, a new combination of symbols was emerging rapidly.

The fact that the kind of ingenuity that characterizes Paul's letters is lacking in the deutero-Pauline writings might be partially explained by the existence of a fairly dense symbolic universe. This is not to suggest that no growth of the symbolic universe took place in the absence of the Apostle. The clear differences between the symbolism visible in the authentic Pauline letters and in Colossians and Ephesians indicates that the universe expanded and was transformed. It is important to distinguish, however, between the kind of change that takes place in the growth of a symbolic universe and the kind of radical innovation that leads to the rejection of at least some aspects of a past symbolic universe, calling for the formation of a sect where a characteristically different symbolic universe is given shape.

The symbolic universe reflected in the epistle to the Colossians may be envisioned as a system of categories which expands to include ideas and practices that can be accommodated and closes to reject those that cannot. The author of Colossians responds to Jewish gnosticizing tendencies in the same way that Paul reacts to the problems in Galatia: community members are reminded of the centrality of Christ. Nevertheless, the author responds to the opponents in a way that suggests that many ideas are shared by both parties. The cosmological significance of Christ as the 'image of the invisible God' and mediator of creation who is above all powers and alone guarantees salvation is underlined (Col 1:15ff).[17] Although Paul himself can speak of Jesus as the ruler of the cosmos (Phil 2:5ff), the cosmological significance given to the Christ event in Colossians far exceeds what we find in the authentic writings. Similarly, Eph 2:11–22, with its cosmic depiction of the reconciliation of Gentile and Jew, and the description of the church as the household of God built upon a foundation of apostles and prophets, indicates that ideas that are non-Pauline can be given a place within Pauline thought.

In Part 1, the close connection between the symbol system reflected in the text and Paul's own conception of his mission to the Gentiles was illustrated. How is it that aspects of this symbol system remained meaningful after the Apostle's death? Berger and Luckmann's sociological insights help explain the survival of symbols detached from the context of their origin.[18] The solidification of the symbolic universe makes it possible for the system of beliefs to be transmitted to a new generation. Paul's experience in relation to the sect to which he is closely bound becomes objectified and is embodied in symbols that can be shared; a kind of language is formed which has the power to survive its creator. Language is passed down to a new generation and the reconstruction of the original process of formation becomes unnecessary.

If one considers the way in which the mystery of the union of Gentile and Jew in one church is portrayed in Eph 2:11−22, it is evident that the tradition is detached from the conflict situation where it was born. It is not so much used to legitimate sect formation as to encourage internal cohesion. This process is even more apparent in Eph 2:7−10 where the author contrasts faith and works without attempting to recreate the actual origins of these beliefs in a situation where it was necessary to contrast faith in *Christ* and works of the *law*. The statement intended to illustrate that faith in Christ is a gift, and is not by human accomplishment, indicates that Ephesians is far removed from the 'innovation-linked' struggles of Paul's Jewish/ Gentile world.

Although as symbols become detached from their original social setting they lose some of their original content, it is only by achieving this objective quality that they are able to survive. In the communities underlying Colossians and Ephesians, the Pauline symbol of the body of Christ appears in a changed form (Col 1:17ff; 2:19ff; Eph 1:22f). The authority of Christ over the church is depicted in the image of Christ as head of the body. As in Paul's letters, the symbol of the body encourages unity in community life, but the head component underlines the authority of Christ in a new way. The symbol of the body of Christ in Colossians and Ephesians points to a simultaneous appeal to tradition and transformation of tradition to 'fit' a new situation.

1.2 The maintenance of the symbolic universe

From Paul's letters it is clear that the Apostle must legitimate the formation of the sect with respect to Judaism. Although it is impossible to deduce how long the communities which are the recipients of Colossians and Ephesians have been in existence, it is evident that the situations requiring ideological justification involve not so much the problems of sect formation as the problems of continued existence. The lengthy discussions about the role of the law have disappeared from view. In attempting to explain the meaning of the Christ event, an increasing appeal is made to tradition. A cry for unity in community life is fervently expressed. Improper conduct is relegated to the outside. An appropriate life-style for the Christian community is outlined. Colossians and Ephesians reflect

the situation of communities dealing with the disappearance of Paul
and with the increased dangers of deviant behaviour that come with
the incorporation of a new generation. Within the text is hidden an
effort to maintain the Pauline symbolic universe and to stabilize the
community life it embraces.

The struggle against false teaching is generally given as the occasion
for the letter to the Colossians.[19] It is clear that the Colossians are
threatened by a philosophy which the author believes is luring
members away from the centrality of Christ (Col 2:8 cf. 2:4). There
are apparently people in the Colossian community who take it upon
themselves to disquality those who do not share their beliefs and
practices, and to lay down regulations concerning eating, drinking
and sacred times (Col 2:16–19). The observation of certain ascetic
taboos is required by the propounders of the false teaching (Col
2:20–3).[20] These people base their authority on visionary experiences involving humility (ταπεινοφροσύνη – perhaps fasting)
and angel('s) worship (θρησκεία τῶν ἀγγέλων) (Col 2:18; cf. Col
2:21–3).[21] The author responds to the opponents by proclaiming
the deliverance community members received as a result of the
Christ event: trespasses were forgiven, ordinances were blotted
out, and powers and principalities were brought into subjection by
Christ (Col 2:13–15). To combat the consequences of mystical
innovations in community life, the author appeals to the authority
of Paul and, through the Apostle's voice, clarifies the implications
of the Christ event in a world where mysterious forces threatened the
lives of individuals.

Underlying the epistle to the Colossians is an effort to deal with
the social disruption that comes with the problem of deviation. Time
has been passing and individuals have been seeking to put into practice
what they perceive to be the implications of the Christ event for life
in the world. The author's judgement is that some are going astray.
Throughout the epistle, recipients are exhorted to hold fast to what
they received. If the passages related to the threatening philosophy
are placed in the context of the epistle as a whole, one discovers a
remarkable concern for consolidation. Members are exhorted not to
be moved from the hope of the gospel which they have heard (Col
1:23; cf. Col 2:6–7) and to hold to the head which is Christ (Col 2:19).
A cosmic reconciliation is reflected in the unity of the congregation
(Col 1:15–23). The community is described in terms of membership
in a unified and thriving body (Col 2:19). Baptism is recalled to remind
members of the implications for life-style connected with this event

(Col 2:11ff; 3:1ff).[22] Long lists of ethical exhortations distinguish between appropriate and inappropriate behaviour in the Christian community (Col 3:5ff; 4:1ff). Behaviour to ensure the well-being of the Christian household is demanded (Col 3:18−4:1).

The uncertainty surrounding the literary character of Ephesians and the lack of reference to concrete communal realities, lead to great difficulties with respect to the investigation of its aim and historical context.[23] Scholarly opinion is divided on these issues. Goodspeed argues that the author of Ephesians was the collector of the authentic letters and that Ephesians was written as a general letter to provide an introduction to the corpus.[24] Noting the difficulty in maintaining that Ephesians was actually intended to be such an introduction, Mitton nevertheless supports the general correctness of Goodspeed's theory. He asserts that the writing sprang from a relationship with the Pauline corpus and from an intention to present the message of the recently assembled letters to a new generation.[25]

A very different approach to the question of the occasion and purpose of Ephesians is taken by N.A. Dahl. He argues that Ephesians was written by Paul to give newly formed Gentile churches instructions on the meaning of their baptism. Eph 1:3ff is, according to Dahl, best understood as based on a blessing uttered before baptism. Members are reminded of the way of life now required as a result of their incorporation into the community.[26] The connection of Ephesians with baptism is also stressed by J.C. Kirby. He investigates the relation between the writing and early Christian rites which he argues were influenced by Jewish liturgical traditions.[27]

E. Käsemann believes that the specific historical situation addressed by the author of Ephesians is disclosed by Eph 2:11ff. The emphasis on the unity of Gentile and Jew here indicates that the danger expressed by Paul in Rom 11:17ff has come true: in the light of the success of the Gentile mission, Jewish Christianity is despised and pushed aside by Gentile Christianity.[28] J.P. Sampley arrives at similar conclusions about the purpose of Ephesians. Through a detailed examination of the traditional material in 5:21−33, he concludes that the use of the Old Testament reflects the author's intention to reply to Gentile Christians who reject, or at least question, their continuity with Jewish Christianity and the old Israel.[29]

The attempt to summarize Paul's teaching in Ephesians largely exhausts the writing's purpose. To hear Paul's voice, to feel his presence, to gain his direction − this is the effect of the letter proclaimed in the midst of the assembly. The liturgical-catechetical style of the writing and the lack of specific reference to community concerns make solid conclusions about the historical situation impossible. Is the writing best described as a letter or as a sermon? However one chooses to describe this puzzling tract, it is clear from its lengthy ethical exhortations that it is meant to say something to individuals who are living in community.

Eph 2:11ff may provide some clues as to the nature of the situation addressed. The argument made by Käsemann and others about Ephesians being directed to Gentile Christians who were in danger of divorcing themselves from their Jewish origins is conceivable. It is important, however, to move beyond speculation about the attitude of Gentile Christians to Jewish Christianity and think about the possible social situation that is presumed by the text: Is the author of Ephesians addressing a mixed community of Jewish and Gentile Christians whom he encourages to live in harmony?

Eph 2:11ff contains no reference to a specific conflict. However, throughout the passage the author reminds Gentile Christians of their past alienation from Israel and present adoption as fellow citizens (Eph 2:12, 19). That the addressees are Gentiles is clear from the author's explicit identification of them as 'Gentiles in the flesh' (Eph 2:11; cf. 2:12, 19, 3:1). Paul here appears to speak as the representative of Jewish Christianity. He announces: 'Through him we both have access by one spirit to the Father' (Eph 2:18, cf. 2:14). In Eph 1:12−13, the contrast between the Gentile Christians and Paul is evident. The 'we' of Eph 1:12 is defined as those who first hoped in Christ. The 'also you' of Eph 1:13 refers to Gentile Christians who, having heard the word of truth, also believed and were sealed with the Holy Spirit of promise. Those who first believed in Christ may be the original Jewish apostles, like Paul and Peter, who are compared with Gentiles brought in as a result of the evangelizing mission. As well as pointing to a contrast between groups in the church, Eph 1:12−13 may represent the efforts of an author located in a predominantly Gentile church to clarify its relation with the central community-building events of the first generation.[30]

It is impossible to tell for certain whether or not the author of Ephesians is a Jewish Christian since he or she has adopted the identity of the Jewish Apostle to the Gentiles. In light of the use of scripture, the you/we contrast in the text and the persistent interest to clarify the relation of the Gentile church to Israel, Jewish Christian authorship is likely.[31] The epistle may represent the voice of the Jewish Christian minority which, along with the growing number of

Gentiles, is devoted to Paul as a leading authority. What can Paul say to a predominantly Gentile community about its relations with Jewish members? How is Paul's teaching on the relationship between Jews and Gentiles to be explained to this new generation of Christians?[32]

The underlying presupposition of Eph 2:1ff is that the Gentiles have entered the commonwealth of Israel. It is striking that in this passage the church appears to be less of an entity distinct from Israel than in Paul's letters.[33] Apart from the possible exception found in Gal 6:16, Paul does not employ the term 'Israel' to refer to the Christian community.[34] Often his thought implies that he considered Christians to be the 'true Israel' (cf. Gal 3, Rom 4, Rom 9), but it is evident that he knows that Israel exists also outside of the sect. In Rom 9:6, for example, he can assert that not all who are descended from Israel actually belong to Israel. Yet in Rom 9:4 he mentions the inherited privileges of the Israelites and in Rom 9:31 he refers to the failure of Israel who pursued righteousness which is based on the law to attain righteousness.[35] Paul's discussion discloses an awareness that there are real Israelites, real Jews, who are not in Christ.[36]

The author of Ephesians clearly recognizes that Jews and Gentiles are different and that to unite them in one community is a major achievement. It remains striking, however, that the author of Ephesians can simply equate the church with Israel. The description of the adoption of the Gentiles into Israel ironically points to the fact that the church has become an even more firmly-established entity distinct from the physical Israel than is evident from Paul's letters. Gentiles are no longer strangers and foreigners but are fellow citizens with the saints and members of the household of God. This household is one built upon the foundation of the apostles and prophets with Christ Jesus as the cornerstone (Eph 2:19–20).

The achieved unity of Gentiles and Jews is one of the most remarkable features of Ephesians. The Gentiles are reminded of the gracious action of God in Christ that resulted in their inclusion as members of the commonwealth of Israel. Language of reconciliation characterizes the description of the union of Gentile and Jew that has taken place in Christ (Eph 2:13–18). The middle wall of partition separating Jews and Gentiles has been broken (Eph 2:14).[37] The fact that the Gentiles are joint heirs (συγκληρονόμα), of the same body (σύσσωμα) and joint sharers (συμμέτοχα) of the promise in Christ Jesus through the gospel, is described in Ephesians as the mystery of Christ (Eph 3:3–6).

The call to Gentile Christians to remember their estrangement from Israel and ultimate incorporation as fellow citizens and joint heirs may point to tensions between a Gentile majority and a Jewish minority in community life. The author of Ephesians may be calling for respect for Jewish Christians and for Jewish origins. The problem of the means of incorporation of Gentiles in the Pauline sect makes no appearance in Ephesians and is probably not an issue at this stage. That does not mean, however, that the issue of how Jews and Gentiles should live together in Christ has been settled.

The problems of Jews and Gentiles living together may be reflected in a writing that bears some striking resemblances to Ephesians both in language and style – the Acts of the Apostles.[38] In his recent book, Philip Esler argues that Luke told the story of the development of the church to serve the needs of his own mixed community of Jews and Gentiles.[39] Esler believes that an effort to conciliate is especially apparent in passages that exhibit a concern for table-fellowship (cf. Acts 10:1–11:18; 15:20, 29; 16:14–15, 25–34; 18:7–11; 27:33–8).[40]

As in Ephesians, the place of the Gentile Christians *vis-à-vis* Israel is considered in Acts. Luke depicts the development of the primitive Christian community of Jerusalem into the more established church made up of cells dotting the eastern Mediterranean world as far as Rome. The pattern of Paul's missionary enterprise – first to the Jews and then to the Gentiles (Acts 13:46; 18:6; 28:28) – underlines the important part played by Israel in God's plan of salvation. Some Jews are in fact converted (e.g. Acts 13:43). However, frequent depiction of Jewish rejection of the gospel which results in a turning to the Gentiles (e.g. Act 13:46) perhaps legitimates the Gentile mission and the increasing Gentile membership in the community.

The social situation evident in 1 Peter may also be somewhat similar to that underlying Ephesians.[41] The image of the members of the community being shaped into a building with Jesus as the cornerstone appears in 1 Pet 2:4–6 as well as in Eph 2:18–22. The notion of God's plan of salvation being unknown to people of other ages but now being manifest in the community appears in both 1 Pet 1:10–12 and Eph 3:2–6. Of particular significance, however, is the remembrance throughout 1 Peter of former Gentile ignorance and isolation from Israel (1 Pet 1:14, 18; 2:10; 4:2–4). The addressees were once not a people, but are now referred to as the people of God (1 Pet 2:10). J.H. Elliott believes that the internal evidence of 1 Peter suggests that a mixed audience of both former Jews and Gentiles is being addressed.[42] Theological legitimation of the break with Judaism and of the mixed character of church membership has become an important concern.[43]

It is impossible to arrive at firm conclusions about the social situation addressed in Ephesians. However, investigating the contact of the letter with other writings stemming from the complex period following the disappearance of the earliest authorities is useful for understanding the general state of affairs addressed in Ephesians. If Eph 2:11ff is placed in the context of the writing as a whole, one discovers its role in an endeavour to encourage cohesion in community life (e.g. Eph 4:3ff, 15f; 5:21ff).

Both Colossians and Ephesians disclose an effort to stabilize community life.[44] In sociological terms, these writings reflect a desire to maintain the symbolic universe that was shaped during the days of Paul's mission. Universe maintenance becomes necessary because of the conflicts and struggles experienced in the communities. Perhaps false teachers are leading community members astray. Perhaps a predominantly Gentile constituency is leading to a neglect of Jewish roots or to the segregation of a minority of Jewish Christians. Paul's teaching is made to speak to new situations. As the symbolic universe is maintained, it is also transformed in response to these situations. The espoused ideology serves to consolidate and preserve the Pauline movement in the absence of the Apostle.

1.3 The growth of the sect

Colossians and Ephesians describe the cosmic significance of the Christ event (e.g. Col 1:15–20; Eph 1:20–3). The use of the image of Christ's body encompassing all (Col 1:17; Eph 1:23; cf. Col 1:19) presupposes the success of the evangelizing mission. Colossians tells of the gospel bearing fruit throughout the world (Col 1:6, 23). In Ephesians, the purpose of Paul's mission is depicted as being to bring to light (φωτίσαι – make all people see) the plan (οἰκονομία) of the mystery hidden in God for ages; that through the church the manifold wisdom of God might be made known to the principalities and powers in the heavenly places (Eph 3:9–10).[45] The world-wide vision of salvation takes on new dimensions in Colossians and Ephesians. If the Pauline sect is indeed expanding rapidly, the problems of managing increased numbers and preserving its identity in the light of new membership may have arisen. This raises the question of how it is able to maintain the boundaries separating it from the outside world. What has happened in the communities of Colossians and Ephesians to the tension discovered in the authentic Pauline letters between separation from outsiders and evangelizing outsiders?

As in the case of the communities reflected in Paul's letters, the cohesion of the communities of Colossians and Ephesians is reinforced by the language of belonging. The members of the group are called saints (Col 1:2, 4, 26; Eph 1:1; 3:18; 5:3). They are described as the elect or the called ones (Col 3:12, 15; Eph 1:4; 4:4). They are loved by God or Christ (Col 3:12; Eph 2:4; 5:1f, 25). The Colossians are referred to as the faithful brethren (Col 1:2) and the brethren in Laodicea are greeted (Col 4:15). The exhortations at the end of the letter underline the intimate connection between Paul and his fellow workers (Col 4:7ff). Both Tychicus and Onesimus, for example, are referred to as beloved brothers (Col 4:7, 9). In the address of Colossians, Timothy is also identified as a brother (Col 1:1). Similarly, in Ephesians, peace is bestowed to the brethren (Eph 6:23). Tychichus, who is the only individual singled out in Ephesians, is referred to as a beloved brother as in Colossians (Eph 6:21). The addressees are described as the children of God (Eph 5:1) and as members of the household of God (Eph 2:19).

The language that speaks of group members as if they were a family is much less frequent in Colossians and Ephesians than in the authentic epistles. In fact, the address 'My brothers ...', which appears frequently in Paul's letters and underlines the Apostle's personal relationship with his communities (e.g. Rom 7:4; 1 Cor 1:11; 2 Cor 1:8; Gal 1:11; Phil 4:1; 1 Thess 1:4), is completely absent from these writings.[46] Because it makes no direct reference to particular communal situations nor mentions an entourage of fellow workers (with the exception of Tychicus), Ephesians stands out especially sharply as lacking the kind of intimate connection between community and Apostle found in Paul's letters.

Absence of Paul is obviously responsible for the reduced intimacy of the language found in Colossians and Ephesians. The pseudonymous nature of these writings means that the author is once-removed from his audience. It is clear, however, that members of the Pauline movement relied on other means employed by the Apostle to promote cohesion. Language of incorporation appears in both Colossians and Ephesians. As in Paul's letters, the expression 'ἐν Χριστῷ' reinforces the boundaries determining where salvation is to be found (e.g. Col 1:2; 2:6; Eph 1:10; 2:10). The use of the Pauline symbol of the body of Christ is transformed to serve what perhaps may be an even more central unity-generating function (Col 1:18–20,

21–22; 2:9–10, 19; 3:15; Eph 1:22–23; 4:15–16; 5:23, 30). Christ now becomes the head, while the members of the communities make up the body. Moreover, the symbol of the body becomes a vehicle for describing the cosmic reconciliation that has taken place in the Christ event. The strength of such symbolism to encourage the cohesion of the community is tied to the depiction of community members as intimately connected to Christ as members of his body and to the description of the authority of Christ as head of the church and of the entire universe.[47]

As in Paul's letters, language of separation in Colossians and Ephesians is found side by side with language of belonging. In both of these writings, the language of separation primarily takes the form of a remembrance of conversion. This remembrance is linked to exhortation concerning the behaviour appropriate for those who have made the transference into the body of Christ. For example, in Colossians, a long proclamation of the reconciliation of the estranged, underlining the significance of the Christ event and the role of Paul in proclaiming the message of salvation, ends with the following admonition: 'As therefore you received Christ Jesus the Lord, walk in him, having been rooted and built up in him and being confirmed in the faith, as you were taught, abounding in thanksgiving' (Col 2:6–7; cf. Col 1:1–2:7). The remembrance/exhortation pattern is also evident in Ephesians. Recipients are reminded that Paul's mission is to proclaim the mystery that the Gentiles are joint-heirs in the same body and partakers of the promise in Jesus Christ through the gospel (Eph 3:6; cf. 3:1–21). This inclusion in the body requires a particular life-style. Above all, there must be unity in community life (Eph 4:1ff).

It is clear from the above discussion that the term 'conversionist sect', employed to speak about Paul's communities in Part 1, remains an appropriate means of describing the communities of Colossians and Ephesians. Members are not exhorted to engage in further evangelization, however, but to demonstrate behaviour that is fitting for a community of the converted. In Part 1, it was noted that Paul's own mission to the Gentiles shaped the exhortations he made to the communities. Communal behaviour that might thwart the possibility of outsiders being won for Christ was discouraged (cf. 1 Cor 14:23f).[48] For the authors writing in Paul's name, the focus falls more strongly on the settled community.[49] The long lists of exhortations distinguishing between appropriate and inappropriate behaviour in the body of Christ point to the continuing process of self-definition (Col 3:5–4:6; Eph 4:25–32; 5:3–7, 17–18; 5:21–6:9).

The rule-like statements found in the household codes disclose the institutionalization of norms concerning Christian life-style (Col 3:18−4:1; Eph 5:21−6:9).

Although one does not find a pronounced desire to evangelize in Colossians and Ephesians, it is clear that the communities underlying the pseudonymous writings understand themselves to be part of a growing movement. In Paul's absence someone is evangelizing. The Colossians are part of a growing and thriving body that is filling the world (Col 1:18−20; 2:9, 19; 3:15). The growth of the Colossian community is linked with the spreading of the word throughout the world (Col 1:6, 23). Furthermore, the connection of the local community with other Christian cells is implied by the exchange of messengers (Epaphras, Col 1:7; 4:12; Tychicus, Col 4:7−8; Onesimus, Col 4:9; Mark, Col 4:10) and by the exchange of greetings (Col 4: 10−18).[50] Greetings are sent to the brethren at Laodicea and to Nympha and the church in her house (Col 4:15).[51] The church of the Colossians is evidently connected with the church of the Laodiceans; they are to exchange letters (Col 2:1; 4:15−16). Throughout the epistle, the Colossians are reminded frequently that the unity they are to cultivate is a wider-than-local unity.[52]

Commentators consistently describe the aim of Col 4:5−6 as the missionary enterprise.[53] The Colossians are instructed to walk in wisdom toward outsiders, making the most of time. Their speech is to be seasoned with salt so that they may know how to answer everyone.[54] The evangelical interest of the passage is supported by the previous two verses where prayer for the success of Paul's mission is requested (Col 4:3−4). A similar request is made in 2 Thess 3:1. Once again, a concern for relations with outsiders is visible. A prayer that the word of the Lord will have free course and be glorified is followed by a prayer that the sect will be delivered from perverse and evil people; for not all have faith (2 Thess 3:1−2).

Col 4:5−6 discloses not only an interest in the evangelization of outsiders, but also recommends caution in dealing with them. The term outsiders (τοὺς ἔξω) points to a clear division between everyone inside the body of those who are being saved and everyone on the outside (cf. Mk 4:11). The term is employed by Paul in 1 Cor 5:12f to make the point that it is the behaviour of those within the sect that is of central concern. The term also appears in 1 Thess 4:12 where, as in Colossians, it is the relationship with outsiders which is the topic of interest. The Thessalonians are instructed to live quietly, to mind their own affairs and to work with their own hands. In this way, they may command the respect of outsiders and be in need of nothing (cf. Eph 4:28). Paul's apparent desire that the Thessalonians win the respect of outsiders may be related to an insistence that communal behaviour not stand in the way of the possibility of winning outsiders for Christ. It may also be related, however, to a desire to reduce tension between outsiders and sectarians.

In 2 Thessalonians the theme of working for one's own living is taken up again in more detail (2 Thess 3:6ff).[55] The Thessalonians are instructed to keep away from those who are living idly, and not according to the tradition which they received from Paul (2 Thess 3:6; 14f). Paul's life-style as a labouring apostle is held up as an example for them to imitate (2 Thess 3:7−9). They previously received a command from Paul that those who would not work should not eat (2 Thess 3:10). There apparently has been a problem in the community with social disruption caused by idleness and busybodiness (2 Thess 3:11). The trouble-makers are exhorted to work quietly so that they may eat their own bread (2 Thess 3:12). It may be that the activity of these early Christians has led to hostile reactions from outsiders. If this is the case, the instructions are aimed at reducing tension between the sect and the outside world.

Consideration of the passages from 1 and 2 Thessalonians is helpful in the attempt to place Col 4:5−6 in a social context. These early Christians came into contact with outsiders in their daily lives. If one began to forgo one's responsibilities in the workshop in an effort to devote more energy to proclaiming that salvation was now in Christ, how would this have been viewed by those with whom one laboured daily? If one's house was noted for its 'secret-filled' meetings, what reaction would one receive from the neighbours? In the conditions of high social visibility of Greco-Roman society, caution was necessary for dealings with outsiders. Social respectability was important in a movement that endeavoured to save all. As the sect became more clearly visible, it stands to reason that outsiders were asking questions. The Colossians must know how to answer everyone. They must take advantage of the opportunity for dialogue, but be careful not to harm their precarious relations with these outsiders. In a similar fashion, the recipients of 1 Peter are instructed to be always ready for defence (ἀπολογίαν) to anyone who calls on them to account for the hope that is within them, but with meekness and fear. They are to keep their consciences clear so that the ones speaking against them and abusing their good conduct in Christ will be put to shame (1 Pet 3:15−16). In the face of slander and abuse, they are to remain open to outsiders.

In contrast to the Colossians, the recipients of Ephesians are not told to act wisely towards outsiders, but simply to act as wise people. Furthermore, the statement about making the most of time in Ephesians has a different meaning than in Colossians; caution is required simply because the days are evil. The instruction about appropriate speech finds no parallel in Ephesians (compare Col 4:5–6 and Eph 5:15–16). Nevertheless, this general statement with respect to acting wisely in the face of evil days does presuppose that caution is necessary in one's dealings with an evil world. This evil is perhaps connected with the action of deceptive teachers. Dissociation from the sons of disobedience is demanded (Eph 5:5–7). In addition, the recipients of Ephesians are instructed to put on the armour of God to be able to stand protected against evil (Eph 6:10–17). The strong language of separation does not, however, lead to introversion.[56] The recipients of Ephesians identify strongly with Paul's evangelizing mission; the mystery of the Gospel ought to be proclaimed boldly (Eph 6:19–20). The description of Paul's own mission in Eph 3:8–13 appears to reflect the perspective of later development. Here Paul's mission to the Gentiles is connected with the role of the church in the world. The church is both powerful and visible; it is surely growing.

Thus, in both Colossians and Ephesians we discover the same tension between a desire to evangelize and a desire to separate from the outside world that we found in Paul's writings. The emphasis on growth of the body in both writings may imply that rapid growth of the sect is taking place. Expansion presupposes greater visibility which, in turn, increases the demands for social respectability. We have yet to consider one aspect of the attitudes to the world/ethics of the communities underlying Colossians and Ephesians that may in fact be indicative of increased pressures for social respectability. In the household codes, we discover the reflection of an ethos that was of central significance for the expansion of Christianity in the Greco-Roman world.

1.4 The household codes and the ethos of love-patriarchalism

While the household codes of Colossians and Ephesians (Col 3:18–4:1; Eph 5:21–6:9) may represent a departure from Paul's style of exhortation, they do not stand out sharply as being non-Pauline. On the one hand, the rule-like statements reflect a more conservative attitude toward the role of subordinate members of the household;

they leave much less room for ambiguity and, consequently, for exceptional activity on the part of certain members. On the other hand, the instructions are not incompatible with Paul's own teaching about women and slaves (cf. 1 Cor 11:2–16; 1 Cor 14:34–6; 1 Cor 7:20–4; Philem 10–20).

In Gal 3:28 (probably a baptismal formula, cf. 1 Cor 12:13), Paul speaks of the abolition of divisions between social groups that has occurred in Christ. As in Gal 3:28, the pattern 'there is neither ...' (οὐκ ἔνι) appears in Col 3:11. In both instances the formula is cited specifically in reference to baptism and with respect to the experience of putting on Christ, or, as he is referred to in Colossians, the new man (Gal 3:27, Col 3:10). The new man is renewed in full knowledge according to the image of his creator; according to Col 1:15, Christ is the image of God (cf. 2 Cor 4:16).[57] In both Galatians and Colossians the idea of a re-created humanity in Christ comes to the fore. In Gal 3:28 the new unity of the community who are all one in Christ Jesus is proclaimed (all are heirs according to the promise, 3:29). In Col 3:11 the contrast between old divisions and the new reality obtained in Christ is underlined; Christ is all and in all.

Despite the obvious similarities between Gal 3:28 and Col 3:11, these passages play different roles within the epistles as a whole. In Colossians, as in Galatians, the contrast between Jew and Greek is maintained. Yet in Colossians, there is an interpretation of this contrast found in the listing of a second pair, circumcised and un-circumcised. In Gal 6:15 Paul himself speaks of the abolition of this difference in terms of a new creation. The contrast between slave and free is also maintained in Col 3:11 (there is no reference to the male/female contrast). The addition to the list of barbarian (the non-Greek) and Scythian is striking. These terms are not juxtaposed antithetically but are enumerated together as representatives of stigmatized groups.[58] The mention of barbarian and of a race known to be especially barbaric is made to stress the fact that old designations referring to the cultural inferiority or superiority of nations are no longer relevant.[59]

Although the baptismal formula in Colossians does recall the abolition of distinctions in Christ, it is not cited in an attempt to draw revolutionary consequences for the relations between members in the social realm. This is clearly what Paul is attempting to do in Gal 3:28 with respect to the entry of Jews and Gentiles into the community. While this verse may be said to encourage unity in the community, Paul's primary interest is to legitimate his understanding of how the community should be built. In contrast, in Col 3:11, as in 1 Cor 12:13, the intention is mainly to generate unity among group members. Circumcision appears no longer to be a central issue of conflict.[60] Despite the mention of the abolition of contrast between slave and free, a few verses later the household code exhorts slaves to obey their masters and to treat their slaves justly (Col 3:22–4:1), illustrating that in Christ this social institution is not abolished. The main purpose of Col 3:11 is apparently to stabilize the relationship between various groups in one body.

The unity-generating function of Col 3:11 is especially visible when one considers its location within a series of ethical exhortations. Numerous virtues are associated with putting on the new man (Col 3:10–14). Unity and harmony are to characterize the one body where the diverse members live and worship (Col 3:15–17). The need for the stabilizing of relations among members is especially visible in the household code of Col 3:18–4:1. If the baptismal formula leaves uncertain how the various groups should interact in one church, these rule-like exhortations set forth a love-patriarchal pattern which provides a guide for life-style.

In Paul's letters one discovers a certain ambiguity as to the implications of new life in Christ. If, in Christ, there is neither male nor female, how should women behave in Corinth? If the slave Onesimus is a brother of his believing master, how should he now be treated by him? Paul's recommendations with respect to women and slaves illustrate how firmly he is rooted in Greco-Roman society. Although he does not make revolutionizing recommendations with respect to male/female relations and slave/master relations, he does seek to reinterpret these relations according to new life in Christ (cf. 1 Cor 7; 11:11–12). The recommendations made to Philemon exhibit a desire to remind the slave owner that something has changed in the nature of the relation between master and slave. The slave is now to be received as a beloved brother (Philem 16). Nevertheless, one may generalize that the nature of the relationship between the various groups in the church is one of love-patriarchalism: social distinctions between members are maintained. Those in authority are to respect and care for the needs of subordinate groups in return for their obedience.

The household codes of Colossians and Ephesians reflect the same love-patriarchal attitude that one finds in Paul's letters. The fact that the instructions take the form of rule-like statements indicates that the ethical position of the Pauline movement is becoming more conservative. The negation of differences between slaves and free (Col 3:11) does not lead to the complete abolition of differences in the community. The code prescribes how the members of the unified body should interact with one another. The author takes for granted that the cohesion of the group should be preserved in the way that it was in ancient society in general − by the hierarchical structure of those who rule and those who are subordinate.[61] Nympha is said to have a church in her house in Col 4:15, which may indicate that the author of Colossians recognizes that women can play an important role as local leaders. However, the exhortation that wives submit to their husbands points to a firmer demarcation of the role of women than is visible in Paul's letters. In the Ephesian Haustafel the marriage relationship is treated in great detail with regard to Christ's relationship with the church (Eph 5:22−33). The fact that the subjection of wife to husband is divinely ordained is stressed. As will be discussed in Part 3, the use of the household code in the Pastorals reflects an even more conservative patriarchal ethos than is found in Colossians and Ephesians. The household code becomes entwined with recommendations with respect to church leadership. Women are explicitly prohibited from undertaking leadership roles (e.g. 1 Tim 2:9ff).

Despite the existence of more conservative tendencies embodied in the household codes, it is important to note the degree of continuity between these exhortations and Paul's teaching. There is clearly some relation between Paul's instructions concerning women in 1 Cor 11 and 1 Cor 14 and the plea that wives be subject to their husbands. In the early days of community-building institutionalization, it is evident that norms are developing as a result of the interplay of the ethical implications of being found in Christ with the standards prescribed by the society of the day. On the one hand, the standards in the sect must be distinguished from those in the outside world. On the other hand, the standards of the outside clearly influence what is appropriate for life on the inside (cf. 1 Cor 5:1). As time passes and groups form, there is a tendency for norms to become formalized or institutionalized. The household code is the product of the institutionalization of norms determining what kind of behaviour is fitting for life in Christ.[62]

1.5 The origin and function of the household codes

The origin of the Haustafel tradition has long interested scholars. They have noted similarities in the outlook and structure of the household codes with elements of the thought-worlds of Stoicism and Judaism. They have debated the question of whether or not the development reflects primarily an adoption of tradition material from the outside world or a specifically Christian creation.[63] Most recently, scholars have been interested in exploring the connections between the household codes and the traditional topos 'concerning household management' which appears frequently in the literature of Greco-Roman society.[64]

David Balch has argued that the topos 'concerning household management' found in Greek philosophical discussion is the antecedent to the New Testament Haustafeln. The most important example of the topos providing a parallel to the New Testament codes is found in Aristotle's *Politics* 1. Here Aristotle states that a discussion of the component parts of the state must begin with a consideration of household management, for every state is composed of households (cf. I 1253b 1–14).[65] Aristotle considers the various household relationships under the rubrics of ruling and being ruled:

> Hence there are by nature various classes of rulers and ruled. For the free rules the slave, the male the female, and the man the child in a different way. And all possess the various parts of the soul, but possess them in different ways; for the slave has not got the deliberative part at all, and the female has it, but without full authority, while the child has it, but in an undeveloped form   (I 1260a 9–14).[66]

Balch illustrates that the topos 'concerning household management' remained at home in the morals and philosophical thought of the Empire. He gives examples of its usage by Stoics, Hellenistic Jews and Neopythagoreans.[67]

The most striking resemblance between the New Testament household codes and the topos 'concerning household management', as reflected in Aristotle's thought, is the presence of the three pairs of relationships: wives/husbands, children/parents and slaves/masters. Moreover, in both cases the pairs are treated expressly as relations of superiors to subordinates. The affinities of the New Testament instructions with the traditional ethics of the ancient world are clear. The topos 'concerning household management' is reflected most plainly in the household codes of Col 3:18ff and Eph 5:21ff (cf. 1 Pet 2:13ff; 1 Tim 2:8–15; 3:4; 6:1–2; Tit 2:1–10; 3:1; Ign Pol 4:1–5:1; Pol Phil 4:2–6:1).

In the Colossian and Ephesian household codes there is no explicit connection made between the household and society at large. Nevertheless, the comparison of the relation of Christ to the church with the relation of husband to wife in Ephesians suggests that the household relations could be seen as reflecting a wider social reality.[68] The household code of 1 Peter is particularly interesting in this regard. It begins with an exhortation that Christians be subject to 'every human institution' – all the representatives of governmental authority. As in the traditional topos, a parallel appears to be drawn between behaviour in the household and in society at large. Similarly, the connection of the household mangement topos with the discussion of the wider *politeia* may be somehow related to the instructions found in 1 Tim 2:1f and Tit 3:1f; submission to governmental authorities is demanded.[69]

Balch argues that the function of the Haustafel of 1 Peter is apologetic. Christians are being accused of promoting deviant behaviour in the household. Consequently, they are exhorted to behave in an exemplary fashion in order to refute the slanders of their antagonists in the larger society. Balch notes that the hierarchical Greek ethic expressed in the household management topos became a standard for household behaviour in the aristocratic segments of Greco-Roman society. This meant that minority religious communities were required to define themselves with respect to this ethic. He gives examples of criticisms made of minority religious groups in Greco-Roman society for upsetting the order of the household, including devotees of the god Dionysus, the goddess Isis and the Jews.[70] For example, the historian Tacitus points to Roman resentment at the social problems caused by Jewish proselytism. He speaks of those who are converted to Jewish ways being taught to despise the gods, to disown their country, and to regard their parents, children and brothers as of little account (*Histories* V.5).[71]

In response to such slanders, Philo and Josephus make statements that underline the stability of the Jewish household.[72] An apologetic use is made of the traditional subordination ethic. In *Apology*, Philo writes:

> Wives must be in servitude to their husbands, a servitude not imposed by violent ill-treatment but promoting obedience in

> all things. Parents must have power over their children ...
> The same holds of any other persons over whom he [a man]
> has authority ...   (*Apology for the Jews* 7.3 and 5).[73]

Similarly, in *Against Apion*, Josephus observes:

> The woman, says the law, is in all things inferior to the man.
> Let her accordingly be submissive, not for her humiliation,
> but that she may be directed; for the authority has been given
> by God to the man   (*Against Apion* II.199).[74]

Josephus then goes on to discuss 'honour to parents' (II.206) as well
as the law and punishment for slaves (II.216). Balch argues that
Josephus' description of the social roles of women, children and slaves
found in *Against Apion* II have close parallels with the apologetic
encomium of Rome given 100 years earlier by Dionysius of Halicar-
nassus in *Roman Antiquities* I.9–II.29 (written 30–7 B.C.E.).[75]

Balch believes that the household code of 1 Peter was intended to
reduce the tension between the Christian community and the outside
society. Although the work was directed to the Christian community,
its aim was to recommend behaviour in the household that would
silence slanderous accusations. That outsiders were indeed expressing
negative opinions about the activity of Christians is suggested by 1
Pet 2:15, where the author exhorts community members to engage
in behaviour that will 'put to silence the ignorance of foolish men',
and 3:15–16, which instructs the Christians to be prepared to make
a defence (an apology) to pagan critics so that those reviling the good
behaviour of Christians would be put to shame. Moreover, Balch
argues that the exhortation to wives in 3:1–6 is both missionary and
apologetic. It is taught here that through her submissive, silent and
chaste conduct, the woman may win her unbelieving husband. The
encouragement not to be terrified given to wives in v.6 points to the
need for apology. The criticisms these women received were not
necessarily due to an attempt to realize Gal 3:28 in the social realm,
but may simply have been because they were converted to a religion
that was other than that of the head of the household. Religious
insubordination led to accusations of social insubordination (cf. 1
Pet 2:12–14).[76]

It is possible to make a much stronger case for the apologetic
function of the household code of 1 Peter than for the codes found
in Colossians and Ephesians. The instructions of Col 4:5–6, however,
recommend a cautious attitude toward outsiders that is grounded in

a missionary interest. It is possible that the exhortation is aimed at reducing tension between community members and outsiders. In Ephesians there is no explicit mention of dealings with outsiders. Nevertheless, the relation between the ethical stance of the topos 'concerning household management' and the apologetic function of the subordination ethic as illustrated by Balch, leads one to question whether the use of the Haustafel in New Testament writings may have been related to an attempt to stabilize relations with outsiders.

In a growing conversionist sect, contact with outsiders is integral to its nature as a group that seeks to encompass the whole world. Yet distinction from the life-style of outsiders is crucial to the preservation of its identity. Recruitment means competition with other movements. At the most basic level, it means being open to dialogue about behaviour which might be considered suspicious. The reinforcement of the household ethic in the Christian community may be related to the social situation of a sect which has a precarious relationship with the outside world. The negative reaction of outsiders can threaten the sect's cohesion, its God-given elect status, and its evangelizing vision.[77] The sect may need to demonstrate that conversion does not necessarily lead to household disruption. In fact, the subjection of wives to husbands, slaves to masters and children to parents may be done in the Lord. As noted in Part 1, the desire to save all is related to the desire to be respected by all. The ethos of love-patriarchalism, rooted in traditional Greco-Roman ethics and embodied in the household codes, undoubtedly played an important role in the missionary inroads into the household.[78]

In focusing on the possible function of the household code in reducing the tension between community members and outsiders, there is a danger of neglecting the effect of the exhortation on relations within the sect. J. H. Elliott has criticized Balch for underestimating the purpose of the code in the integration of community life.[79] Unlike the examples cited by Balch of the use of the household management topos outside Christian circles, the household code is directed solely to insiders. The kind of behaviour that is recommended has important ramifications with respect to how members will treat one another. This is especially visible in the household codes of Colossians and Ephesians where all three pairs of relationships are the subject of exhortations. This is not, however, to deny the value of Balch's insights on the apologetic functions of the Haustafel in 1 Peter for understanding the function of the household codes in general. What is done inside the conversionist sect is always done with a view to what is going on outside. Encouraging internal harmony means stabilizing relations with outsiders. The community's openness to outsiders must be preserved, but its separate identity must not be destroyed.[80]

Related to Elliott's emphasis on the internal perspective of the Haustafel of 1 Peter, is David C. Verner's discussion of the household codes in terms of specifically Christian tradition. He notes that in comparing the Christian codes with other examples of the use of the topos 'concerning household management', their uniqueness is sharply evident. Verner believes that the topos appears to have been given a characteristic shape within the Christian community − a shape that stands out even beyond such characteristic phrases as 'in the Lord'. He argues that there are recurring key features, especially syntactical features, which are not accounted for by this topos. He notes that the individual exhortations of the various Christian household codes appear to be structured according to a predictable schema which is not associated with the household management topos anywhere except in the Haustafeln themselves.[81] According to Verner, the 'station code' schema has primarily to do with the structure of individual exhortations and secondly with the way these exhortations are characteristically linked. Through careful analysis and the citation of various examples, Verner notes four recurring elements belonging to the structure:

1.   an address;
2.   an imperative;
3.   an amplification; and
4.   a reason clause providing motivation or theological justification.[82]

Verner believes that it is possible to trace a pattern of development in the use of the station code schema. In the later Haustafeln, there is an increasing tendency to make connections between the various pairs. Furthermore, reason clauses and amplifications become longer. Other exhortations become sandwiched between the household exhortations, groups are addressed indirectly and the schema is employed more freely.[83]

In his comparison of the various household codes, Verner has convincingly illustrated the flexibility of both the household management topos and the station code schema. This raises important questions about the relationship between the household codes and particular communities. Both the household management topos and the schema are traditional influences evident in the household codes. The topos 'concerning household management' originated outside the early church, but nevertheless affected the teaching of the early church through the Haustafeln. The station code schema on the other hand, which appears to have undergone a traceable evolution within the church, must be attributed to Christian influences. Yet the differences between the various household codes (including the changes in schema) that occurred as time went on, cast doubt on approaches to the study of these exhortations that attempt to disconnect this traditional material from any real base. The Haustafel tradition was apparently subject to revision in individual communal contexts. Verner is correct when he points out that the form of the household codes strongly suggests that they address concrete, and in some cases persistent, social needs within the church.[84]

1.6 The Colossian household code and its social context

The compact nature of the Colossian Haustafel (Col 3:18−4:1) is often noted by scholars. This household code, with its emphasis on subordination and order, as well as mutual responsibility in the Lord, may be contrasted both with Eph 5:21−6:9 and 1 Pet 2:13−3:17 on account of the purity of its form and its content. If one were present in the first-century household gathering (in Nympha's house perhaps) where this exhortation was read, one's attention would be grasped. No matter what social group one belonged to, one would be provided with a pattern for Christian life-style. The way one should relate to fellow members of the body of those who are being saved would be clarified. The call for reciprocity of responsibility would be powerfully impressed by the concise nature of the instructions. Even if one were a Christian wife who was coming under the pressure of a non-believing husband, or a slave who was being persecuted by a non-believing master, one would presumably be provided with a guide for living. Subjection and obedience to one's husband or master were appropriate for life in the Lord. After all, from the Lord one would receive the reward of inheritance. The wrongdoer would be paid back for the wrong he or she had done. There is no partiality; all groups come under judgement.

The Colossian household code clearly encourages harmony in community life, but does it respond to a specific conflict? James E. Crouch believes that the Colossian Haustafel reacts against enthusiasts who appealed to such slogans as Gal 3:28.[85] In light of his interpretation of the passages on women and slaves in 1 Cor 7, 11 and 14, he proposes the working hypothesis that the Corinthian disorders constituted a local expression of enthusiastic tendencies in a significant segment of the Hellenistic church which necessitated the incorporation of the Haustafel into Christian paraenetic material.[86] Crouch believes that, in the Colossian community, the slave question presented the most difficult problem. He argues that it is the same restlessness which is mirrored in 1 Cor 7:20ff which necessitated the direction of the Haustafel towards slaves.[87]

The main problem with Crouch's thesis about the social context of the Colossian household code is that there is no solid evidence to support his contention that the community is being troubled by the social unrest of slaves. Although the long exhortation to slaves (Col 3:22–5) does imply that the author took special care to exhort them, this does not mean that slaves were seeking their freedom. Moreover, Crouch's argument that the exhortation in 1 Cor 7:20ff implies that expressions such as Gal 3:28 stimulated unrest among slaves, has little foundation.

In his study of the relationship between the exhortation to slaves in 1 Cor 7 and the institution of slavery in the Greco-Roman world, Scott Bartchy arrives at the opposite position to Crouch.[88] According to Bartchy, the ambiguous exhortation to slaves in 1 Cor 7 including the advice which might be summarized as 'Don't worry about it', can only be understood in the light of a consideration of the position of slaves in the society where Paul lived. Bartchy does not deny the fact that freedom was more desirable than slavery in Paul's society. In fact, most slaves expected to be manumitted at one time or another. However, it is also evident that manumission was not a possibility that slaves could accept or reject; it was for the most part out of their control except for the fact that hard work might increase their chances of becoming manumitted. The desirability of manumission served to encourage the efficiency of those who remained in slavery. Bartchy concludes that the general climate of unrest that has been assumed by some biblical scholars simply did not exist in the first century.[89]

In light of these considerations, Bartchy believes that in 1 Cor 7:21, where Paul apparently urges slaves who are able to become free to do so, the Apostle is truly addressing slaves who have already been set free by their owners; he instructs the Christian slave to use the new opportunity. Bartchy argues that Paul was urging any person in the Corinthian congregation who had received the call of God in Christ when in slavery to continue to 'use' (in the sense of 'live in' or 'obey') this call after manumission, i.e. after receiving the new status as a freedperson.[90] In attempting to answer the question of what prompted Paul to mention the question of slavery, Bartchy argues that Paul used the slave/free case (1 Cor 7:21–2) and the circumcision/uncircumcision case (1 Cor 7:18–19) not because they were issues of conflict in Corinth. Rather, they are employed to illustrate Paul's theology of calling which functions as one of the principal theological arguments in 1 Cor 7 against what appears to be the specific problem addressed by Paul in this chapter, the pneumatic understanding of the male/female relationship.[91]

Bartchy is correct in his contention that there is no concrete evidence to suggest that the master/slave relationship was disturbed by the pneumatic Christianity of the Corinthians. In addition, as he points out, the conflict in Corinth probably has more to do with sexual practices and the role of women (cf. 1 Cor 5; 6; 7; 11; 14).[92] Thus, Bartchy's work casts doubt on the link made by Crouch between the Colossian Haustafel and the restlessness of slaves in Corinth. Bartchy argues that nothing is said in Col 3:22–5 which indicates that they needed to be admonished because of striving to become manumitted. Rather, they are addressed concerning their role in the family structure as are wives, husbands, children, parents and masters.[93] Bartchy is undoubtedly right when he points out that there is no evidence of unrest in the Colossian congregation. Yet his explanation does not account for why so much of the Colossian Haustafel is devoted to the exhortation of slaves in comparison to the brief exhortation to other groups. Why did the subordination of slaves receive so much attention?

The two main points of Col 3:22–5 appear to be that enthusiastic obedience of servants to their masters is appropriate for life in the Lord and that service to 'fleshly' lords (τοῖς κατὰ σάρκα κυρίοις – v.22) is a means of serving the Lord Christ (v.24). The slaves are promised that they will receive the reward of inheritance, but are also reminded that those who have done wrong will be judged. The statement that there is no partiality is probably intended to remind slaves that all will one day be judged equally. It is not inconceivable that slaves heard in this statement a promise that the injustice of masters will be reckoned with on a day when there will be no distinction between masters and slaves. This is supported by the fact that masters are reminded in Col 4:1 that they themselves have a master in heaven.[94]

The strong plea for subordination and the accompanying promise

of salvation must have brought hope to slaves who were being persecuted by unbelieving masters. As Balch's analysis indicates, a slave
who gave up worshipping the traditional gods of the paterfamilias
could very well receive harsh criticism for being insubordinate.[95] The
exhortation would legitimate the slave's present position in subjection
to the master while at the same time promising recompense for
suffering. In addition, by encouraging slaves to serve their masters
enthusiastically, indeed as though they were serving the Lord himself,
tense relations with outsiders could be considerably stabilized.

It is apparently the Christian slave/master relationship that is the
object of concern in the Colossian Haustafel. Both masters and slaves
in the community are exhorted. If the paterfamilias was converted,
one would expect that his whole house would enter the body of those
being saved as well. The relationship between Christian masters and
slaves is clearly love-patriarchal; slaves are to serve their masters
heartily and masters are to treat their slaves justly. The strong are
not to abuse their authority over the weak. It is clear from this passage
that in Christ the social structures of the society maintain some of
their relevance. This is hardly surprising, however, considering the
conversionist nature of the sect. In a sect whose members continued
to mingle with outsiders in their work-a-day world and whose vision
was to encompass the whole world, societal structures could not easily
be discounted.

Crouch argues that in contrast to 1 Corinthians, which reflects the
situation in the gathering of the church, the Colossian Haustafel
reflects a threat to the social order. He writes:

> It is one thing for a Christian slave to act equal in the gather-
> ing of the church. It is quite another situation, however, when
> the same slave asserts his equality in society.[96]

One wonders if Crouch may have the slave problem in Colossae
somewhat backwards. If, for instance, the unrest of slaves with respect
to their position in the outside society was not a problem in Corinth
or Colossae, might not the tightening of structures we witness in the
household code be connected with the role of slaves in the house
church? There is no reason to doubt that slaves performed functions
in the Pauline churches that gave them authority and provided them
with at least minor leadership roles. However, the emphasis on subordination in the Colossian Haustafel makes it plainly evident that
in the Lord, slaves are to be subject to their masters. One wonders
if this means that slaves are to turn to their masters for guidance

about which teaching is to be followed (an apparently potent issue in Colossae), how one should relate to outsiders, and generally how one should live one's life in the Lord. Could this appeal for sub-ordination, which places power more firmly in the hands of masters (also husbands and fathers), represent an attempt to consolidate the leadership of a church threatened by false teaching and experiencing adjustments connected with the death or absence of Paul?

1.7 The Ephesian household code and its social context

The Ephesian Haustafel (5:21ff) appears to fit more naturally within the writing as a whole than the Colossian Haustafel. The exhortations intended to generate unity in the household fit well within a writing devoted to the encouragement of unity in the community as a whole. It is the husband/wife relationship that receives most attention in the Ephesian household code. Whereas thirteen verses are devoted to this relationship (5:21−33), only nine verses are allotted to the remaining groups.[97] It is especially in the exhortation to wives/husbands that we discover an interest in the early Christian household on the one hand, and in the church understood on the model of the household on the other.

In 1 Cor 6:9−11 Paul reminds the Corinthians that some of them partook in sexual immorality and other vices, but they have now transferred into a 'clean' sect. They have been washed and sanctified in the name of the Lord Jesus Christ (cf. Rom 6:19; 1 Thess 4:3−7). Similarly, in Ephesians, we discover a strong plea that sexual im-morality and all impurity belong outside, coupled with a remembrance of transference (Eph 5:1ff; cf. Eph 4:17ff; Col 3:1ff). The list of vices is followed by the reminder that community members are no longer in darkness, but should walk as children of light (Eph 5:8ff). The household code comes shortly thereafter, drawing special attention to the marriage relationship as a means of understanding the relation-ship between Christ and the church (Eph 5:21−6:9). Like the com-munity as a whole, the pure bride is sanctified and cleansed by the washing of the water by the word (baptism?).[98] As a reflection of the holy and unblemished church, she stands in contrast to the decadence of the outside world (Eph 5:25−7).

In Ephesians, as in Paul's letters, woman is presented as a special reflection of the purity of the sect. When Paul wishes to chastise the Corinthians for their immoral behaviour, he reminds them that in having intercourse with a prostitute, they become one body with her.

In engaging in such activity, members are desecrating the body of Christ (1 Cor 6:15−20). Similar ideas operate in Paul's discussion of the problem of mixed marriage (1 Cor 7:12−16). The likely outcome of Paul's line of reasoning in 1 Cor 6, when applied to the problem of mixed marriage, is that union with an unbeliever will desecrate the church. However, here Paul reverses the argument and makes mixed marriage a possible source of sanctification for the unbelieving partner. Exhibiting an interest in the preservation of household relationships and his usual zeal to leave every possible door open for conversion, Paul gives members engaged in mixed marriages a choice: they may separate or remain together. The validity of the marriage is connected with the consent of the unbelieving partner to remain married to the believing partner. The unbelieving partner who consents to remain married to the believing partner will be made pure; moreover, the children of such a mixed marriage will be made holy (1 Cor 7:14).[99]

Throughout his exhortations concerning marriage in 1 Cor 7, Paul is careful to underline the mutual responsibility of men and women. Instructions to men are carefully balanced with instructions to women (e.g. 1 Cor 7:3−4). However, in light of the role of the male head of the Greco-Roman household, one wonders whether the problem with respect to mixed marriage has to do mainly with believing women involved in such relationships. One would expect the wife of a male believer to be under considerable pressure to 'convert' as well. On the other hand, the conversion of a wife would by no means necessarily lead to the conversion of the husband. Moreover, the rejection of traditional gods would result in the woman coming under considerable pressure in the household. Paul's emphasis on 'consent' may be an attempt to stabilize difficulties experienced in community life with respect to mixed marriage − to legitimate the continued membership of a believing wife in a non-believing household − rather than to describe a real option open to women. For example, although women could initiate divorce in Rome and in the eastern provinces, this was only possible with the permission of a guardian, who was usually a father or another male relative.[100] In this context, the exhortation in 1 Peter 3:1ff to women to be models of subjection so that they may win their unbelieving husbands is suggestive.

The activity of the women in Paul's communities may have been understood as a visible sign of the nature of the Pauline sect. This is implied by Paul's reaction to women being unveiled at worship (1 Cor 11:3−16). The reason clause, 'because of the angels', given by Paul to explain the need for a woman to be veiled (1 Cor 11:10), points to a possible connection between the activity of women and the concern for purity. This phrase appears in the writings of Qumran in connection with purity prohibitions.[101] Newton argues that in light of the evidence from Qumran, it is possible that Paul's phrase 'because of the angels' also refers to those angels which signify a divine presence in the community and which would remove themselves in the face of any impurity.[102] In 1 Cor 11:5, Paul argues that the woman who prays or prophesies with her head uncovered dishonours her head. In 1 Cor 11:3, Paul writes that the head of woman is man and the head of man is Christ. Thus, in 1 Cor 11:5 he is probably arguing that the woman who dishonours her head is dishonouring her husband (cf. 1 Cor 14:35).[103] The activity of women can lead to the desecration of the marriage relationship. As in Ephesians, the marriage relationship appears to take on special significance as a reflection of the nature of the community. The activity of women can lead to the desecration of the community.

Num 5:13−18 states that for a woman's hair to be loosed is a sign of an adulteress. It is possible that Paul is sensitive to this tradition, believing that if a woman has an uncovered head she will dishonour her husband and bring shame on herself.[104] From 1 Cor 6:15−18, it is clear that relations with a prostitute can lead to the desecration of the community. Like the prostitute, the woman who appeared as an adulteress would be considered impure and defiled.[105] The corruption of the outside world would consequently gain entry into the sect. In 1 Thess 4:4−5, Paul instructs the Thessalonians that everyone should take a wife (σκεῦος) in holiness and honour and not in the passion of lust, like the Gentiles, who do not know God.

Paul's instructions about the marriage relationship exhibit an interest in the preservation of purity, both by distinguishing the activity of sectarians from those on the outside and by keeping the sacred space free of polluting influences. The connection of the purity imagery with household ethics in Ephesians underlines how firmly New Testament texts are rooted in their first-century setting. The subjection of wife to husband becomes a sign of an 'honourable' marriage in the Lord. The honourable marriage becomes a sign of the pure sect.[106]

The exhortation concerning marriage in Ephesians 5:22−33 exhibits many ideas similar to those found in Paul's letters. As in Paul, we discover the description of husband as head of the wife (Eph 5:23), the image of woman as a reflection of the purity of the church (Eph

5:26–7), and a strong impression of the sanctifying possibilities of physical union (Eph 5:28–31). The woman who is joined to the man becomes part of his body (Eph 5:28–9). For the author of Ephesians, marriage provides an excellent image for the relationship of Christ to the church. The subjection of wife to husband is compared to the subjection of the church to Christ. The cleansing of the bride is compared to the purification of the church that has taken place in Christ. The intimate attachment of wife to husband is compared to the connection of members of the church to Christ as members of his body. The sanctity of this union is legitimated by the author of Ephesians with a quotation from Gen 5:31 which terminates in the phrase: 'and the two shall become one flesh'.[107] The union is described as a great mystery, a mystery concerning Christ and the church (Eph 5:32).[108] When the author of Ephesians speaks of a great mystery, it is impossible to tell whether he is referring specifically to marriage or to the relationship of Christ and the church, but this apparent lack of clarity is suggestive of the close connection between the two in the author's own mind.

In light of the elaborate description of the relationship of husband and wife as a reflection of the relationship of Christ and the church, it is easy to lose sight of the author's clearly stated aim. The author intends to justify and clarify his exhortation that wives be subject to their husbands (Eph 5:22, cf. v.23–4). The ethos of love-patriarchalism is clearly reflected in the instructions to husbands and wives in Ephesians. The subordinate wife is to respect her husband and the husband, in turn, is to nurture and care for his wife (cf. Eph 5:33).[109] These ideas are easily encompassed within a Pauline symbolic universe. However, the idealization of marriage as a reflection of the relationship of Christ and the church stands at some distance from Paul's 'celibacy is better' position evident in 1 Cor 7.

By the time of the writing of Ephesians, marriage apparently had a central role in community life. It is likely that the audience addressed in Ephesians would have understood the exhortation to be an encouragement to marry 'in the Lord'. It is impossible to arrive at definite conclusions as to the historical circumstances providing the impetus for the idealization of marriage by the Paul of Ephesians. However, the statement in Eph 5:29 that no man ever hates his own flesh but nourishes and cherishes it as Christ does the church, may provide a clue. Could this be a response to ascetic extremism? The Colossian Haustafel is also found in a letter warning of the dangers of asceticism (e.g. Col 2:20–3). Similarly, in Heb 13:4 a proclamation is made that marriage should be held in honour. The kind of recommendations made by Paul himself with respect to marriage may have been labelled as dangerous by authorities in later communities.

In his discussion of Eph 5:21–33, J.P. Sampley argues that the passage is suggestive for determining the author's overall purpose. He believes that emphasis in Eph 2:11ff on the unity of Jew and Gentile in the church is mirrored in 5:21–33 with its proclamation of the unity of husband and wife. 5:21–33 represents the author's specific application of the theme of unity to the smallest unit into which the church may be divided. According to Sampley, in the author's talk about marriage, he remains faithful to his commitment that the Gentiles cannot understand their place before God apart from Israel. He argues that in Eph 5:21–33 the marital relationship is shown to be patterned on Yahweh's marriage to Israel, as reflected in Christ's relationship to the church.[110]

Although Eph 2:11ff and Eph 5:21–33 disclose a strong intention to generate unity in community life, Sampley's linking of the passage on marriage with the specific purpose of harmonizing Jewish/Gentile relations is difficult to defend. The use of scripture and the possible influence of ideas concerning the marriage of Yahweh to Israel do not provide enough evidence to support Sampley's contention that in his exhortation to husbands/wives, the author had his eye on the Jewish/Gentile question. It seems that in his study, Sampley has overlooked the obvious application of the husbands/wives exhortation to relations between married partners in community life. He has not considered, for example, what the exhortation that wives should be subject to their husbands as the church is subject to Christ would have meant for female members of the community.[111] What are the implications of the fact that so much of the Ephesians Haustafel is devoted to exhorting husbands and wives and exploring the significance of their relationship in the household of God?

In Paul's writings, one finds a somewhat ambiguous position toward women. Although Paul by no means encourages a revolutionizing of male/female roles in the social realm, the involvement of certain women in the community points to the fact that they were able to occupy important leadership roles.[112] On the one hand Paul commends female fellow workers, but on the other hand his teaching with respect to women in 1 Cor 7, 11, 14 illustrates his traditional point of view. As noted earlier, the household codes represent a more conservative application of the ethos of love-patriarchalism than is found in Paul. The rule-like statements place women in the community more firmly under the auspices of male householders. If one compares the position of women in Paul's communities with that evident in the Pastoral Epistles, it seems that women were gradually being eliminated from leadership roles in some communities. The household codes of Colossians and Ephesians may represent an intermediate step in this process. In Colossians, the leader of the household church, Nympha, is mentioned (Col 4:15). In Ephesians there are no explicit references to women. One could argue that this does not say very much, since the only individual mentioned in Ephesians is Tychicus (Eph 6:21). However, in light of the elaborate argumentation made to support the subjection of wife to husband and to elevate the married state, it seems likely that the development visible in Ephesians represents an important step in the patriarchalization of Pauline communities. The women in the Ephesian community or communities who heard the household code were being given clearly defined roles in the household which undoubtedly had ramifications for their roles in the church. The significance of their subjection to their husbands for the church is triumphantly expressed by the author.

It is possible to make a similar argument about women in Ephesians, as that made about slaves in Colossians: power is being placed more firmly in the hands of household rulers. As an important locus for the purity of the community, the activity of women was considered of great significance for the sect's self-definition, as well as for the maintenance of distinctions from the outside world. As the sect became more visible, the activity of its women likely came increasingly under attack. The conversion of a woman from a non-believing household would carry with it certain risks. Thus, the household code may have been an important guide for how authority should be distributed within the community as well as a possible source for the stabilization of relations with outsiders. Harmony in the household of God (Eph 2:19) would act as an important means of preserving identity.

1.8 Conclusion

The level of institutionalization reflected by Colossians and Ephesians is aptly described by the phrase 'community-stabilizing institutionalization'. This stage of development is connected with the absence of Paul. The pseudonymous efforts of the writers of Colossians and Ephesians are made in an attempt to bring Paul's presence and authority to bear on community life.

Both Colossians and Ephesians rely heavily on traditional material. Ephesians, in particular, appears to exhibit a need to provide a comprehensive summary of Paul's teaching for a new generation. With the existence of a fairly solidified symbolic universe, creativity is no longer necessary, nor perhaps even possible, in the same way. Nevertheless, the symbolic universe can clearly be transformed in relation to new situations.

Colossians and Ephesians demonstrate a concern for the maintenance of the symbolic universe. The growth of the sect and the incorporation of a new generation bring new problems to community life. In the Colossian community, false teaching threatens. The historical circumstances underlying Ephesians are more difficult to determine. However, the stabilization of Jewish/Gentile relations in a growing Gentile church may be a concern of an author intent on proclaiming unity.

As in the case of the authentic epistles, the communities of Colossians and Ephesians may be described as conversionist sects. The mission of universal salvation is given cosmic scope in both of these writings. Both appear to disclose an awareness of the growth of the movement. Increased visibility of the sect may have been an important factor influencing the direction of the institutionalization of communal norms.

The ethos of love-patriarchalism is embraced in the Colossian and Ephesian Haustafeln. These rule-like statements are a more conservative demonstration of the ethos than is found in Paul's letters – they leave less room for exceptional behaviour. The New Testament Haustafeln are influenced by the ethics of Greco-Roman society as exhibited in the topos 'concerning household management'. Their characteristic structure, however, points to the existence of a schema that was given shape within Christian communities. The variations within the household codes point to the flexible use of tradition in varying social contexts.

The Colossian and Ephesian household codes appear to be employed primarily to manage internal communal relations, but possibly also to stabilize relations with outsiders. The rejection of traditional gods on the part of subordinate members of Greco-Roman households may have led to the criticism of members of the early Christian communities. The household codes would provide a pattern for life-style that could contribute to the easing of tensions with outsiders and that would be compatible with the evangelizing mission. The Colossian and Ephesian Haustafeln represent a placing of power more firmly in the hands of the rulers of the households (husbands, fathers, masters), ensuring that leadership positions fall to members of this group.

2

MINISTRY

The following investigation focuses especially on the way in which Paul's authority was exercised in his absence. The leadership structures constructed to cope with the disappearance of the charismatic leader are analysed. The relationship between ministry in these communities and the social realities of the Greco-Roman household is investigated.

2.1 Images of Paul

The above sub-title was inspired by an article by M. de Boer entitled 'Images of Paul in the Post-Apostolic Period'.[113] In his essay, de Boer investigates those communities for whom the person and achievements of Paul remained of significance after the disappearance of the Apostle.[114] He focuses on the four major New Testament witnesses to this reliance on Paul and his achievements: Colossians and Ephesians, Acts and the Pastoral Epistles.[115] De Boer repeats the insight of H.M. Schenke who argues that a 'legend' of Paul became current prior to any widespread knowledge of the existence of his letters or a collection thereof; Schenke points to the omission in Acts of any reference to Paul's letters as evidence for this.[116] The existence of such a 'legend' of Paul would perhaps explain why images of Paul contained in Colossians, Ephesians, Acts and the Pastorals exhibit many similarities. De Boer identifies six common elements of the images of Paul in Pauline Christianity after the death of the Apostle:

(1)   *the* apostle (or, in Acts, *the* missionary)
(2)   to the Gentiles of nations (τὰ ἔθνη)
(3)   who brought the gospel to the whole world
(4)   and suffered to make this possible.
... Paul is
(5)   the redeemer persecutor
(6)   and the authoritative teacher of the church.[117]

Hans Conzelmann also refers to the construction of similar pictures of Paul in deutero-Pauline writings.[118] Furthermore, he speaks of a Pauline school where traditions about Paul were articulated:

> Es wird als Arbeitshypothese (mehr is nicht möglich) vorgeschlagen: Es gab eine Schule des Paulus, die von ihm selbst gegründet wurde und über seinen Tod hinaus bestand. In ihr wurde 'Weisheit' gepflegt. Die Deuteropaulinen spiegeln Themen und Denkstil, Kol und Eph auch einen ausgeprägten Sprachstil.[119]

Although Conzelmann sees evidence of the existence of a Pauline school in Acts and in the Pastorals, he concentrates particularly on Colossians and Ephesians because of their closer affinity with the language and thought of the Apostle.

For the members of the Colossian community who had never seen Paul's face (Col 2:1), the letter from the imprisoned Apostle (Col 1:24; 2:5; 4:3, 10, 18) carried his authoritative word. It is probable that the members of the Colossian community did not know that their letter was not by Paul.[120] The pseudonymous epistle may, for example, have been presented to the community by a prominent local leader known to have personal connections with the Apostle. The setting of Ephesians is also Paul's imprisonment (Eph 3:1, 13; 4:1) and the tone is one of encouragement in Paul's absence. It is perhaps more likely than in the case of Colossians that the audience addressed by Ephesians knew that Paul was dead. Perhaps this letter from prison was presented as the last of Paul's teaching.

The attempt to reproduce Pauline thought and modes of expression in Colossians and Ephesians indicates a continuation of the Pauline movement beyond the boundaries of the Apostle's lifetime; it suggests a desire on the part of his associates to communicate his authoritative word when he no longer was able to do so and a readiness on the part of the communities on the mission route to recognize this word as authoritative. As noted previously, the expansion and transformation of the Pauline symbolic universe took place as it stood in dialectical relation to the new situation determined by the death of Paul and other early authorities. However, not only were elements of the belief system changed, but the ways through which authority was asserted were also transformed. The death of Paul led to a certain idealization of his identity. The presence of the six elements isolated by de Boer in the depiction of Paul in Colossians and Ephesians points to the formation of images of the Apostle that underlined the authoritative nature of his teaching for community life.

Throughout the authentic Pauline letters, it appears to be necessary for Paul to defend his apostleship (e.g. 1 Cor 15:3–11; 2 Cor 10–13; Rom 1:1–5; Gal 1:15–17; 2:7–9). In Colossians and Ephesians there is no evidence of doubt surrounding Paul's identity (Col 1:1, 23,25; Eph 3:1–13). In fact, in these letters Paul's apostleship is depicted in cosmic terms (Col 1:23–9; Eph 3:1–21). The confidence with which Paul is depicted as the apostle to the Gentiles is likely related to the growth of the Gentile churches, but also to the authority of the Apostle to regulate community life.

The suffering of the Apostle is a key element of the picture of Paul in Colossians and Ephesians. In short, the gospel is able to penetrate the world because Paul suffers (Col 1:24; 4:3, 10, 18; Eph 3:1, 13; 4:1). The suffering of Paul is closely linked with the purpose of the church in the world (Col 1:24; Eph 3:13). Eph 3:13 states that Paul's suffering is the addressees' (i.e. the church's) glory. Suffering is glorified in a way here that is foreign to the authentic Paul. Particularly striking, however, is Col 1:24. Paul is said to be suffering for the sake of the Colossians; he is said to be completing in his flesh what is lacking in Christ's afflictions for the sake of his body, that is, the church.[121] The idealization of Paul's suffering may be the result of an attempt to ensure the Apostle's firm connection with the Colossian community (cf. Col 2:1). One must listen to the voice of the one who suffers for the sake of the church. Suffering is a sign of an authentic apostle (e.g. 1 Cor 4:9–13; 2 Cor 11:23–33; Gal 6:17; cf. Acts 9:15–16; 20:19–23). Moreover, in a community that longs for Paul's presence, his absence and suffering in bondage must be explained and justified. The continued efficacy of the universal vision of salvation must be legitimated (cf. Phil 1:12–14): Should one not separate oneself completely from a world that can imprison the Apostle to the Gentiles?

Another common element of the images of Paul found in deutero-Pauline writings, as indentified by de Boer, is that of the redeemed persecutor. There is no doubt that Paul himself believed this to be an integral factor of his apostleship (e.g. Phil 3:5–11; 1 Cor 15:8–11). This expression of Paul's identity is explicit in Eph 3:8, but is found nowhere in Colossians. In Eph 3:8, Paul describes himself as the least of all the saints who received grace to preach to the Gentiles. The expression 'least of all the saints', rather than 'least of the apostles', perhaps expresses a sense of solidarity between Paul and the early

Christians. It is not difficult to understand why those who had transferred from the corruption of the outside world would be able to identify with an authoritative leader who was himself a redeemed persecutor.

A final aspect of the images of Paul found in Colossians and Ephesians is his role as teacher. In both letters the authority of the Apostle is set up against false teaching (e.g. Col 2:8ff; Eph 4:13−16). The predominant fear appears to be that community members will be led astray from the Pauline gospel (Col 1:23; Col 2; Eph 4:13−16, 20−4; 5:6−7). A need for continuing education is apparent. Paul is an authoritative teacher who stands firmly against any deviation from the truth he teaches.

Thus, in Colossians and Ephesians, one discovers a vision of Paul as the Apostle to the Gentiles who brought the gospel to the whole world and suffered to make this possible. Paul is a redeemed persecutor (Eph) and an authoritative teacher of the church. The picture of the Apostle suffering as he carried out his universal vision of salvation may have been of utmost significance to the Pauline sect which struggled to keep its doors open to Greco-Roman society, while at the same time experiencing difficuties in its dealings with outsiders. The image of the Apostle as the redeemed persecutor may have been employed in relation to an attempt to remind addressees of the significance of their transference into the body of Christ in terms of the life-style now required of them. The role of Paul as an authoritative teacher was articulated in an effort to clarify which teaching was appropriate for life in the Lord and was employed by early church leaders to curtail deviant behaviour. In order to consider more specifically how Paul's authority was exercised in the communities of Colossians and Ephesians, however, it is essential to consider the particular authority-asserting exhortations found in these writings.

2.2 Governing in the absence of the Apostle: Colossians

The fact that Paul is first and foremost a missionary, and was not rooted in any one community, meant that the small cells of Christians along his mission route needed to be somewhat independent. Nevertheless, it is evident that the groups were dependent on him for guidance. 1 Corinthians indicates that direction would be given by the Apostle about how leadership should be exercised if problems arose. With the death of Paul, it became clear that this style of governing could not persist. Communities were faced with the realities of a new kind of independence. Further institutionalization was required to deal with the new problems of management surrounding the absence of the charismatic leader and the incorporation of people farther removed from the events that called the sect into being.

The kind of social situation that would have resulted from the death of Paul deserves attention. Paul's letters presuppose an intimate relationship between the Apostle, his network of fellow workers, and the members of local communities. For those associates who worked with him on the mission route or for local leaders who offered him hospitality, the disappearance of the Apostle may have caused a considerable crisis. How would they deal with the death of this authoritative figure? One obvious answer to this question, in light of the existence of pseudonymous letters, is that they would attempt to make Paul's presence a continuing reality within the community.

Weber's understanding of the routinization of charisma is enlightening for investigation of the social situation created by the absence of the Apostle. According to Weber, the problems surrounding the death of the original charismatic leader give rise to the routinization process. The absence of the charismatic leader creates the problem of succession: to whom should we now listen? Those who have been followers of the leader naturally have an interest in preserving their identity. The staff, which is closely associated with the charismatic leader, is interested in securing its leadership positions.[122] The problems surrounding the death of the charismatic leader generate the formation of more clearly defined authority structures. Beneath the pseudonymous writings of Colossians and Ephesians, one discovers the efforts of the Pauline sect to deal with the absence of the original charismatic leader. The authority-asserting exhortations in each of these writings give some indication as to how community members are dealing with the inevitable problem of how to live 'in Christ' in the absence of Paul.

The letter to the Colossians promises Paul's continuing presence in the community despite his physical absence. Here we find evidence for the evangelizing activity of Paul's associates. Paul is presented as struggling on behalf of the Colossians, Laodiceans and all those who have not seen his face in the flesh (Col 2:1; cf. Col 1:29). Communities apparently exist which appeal to the Apostle's authority, but who have never seen him. Some other members of the Pauline movement have evidently been responsible for the establishment of such communities. It is significant that Paul does not promise to visit the Colossians in the near future, as he does the Romans (Rom 15:24). The importance of the exhortation is underlined by the address: 'For I wish you to know ...' (Col 2:1; cf. 1 Cor 11:3). The attention of the audience is captured. What Paul is about to teach deserves careful attention.[123]

The purpose of Paul's involvement with those who have never seen his face is to provide encouragement (παρακαλέω Col 2:2). From the context, it appears that this encouragement takes the form of teaching. In Paul's letters the term 'παρακαλέω' can refer to admonition (e.g. 1 Thess 4:1).[124] Paul desires that their hearts be comforted and that they be joined together (συμβιβάζω) in love. The verb 'συμβιβάζω' can be employed by Paul in the sense of giving instruction (1 Cor 2:16). In Col 2:19 the verb literally means 'joined together'.[125] But in Col 2:2ff, the joining and teaching ideas go together. Wishing that the community be joined together in love is dependent on their receiving, and their being rooted in, the Pauline gospel. The stress on understanding, knowledge, and wisdom in Col 2:2–4 also supports the fact that teaching is of major concern in Colossae.

In Col 2:4 Paul gives the reason for his admonition. He wishes no one to be deceived by persuasive speech. Such a warning is related to the reality of Paul's absence (Col 2:5). Paul's presence is apparently understood as being crucial to the prevention of members being led astray. The addressees are reassured: Paul may be absent in the flesh but he is with them in the spirit.[126] He rejoices in their order and in the firmness of their faith in Christ Jesus. The Colossians are apparently praised for their well-ordered community life – they are governing themselves well. It is significant that this order is associated with what appears to be a central concern of the argument of Colossians against the false teachers – the centrality of Christ.[127] The author's arguments elsewhere indicate that he believes that not all recognize the central authority of Christ in the community (cf. Col 2:8ff). This seems to have led to disorder in community life (Col 2:16–18). In Col 2:2–7 the intention of Paul's instructions is straightforwardly expressed. He desires to remind them of what they have been taught (cf. 1 Thess 2:13; 4:1, 1 Cor 11:2).

The Colossians did not receive the gospel from Paul himself, but from Epaphras (Col 1:7). Paul commends Epaphras in a way that underlines his close identification with the Apostle and his authority in the Colossian community. Epaphras is a fellow servant and a faithful minister (διάκονος) of Christ (cf. Philem 23).[128] He is presented as an intermediary between Paul and the Colossian community. He has brought news about the life and conduct of the community to the Apostle (Col 1:8). The result of this reporting is that the Apostle continuously prays for the Colossians. Wisdom, knowledge, and spiritual understanding which unfold in every good work are his desire for them (Col 1:9–10).

It appears that, in Colossians, the community is being reminded of what they received from Paul's fellow worker, Epaphras, in order to impress on them the importance of holding fast to such teaching (cf. Col 1:23).[129] The role of this fellow worker is instrumental in the instruction of the community in the word of truth, the gospel (Col 1:5ff). In Col 1:7, as well as in the list of messages and greetings in Col 4:7ff, the reliability of Paul's fellow workers and the importance of their roles in maintaining communication between the Apostle and the community are emphasized. Tychicus and Onesimus (who is described as one of the Colossians) are singled out as those who will report news of Paul to the community.[130] Tychicus is apparently the bearer of the letter to the Colossians. His connection with the Colossian community is similar to that of Epaphras (Col 1:7). Tychicus' mission with respect to the Colossian community is in fact identical to Paul's mission; he is to encourage their hearts (cf. Col 2:1; Col 4:8). Many fellow workers send their greetings to the Colossian community (Col 4:10ff). Once again the role of Epaphras is singled out for mention (Col 4:12–13). He is described as one of the Colossians and is fervently commended by Paul for his work on behalf of the Colossians and those in the neighbouring communities of Laodicea and Hierapolis. His authority (perhaps against the proponents of the Colossian philosophy) in community life is legitimated.[131]

If one compares the list of messages and greetings of Rom 16 with those found in Colossians, a difference of perspective is evident. The Romans list is comprised mainly of the greetings which Paul sends to fellow workers and associates, mentioning only a few greetings from others in the conclusion (Rom 16:21–3). But in Colossians, it is the greetings of Paul's helpers which are reported first and in the greatest detail.[132] The emphasis on the reliability of the fellow workers in Colossians is made even more significant through a comparison with parallel passages in Philemon. Almost all the names which appear in Colossians also appear in Philemon.[133] Due to the consistent agreements found between the two lists of greetings, it appears as though Colossians must have been composed by one of Paul's students who knew and used Philemon. Colossians must have been written after Philemon on account of the clear expansion of Paul's list in Philemon by the author of Colossians through the addition of information.[134] To name only one of numerous examples, in Philemon, Archippus is designated as a co-recipient of the letter and as a fellow soldier (Philem 2). In Colossians, however, his name occurs at the end; he is admonished to fulfil the ministry which he has received in the Lord (Col 4:17).[135] In employing Philemon's list of greetings and making it more vivid, the author of Colossians may have sought to ensure that the letter would gain a hearing as a message from Paul.[136]

Colossians may represent the efforts of one of Paul's associates to reinforce the authority of fellow workers in Colossae and in other Pauline communities. Epaphras and Tychicus are described as ministers (διάκονος Col 1:7; 4:7). Archippus is exhorted to fulfil the ministry (διακονία Col 4:17) which he has received. In Col 1:23 Paul is described as a minister (διάκονος) of the gospel — a ministry that is intimately connected with the purpose of the church in the world (Col 1:23−9).

Colossians reflects the problems of governing in the absence of Paul. The disappearance of the Apostle would surely have left a gap in the leadership of the Pauline sect. The Apostle could not be present in the community, but his associates could speak in his name. They could make his presence felt — bring comfort in his absence. Paul's disciples were faced with the problem of succession described by Weber. In order to be able to carry out the work of the charismatic leader, they had to legitimate their own authority in terms of the authority of the Apostle. They believed in the Pauline mission and sought to preserve its identity. The defence of their own leadership positions as being closely connected to the Apostle's mission would naturally accompany an attempt to ensure the continued existence of the Pauline sect. The reliability of the witness of associates was stressed by other writers in the New Testament. In Eph 6:21 a promise is made that Tychicus will communicate all things to the addressees, which resembles the exhortation found in Col 4:7−8.[137] In 1 Pet 5:12 Silvanus is described as the faithful brother to the community; it is through him that Peter is said to write.[138] In the Pastoral Epistles, the communities are addressed through Paul's delegates, Timothy and Titus. These examples reflect an effort on the part of fellow workers to organize and care for the churches the apostles established.

2.3 Governing in the absence of the Apostle: Ephesians

The description of the unity of Gentiles and Jews in Eph 2:11ff ends with a proclamation that they are fellow citizens with the saints and members of the household of God which is built on the foundation of the apostles and prophets with Jesus Christ as the cornerstone (Eph 2:19−20). The mention of apostles (which include Paul, Eph 1:1; 3:1−13) and prophets as a foundation likely reflects the perspective of a 'built-up' church looking back to its origins. The tone implies considerable distance between the addressees and the earliest leaders.[139] The apostles and prophets are at the base of the relationship between the members of the household of God and Christ.[140]

In 1 Cor 12:28 the apostles and prophets stand at the head of the list of the church leaders given by Paul. In Acts 13:1, Paul, Barnabas, Simeon, Lucius and Manaen are listed as members of the group of prophets and teachers who are leaders of the church at Antioch.[141] In Acts, prophets are depicted as wandering charismatic teachers who are connected with the Jerusalem church (Acts 11:27−28; 15:22, 27, 32; 21:10−11). Through the action of the Spirit, Agabus predicts the future (Acts 11:28; 21:10−11). Judas and Silas are depicted as exhorting the (Gentile − Acts 15:23) brethren at Antioch (Acts 15:32).[142] It is by the action of the Holy Spirit that Paul and Barnabas are set apart for their mission (Acts 13:2−4). God performs many signs and wonders through them among the Gentiles (Acts 15:12).

Luke's picture of the early church being composed of the apostles (those who had known the historical Jesus), elders (authoritative local leaders) and prophets (wandering teachers) was probably painted in a way that would speak to the members of his own community. The account of the confusing events of those early days appears to have been given with the aim of having Paul proclaim the message: 'Let it be known that this salvation of God has been sent to the Gentiles; they will listen' (Acts 28:28). Although Peter and James play roles in legitimating the Gentile mission (Acts 10:1−11:18; 15:7−11, 13−21), it is Paul who actually carries out the mission. The placing of Paul among the group of prophets serves to clarify his role. Paul was set apart by divine intervention to carry out his mission (Acts 9:1−20; 22:4−16; 26:9−18). Not only is his teaching in various locations effective, but he is able to perform spectacular miracles (Acts 19:11−20; cf. Acts 15:12).

The mention of apostles and prophets as the foundation of the church in Ephesians resembles the emphasis on origins one finds in Acts. As noted earlier, both Acts and Ephesians may have addressed the problems surrounding a mixed community of Gentiles and Jews. It is the breaking down of hostility between Gentiles and Jews which culminates in the construction of the household of God built on the foundation of apostles and prophets (Eph 2:11ff). The author of Ephesians apparently considers the witness of this group of leaders as being central to the origin of the Gentile mission. Moreover, this group is connected with the beginning of the movement which has its roots in Judaism. Gentile Christians are perhaps being reminded of their heritage. That these associations accompany the expression 'the apostles and prophets' is made even clearer by its appearance in Eph 3:5: the mystery of Christ has been revealed to his holy apostles and prophets in the Spirit. On account of their proclamation, the mystery is made known throughout the world. The mystery is that the Gentiles are now fellow heirs, members of the same body, and partakers of the promise in Christ Jesus through the gospel (Eph 3:6). Paul proclaims that it was of this gospel (this original gospel), that he was made minister (Eph 3:7). The effect of Paul's grounding of the church in the authority of the prophets and apostles is clearly to establish his own authority over the addressees. It is his understanding of the unity of Gentiles and Jews in the Church which must be preserved.

The apostles and prophets appear a third time in Eph 4:11. Here, however, a concern for the organization of the community is more clearly evident. Eph 4:1–16 is a proclamation of the unity of the community. Various ministries are performed for the preservation of the body. To each is given grace according to the measure of the gift of Christ (Eph 4:7). The point of the citation of Ps 68:18, with accompanying interpretation in Eph 4:8–10, is to emphasize the initiative of Christ in the giving of gifts.[143] The gifts given by the ascended Christ to believers for service to the church have led some to be apostles, some prophets, some evangelists and some shepherds and teachers (Eph 4:11). This giving of gifts takes place to perfect the saints for the work of ministry and for the edifying of the body of Christ. Although the passage in Ephesians is unique in stressing the initiative of Christ in the giving of gifts, it closely resembles Rom 12:5ff and 1 Cor 12:28.

The list of gifts reveals even less about the differentiation of roles in the community or communities of Ephesians than similar lists in

Paul's own letters. All of the ministers listed perform functions of preaching or teaching. We hear nothing of the more practical functions of administration or caring for the needs of the poor. Only the terms evangelist (εὐαγγελιστής) and pastor (ποιμήν) have no counterpart in Paul. In Acts 21:8, Philip is described as an evangelist. He is apparently a wandering teacher (Acts 8:5, 40). In 2 Tim 4:5, Timothy is instructed to do the work of an evangelist; he is to persevere despite the rise of the false teaching (2 Tim 4:1ff). The role of pastor may also be connected with teaching. In Acts 20:28 shepherding (ποιμαίνω) is given as one of the tasks of the elders of Ephesus (cf. 1 Pet 5:2; Jn 21:16). Shepherding is apparently to protect the community from false teachers that threaten to appear (Acts 20:29–31).[144]

Although this teaching/preaching role, characteristic of the ministries listed in Eph 4:11, may tell us little about the concrete functions of leaders, it may nevertheless reveal a great deal about the overall significance of the teaching leadership. The author, in fact, appears to connect the ministries with the protection of the church from false teaching. The hope is that the community will mature in the unity of faith and in the knowledge of the son of God. They are no longer to be children tossed to and fro by deceitful teaching. But speaking in truth, the members of the body are to grow and thrive, each part performing in harmony with the others. With Christ as the head, the body is to build itself up in love (Eph 4:13–16).

The Gospel of Matthew has some interesting similarities with Ephesians in terms of the centrality of teaching. It is significant that the only instances of the term 'ekklesia' in the gospels occur in Matt 16:18 and 18:17. Both of these passages speak of the act of binding and loosing.[145] In Matt 16:18–19, Peter is presented as the authoritative teacher of the universal church. While the notion of admitting and excluding from the church may be present here (the main interest of Matt 18:15–20), it is Peter's authority to declare acts licit or illicit according to Jesus' teaching that is stressed.[146] It is uncertain whether Matthew perceived an individual acting in the Petrine role in his own day. It is evident, however, that in referring to the role of Peter, he grounds the community in foundational teaching. It is on Peter, the rock, that Jesus will build his church (Matt 16:18). In Eph 2:20 the apostles and prophets provide the foundation for the universal church.

In Matt 18:15–20, Jesus gives instructions concerning disciplinary action in the local church. The binding and loosing of Matt 18:17

refers explicitly to the power to admit or exclude from the local church. The problem of sin is to be settled in private if possible, but as a last resort, the local church may be called together to make a decision. If the sinner refuses to abide by the decision, he or she is to be excommunicated.[147] The fact that structures have been constructed to deal with sinners suggests that those who are going astray present a substantial problem for the community. The threat of corruption is heightened by the openness to new members that accompanies a vision of universal salvation (Matt 28:18–20; cf. Matt 24:14; Matt 26:13).[148] Matthew apparently responds to the problem of deviation by presenting the church as a mixed body. As the explanation of the parable in Matt 13:36–43 illustrates, it is only the Last Judgement which will reveal those who are chosen for God's kingdom (cf. Matt 22:10–14; 25:31–46). In addition to depicting the church as a mixed body, Matthew responds to the problem of deviation by stressing the possibility of repentance. Matt 18:15–20, with its instructions about excommunication, is inserted between Matt 18:10–14 and 21–35, so that it must be understood within the context of an admonition to do everything possible not to lose any of the 'little ones' – to go after everyone and forgive them.

What is especially notable about Matt 18:15–20 is that in the matter of discipline, the church is called upon to act as a whole. Perhaps Matthew seeks to ensure that in making such an important decision as the excommunication of a member, the whole community will be involved. This effort may be related to a kind of anti-clericalism that can be deduced from instructions found in the long tirade of Matthew 23. The warnings against ostentatious actions and clothing (23:5), the desire for first seats at religious gatherings (23:6) and the desire to be addressed with the special titles of rabbi, teacher, father and master (23:7–10), make little sense unless such behaviour was a possibility, or to some extent a reality, in Matthew's community.[149] The target of the attack are the scribes and Pharisees as the authoritative teachers of the people (Matt 23:2, 3), but it seems likely that the pointed statements are intended to censure leadership tendencies in the local community. A group of prophets and teachers (scribes and wisemen) may have formed the leadership in Matthew's church (Matt 13:52; 23:34). Matt 5:19 warns against teaching individuals to relax commandments. Matt 7:15–20 contains a warning against false prophets. Even the most active and colourful prophets, exorcists and wonder-workers are not guaranteed entry into the kingdom of heaven (Matt 7:21–3).[150]

Study of Matthew's gospel is particularly valuable for understanding the emergence of ministry roles in the early church for it provides information about the kind of struggles that led to the tightening of leadership structures.[151] 'What can we do about a deviant community member?' and 'How can we determine authoritative teaching?' are questions of primary concern. These problems are not of the kind often identified by scholars as being determinative for the formation of ministerial offices. They do not involve a type of mental anxiety such as that surrounding the realization that the kingdom is not coming or an awareness that a system must be formed to combat a threatening heresy. Rather, the communal realities that call for an exercise of control in Matthew's gospel have to do with such practical problems as how one should deal with a leader who seems more concerned with the preservation of a title than the task of ministry; how one should relate Jesus' commands to community life; how one should determine which teacher's word is authoritative; and how one should deal with a brother or sister who has gone astray.

Matthew leaves his modern readers with many puzzles with respect to the organization of his community. His gospel discloses a certain recognition of the necessity for more established leadership. Community life may have taught Matthew to be cautious, however, for he appears to be aware of the problems such leadership could bring. On the one hand, he recognizes the authority of prophets and teachers who apparently acted as leaders in his community, but on the other hand, he is wary of the external trappings that can come to be associated with established leadership. He holds up Peter as an authoritative figure for the guidance of the church, but appears to be unwilling to have a local counterpart as an authoritative teacher, insisting that the whole community be involved in such important decisions as excommunication. This apparent ambivalence may be related to the fact that Matthew's church is a church in transition.[152]

Like Matthew's gospel, Ephesians may be placed in that period sometimes described by New Testament scholars as the 'third generation'. This is the period prior to the establishment of hierarchy when organizational structures are in the process of becoming more clearly defined.[153] Churches engage in the process of community-stabilizing institutionalization. The authoritative figures of the past serve to ground the communities in authoritative teaching. A greater reliance on tradition is related to an attempt to prevent deviance in community life. The crucial role of the teacher is underlined. The craftiness of the false teacher is stressed. The mutual responsibility of the community with respect to ministry is proclaimed.

If one compares Ephesians with the Pastoral Epistles, or Matthew with Ignatius of Antioch, it appears that the solutions offered in this 'in-between' period to the question of organization of community life had little survivability.[154] The historical circumstances faced by many communities as they made their way into the second century, appear to have led to a tightening of leadership structures to an even greater degree. The legitimation of the authority of officials became the primary means of ensuring the continued existence of communities.

2.4 The household codes and leadership

The household codes of Colossians (Col 3:18−4:1) and Ephesians (Eph 5:21−6:9) reflect authority structures. As noted earlier, in comparison to the instructions found in the authentic epistles, the Haustafeln of Colossians and Ephesians represent a placing of power more firmly in the hands of the husband/parent/master. This has important consequences for determining eligibility for leadership roles. As in the individual household, the subordinate members of the house church are required to submit to the authoritative householder/leader.

The connection of the household codes with leadership structures is especially evident in the instructions found in 1 Pet 5:1−5. Here the elders and the ones that are younger are instructed. Like the wives with respect to their husbands (1 Pet 3:1, 5) and the slaves with respect to their masters (1 Pet 2:18), the younger ones are instructed to submit to the elders (1 Pet 5:5). There is clearly a connection here between leadership roles and senior status in the household. The members' respect for one who is experienced in the direction of community life may be related to his position as head of the household.[155] With the passage of time, the authority of a respected household/leader would probably become more firmly established. Having placed his household at the disposal of the community for many years and being known as one of the first householders converted in a given area, the authority of the householder/leader would progressively strengthen. Von Dobschütz, in 1904, made a great deal of sociological sense when he pointed to the significance of the formation of a class of 'old experienced Christians' for development beyond the first generation.[156]

The Haustafeln exhibit an interest in household relationships on the one hand, and in the church understood on the model of the household on the other. If a slave is instructed to be subject to his or her master in the Lord, this carries with it certain implications for the slave's behaviour not only in the outside society, but also within the sect. The slave of a believing householder would respect the leadership of one who places his home at the disposal of the members of the household of God. As noted previously, it is evident from Paul's letters that the household may have acted as an important model for the formation of the ekklesia. Meetings were held in individual house churches and one's position in the household was probably related to the role adopted in community life. In Colossians and Ephesians one discovers signs of the continued articulation of the implication of this household-rooted church life.[157]

In addition to the household code (Col 3:18−4:1), Colossians makes reference to the existence of a house church (Col 4:15). Although we find no such reference in Ephesians, the church is named explicitly as the household of God (Eph 2:19−20; cf. Eph 2:21−2; Gal 6:10). This expression appears both in 1 Peter (1 Pet 4:17; cf. 2:5) and in the Pastoral Epistles (1 Tim 3:15). Moreover, the description of Paul's mission in Eph 3:14−15 culminates in an announcement of the Apostle's adoration of the Father from whom every family (πατριά) is named. The place of the household in God's plan of salvation is proclaimed.[158] In the Haustafel of Ephesians (Eph 5:21−6:9), the foundational relationship of the household − marriage − is seen to reflect the relationship of the church to Christ. Here we see the inseparable link between social structures and symbolism. Life shaped by realities of the Greco-Roman household affects the articulation of beliefs, while beliefs colour life in the household.

The influence of household structures evident in the Haustafeln of Colossians and Ephesians is significant for understanding the nature of ministry in the communities underlying these writings. The household codes represent more firmly established authority structures than are evident in Paul's letters. The significance of the household code for leadership in Pauline communities will become even clearer in the consideration of the Pastoral Epistles, where household ethics and the delineation of criteria for determining who is eligible for leadership positions go hand in hand.

2.5 Conclusion

The pseudonymous character of Colossians and Ephesians points to efforts on the part of associates to make Paul's presence a continuing reality in community life. The images of Paul found in these writings are clearly related to an attempt to reinforce the authority of the teaching of the Apostle to the Gentiles. It is useful to imagine the kind of social situation created by the absence of Paul. It is reasonable to assume that the newly attained independence of communities would have created a certain crisis of management. In addition, the entourage of fellow workers and associates one hears about in Paul's letters, bereft of this authoritative charismatic leader, must surely have been forced to organize themselves in the light of the new social situation. The existence of the pseudonymous writings of Colossians and Ephesians, which are closely related to the authentic epistles, indicates that the Pauline movement continued to be active beyond the death of the Apostle.

In Colossians, the authority of Paul's fellow workers − their connection with Paul and with the Colossian community − is stressed in order to reinforce the authority of Pauline teaching. In Ephesians, the authority of Paul's gospel is highlighted by means of a looking back to the past. The church is built on the foundation of apostles and prophets. The original gospel must be protected. A teaching ministry in the church is apparently legitimated.

Many historical factors appear to have acted as catalysts to the changes in the organization of Pauline communities after the death of the Apostle. The absence of the Apostle, coupled with the problems of growth and increased remoteness of origins, led to efforts to stabilize community life. The relations between members of different social backgrounds needed to be harmonized. The focus fell more specifically on the settled community. The danger of members being led astray by false teaching seems to have been understood as especially threatening in these communities.

Governing in the absence of Paul was facilitated by the household codes. These instructions indicate the existence of more solidified authority structures than in the authentic epistles. They carry implications for behaviour both inside and outside the sect, as well as for eligibility for leadership positions. The Haustafeln exhibit interest both in household relations and in the church understood on the model of the household.

3

RITUAL

The following study considers the ritual context of Colossians and Ephesians. The function of hymns in the integration of the communities is examined. The importance of ritual forms for the education of community members is highlighted. The investigation also considers the significance of the frequent allusions to baptism in both Colossians and Ephesians. The connection between the cosmic symbolism, apparently rooted in baptismal experience, and the ethical positions recommended by the writings is of particular interest.

3.1 Psalms, hymns and spiritual songs: communication and integration

In Part 1 it was useful to consider Paul's letters in terms of the ritual context of communities. Ritual was defined, in the language of Clifford Geertz, as 'consecrated behaviour' − behaviour set apart for contact with the sacred.[159] Colossians and Ephesians possibly disclose more evidence of a ritual context than the authentic epistles. Both of these writings are heavily influenced by existing hymns and make frequent allusions to baptism. The proclaiming tone of Ephesians gives the reader the impression that the writing is closely linked to the gathering of a community for worship.

In Col 3:16 the addressees are told to let the word of God dwell in them richly, teaching and admonishing one another in all wisdom, and singing psalms, hymns and spiritual songs with thankfulness in their hearts to God. Whatever they do, in word or deed, must be done in the name of the Lord Jesus, giving thanks to God the Father through him (Col 3:17). In the parallel text of Eph 5:18−20, the author also refers to psalms, hymns and spiritual songs and to the importance of giving thanks. It is impossible to differentiate precisely between the psalms, hymns and spiritual songs. Together they appear to refer to the full range of singing which is prompted by the

Spirit.[160] It is probable that the psalms, hymns and spiritual songs were patterned according to Jewish liturgical traditions.[161] The 'psalms', for example, may include some from the biblical psalter.[162] However, the fact that the singing was seen as evidence for the presence of the word of Christ (Col 3:16) and the Spirit (Eph 5:18), points to the innovative tendencies characterizing such activity (cf. 1 Cor 14:26). As Rev 19:1–8 shows, phrases and themes from scripture could be proclaimed in a form adapted to a contemporary situation in the early church.[163]

The evidence of 'hymnic' influences in the texts of Colossians and Ephesians points to the existence of traditional material connected with community worship.[164] The blessing/thanksgiving of Eph 1:3–14 (cf. 2 Cor 1:3; 1 Pet 1:3) is often considered in terms of liturgical setting.[165] Mitton is correct when he argues, however, that the obvious dependence of this passage on Colossians and the genuine Pauline letters makes it difficult to hold that this piece had an independent liturgical life prior to the composition of Ephesians.[166] Nevertheless, the flavour of Eph 1:3–14 is clearly liturgical (cf. Eph 3:14–21). Against Mitton, it must be said that dependence on other Pauline works does not exclude the possibility of liturgical influences, if one views all the Pauline writings as being connected to a ritual context.[167] Colossians, in particular, is heavily influenced by ritual forms. The adoption by the author of Ephesians of much of the language of Colossians implies that he or she understood it to be of relevance to the addressees. Dahl argues that Eph 1:3–14, which sets out the central ideas of the epistle, may reflect a benediction before baptism.[168] While Mitton's arguments concerning the independent existence of Eph 1:3–14 as it stands are convincing, there is no reason to reject the notion that Eph 1:3–14 resembles what the early Christians may have heard at the time of their baptism into the Pauline sect or in subsequent community gatherings. The repetition of Pauline liturgical traditions would certainly be in keeping with the author's desire to remind community members of their origins rooted in the Pauline gospel and to preserve the authority of the Apostle. To negate the possibility of liturgical influences in Ephesians is to disconnect it from a communal setting.[169]

There is a wide agreement among scholars that Col 1:5–20 is a traditional Christ hymn that was inserted within the epistle to the Colossians in order to reinforce the argument of the letter.[170] It appears, however, that the author of Colossians made short interpretative additions to the hymn. In the first place, the identification of Christ as the head of the body, the church, found at the end of the first cosmological strophe (Col 1:15–18), leads one to believe that the statement, 'of the church', was added by the author. Moreover, the repetition of 'through him' found in Col 1:20 suggests that the words, 'through the blood of his cross', were also inserted.[171] The purpose of these two glosses is apparently to give the cosmological hymn solid historical reference. The reconciliation of the whole world is connected with the death of Christ. The rule of Christ is a present reality in the church.[172] This is supported by the interpretation of the hymn given in Col 1:21–3.[173] The author seems to have adopted a hymn familiar to his audience and interpreted it in order to clarify its relevance for community life.

The Christ hymn in Col 1:15–20 and accompanying interpretation in Col 1:21–3 occupy a central position in the epistle as a whole. The hymn provides the author with a basis from which to launch the argument against the philosophical opponents. The author apparently seeks to remind the addressees of what they already know.[174] This recalling function is also visible in the preceding thanksgiving passage of Col 1:9–14 which also has a hymnic flavour. The combined effect of Col 1:9–23 is to link the conversion experience with God's activity in Christ. The passage serves as an effective tool for the author because it roots the addressees in the ritual context – it calls to mind the arena of worship where they discover and renew their experience of the Lordship of Christ. The citation of the hymn draws attention to what they have probably often heard or sung. But perhaps most importantly, it reminds them of their conversions on the basis of how God has acted in Christ, while at the same time clarifying who Christ is and his relationship to the church and the world. The passage takes the members of the sect back to the beginning and recommends a particular world view; it seeks to stabilize and integrate. The fact that the hymn is removed from its context in song or prayer and is placed in an epistle means that the focus is not on a communal acting out of belief, but on the content of what is believed. Concentration on 'content' becomes especially necessary when a community is threatened by some form of 'empty deceit' (Col 2:8).[175]

The 'hymnic' influences found in Colossians and Ephesians are employed in connection with an attempt to underline certain fundamental beliefs and to recommend a particular life-style. In Col 3:16 the singing of psalms, hymns and spiritual songs is described as a vehicle for teaching and admonishing. A similar meaning is implied by the instruction to the addressees in Eph 5:18 to speak to one another by means of such ritual forms. Although singing is addressed 'to God' (Col 3:16) and 'to the Lord' (Eph 5:19), it is also perceived as a means of educating community members.[176] Paul's remarks in 1 Cor 14 come to mind. The kind of stress given by Paul to the teaching rituals seems to have persisted in the communities that appealed to his authority after his death.

3.2 Baptism: interpretation and life-style

In Part 1, baptism was investigated in terms of its role in the formation of the Pauline sect (cf. Gal 3:26−8).[177] However, the language referring to baptism in Colossians and Ephesians appears less concerned with legitimating the innovation involved in the gathering of the newly-converted in Christ, than with a remembrance of this event to encourage a certain kind of behaviour in Christ (cf. Col 1:12−14; 2:9−15; 3:1−3, 10−11; Eph 1:11−14; 2:1−6; 4:4−6, 22−4, 30; 5:25−7 and possibly 2:11−22 and 5:8−14). For example, in Col 3:1ff, having been raised with Christ (apparently a reference to baptism, cf. Col 3:12) is understood to have implications for life-style. In Eph 4:22ff the putting off of one's old nature (probably an allusion to baptism, cf. Rom 6:6; Col 3:9−10) is recalled in relation to a plea to put away various vices. Thus, in this sub-section the focus will not be on the relationship between baptism and sect formation, but on the link between baptism and sect consolidation.

In Colossians and Ephesians the ideas of unity and restoration are given cosmological dimensions in a way that far exceeds what is found in the authentic letters.[178] In Paul's writings, one discovers an image of the heavenly enthronement of Christ (Phil 2:9ff; cf. Rom 8:34ff; Rom 11:36; 1 Cor 8:6). Likewise, in Colossians, Christ is depicted as triumphing over all powers. However, going beyond Paul, he is described as the body which contains all fullness. Christ's body becomes the locus for cosmic reconciliation (Col 1:5−20). Similar ideas are found in Ephesians (cf. Eph 1:10, 21−3; 3:10). Moreover, the description of the unity of Gentile and Jew (a frequent theme found in baptismal formulas, Gal 3:28; 1 Cor 12:13; Col 3:11) also has a cosmological colouring in Ephesians (Eph 2:11−22); this disciple of Paul apparently sees the inclusion of Gentiles in the people of God as the primary manifestation of God's plan for the fullness of time.[179] The union is described in terms of reconciliation in one body; peace is the result of the creation of one man in the place of two (Eph 2:15−16; cf. 2 Cor 5:17).

Along with the description of the cosmic reconciliation encompassed within the body of Christ, Colossians and Ephesians both describe
a kind of heavenly enthronement of Christ which is presently shared
by the believer. The connection between this symbolism and the
experience of baptism is clear. The emphasis in Col 3:1−4 is on the
present salvation of community members.[180] Because the Colossians
have been raised with Christ (reference to baptism, cf. Col 2:12), they
are to seek the things which are above where Christ sits on the right
hand of God. They themselves are dead − they have been changed,
re-created. Their lives are hid with Christ in God. When Christ
appears, they also will appear with him in glory. The emphasis on
a present enthronement of the believer is even stronger in Eph 2:6.[181]
Here believers are described as having been raised and seated together
in the heavenly places in Christ Jesus. The past tenses in this verse
indicate that something has already happened. The emphasis on present reality is strengthened by the fact that believers are described as
having been saved in Eph 2:5, 8. Although one must remain cautious
about building too strong a case on these few verses, it remains notable
that Col 3:1−3 and Eph 2:6 come close to suggesting the kind of
realized eschatology that Paul seems to struggle against in 1 Cor 4:8
and throughout 1 Cor 15.

It appears that when the recipients of Colossians and Ephesians
were immersed in, and raised out of, water, they had a strong
awareness of the cosmological implications of God's activity in
Christ. The universe was now encompassed in his body. Through their
sharing in his death and resurrection, they themselves were lifted up
into the realm of salvation. One can easily see the relation between
such ideas and the proclamation of Christ's rule over the universe in
the hymn of Phil 2:5−11, or the description of baptism in terms buried
with Christ in Rom 6:3−11 (although Paul never explicitly states
that believers have already been raised with Christ). Nevertheless, the
symbolism associated with the present salvation of believers in
Colossians and Ephesians appears to be less restrained than in the
authentic epistles.[182]

An analysis of the conflict at Colossae reveals that the experience
outlined above was not free from ambiguity. The author of Colossians bases the argument against the philosophy on an exposition of
the meaning of baptism (Col 2:11−15). By appealing to this common
experience, the author apparently believes that the recipients will be
convinced of the mistaken nature of the false teaching.[183] It seems
that for some of the members of the Colossian community the

removal of a 'fleshly' body (Col 2:11) was continuously being realized by means of various activities. A system of regulations concerning ritual and ascetic practices had apparently developed and this led to the emergence of a type of elitism in community life (Col 2:8, 16–18, 21–3). Against all this, the author insisted on the finality and completeness of the Christ event and the defeat of cosmic powers by recalling baptism – the dramatization of the once and for all saving event in which all the recipients of the letter had participated (Col 2:9–15). The life which is somehow outside of this world (Col 2:20) is to be attained through membership in a strongly unified community in Christ and the adoption of a life-style which is fitting to this membership.[184]

The conflict at Colossae has to do with the question of purity. In Part 1, the significance of baptism as a means of purification was considered.[185] The disagreement at Colossae has to do with the protection of the boundaries surrounding the sacred space of the community. It seems that it was not immediately apparent in this first-century world that baptism provided adequate security against evil forces. The members of the community who adhered to the philosophy condemned by the author of Colossians probably desired simply to bolster their faith in Christ with added protection against the evil forces that threatened to penetrate their lives.[186] The author argued, however, that baptism marked the forgiveness of sins, the end of regulations and the triumph over principalities and powers (Col 2:13–15). Salvation required no additional appeal to cosmic agencies, no participation in mysterious rites and no adherence to special rules.

Despite his condemnation of ascetic and ritual practices, however, the author of Colossians does present the addressees with requirements pertaining to their life-style. These requirements are presented as the logical implications of having been raised with Christ (cf. Col 3:1ff). All ethical impurity is to be kept outside the sect. Attitudes of love and forgiveness which lead to communal harmony are to be preserved. An ethos of love-patriarchalism is to characterize household relations. To the question of how the purity of the community is to be maintained, the author of Colossians responds by listing a series of virtues and vices (Col 3:5–4:6; cf. Eph. 4:25–5:9).

Throughout the exhortations, the author of Colossians grounds the community in this world, drawing attention in particular to the historical consequences of the Christ event. A similar grounding occurs in Ephesians. Cosmic imagery rooted in the baptismal experience is found in a writing where a concern for the human congregation is everywhere apparent. The saints may have the power to comprehend the breadth, length, height and depth (Eph 3:18), but they must also lead a life worthy of their calling (Eph 4:1).

The question of how one lives community life in this world was of crucial significance for the authors of Colossians and Ephesians, as it was for Paul. The authors of these deutero-Pauline writings possessed certain guidelines concerning community life which they had acquired during their association with Paul and their membership in the Pauline movement. As communities were built, traditions were formed; the symbolic universe solidified. The arguments in Colossians which see ascetic practices, legal regulations, and esoteric ritual as taking Christ away from the centre of the community and endangering community stability, in fact, stand within the Pauline tradition. The emphasis in Ephesians on relating the Christ event to the life of the church does not come as an unexpected message from the disiciple who sought to bring a summary of his teacher's instruction to a new social situation. Colossians and Ephesians preserve insights that were determinative for the formation of the Pauline sect. It is evident that the symbolic universe has become significantly transformed, but continuity nevertheless exists.[187]

In light of the enthusiastic use of baptismal traditions in Colossians and Ephesians, it is somewhat striking that a more conservative love-patriarchal ethos is expressed than is found in Paul's letters. The authors of Colossians and Ephesians are concerned with the ethics of the communities and recall baptism as a means of reminding addressees of the behaviour that is appropriate for membership in the church. The ethics of the community are evidently related to what is experienced in the midst of ritual. The notion of a unified and re-created humanity, as expressed in the baptismal formula of Gal 3:28, appears to have become more narrowly defined with the passage of time in the Pauline movement. A similar passage appears in Col 3:11, but it functions not so much to legitimate a revolutionary change in the relations between groups (as in Paul's teaching in Galatians with respect to Jews and Gentiles) as to encourage unity in a community comprised of different groups. It appears that cosmic symbolism may have been related to a shift away from an apprehension of the abolition of differences between individuals to an awareness of the re-created universe under the authority of Christ. A strong belief in Christ as the head of all things becomes reflected in an ethos where the subjection of individuals to authoritative members of the household is demanded. The love/authority of Christ becomes a reference point for the carrying out of household relations according to the designs of the ethos of love-patriarchalism. For example, the union of man and woman becomes linked with the cosmic symbol of the union of Christ and the church, while traditional definitions of masculine and feminine roles are at the same time reinforced (Eph 5:21–33).

3.3 Conclusion

The evidence of hymnic influences in Colossians and Ephesians points to the close connection between each of these writings and a ritual context. The citation of the Christ hymn by the author of Colossians is part of an attempt to combat the adherence to false teaching in the community. By removing it from its usual locus in the song or prayer of the community and placing it in a letter, the author wishes to draw attention to its content. The importance of hymns for the life of the communities of Colossians and Ephesians is implied by the encouragement to sing psalms, hymns and spiritual songs. Such activity is connected with teaching in both of these letters. The education of community members is an important means of ensuring cohesion.

The allusions to baptism in both Colossians and Ephesians are also coloured by educational motives. The authors recall baptism as a means of clarifying the meaning and communal consequences of the Christ event. The conflict at Colossae points to ambiguity surrounding the interpretation of baptism. In both Colossians and Ephesians the baptismal experience is expressed with cosmological symbols in a way that far exceeds what is found in Paul's authentic letters. At the same time, the writings disclose a strong interest in community life. In Colossians, the historical consequences of the Christ event are underlined. In Ephesians, the connection between the Christ event and the reality of the church is stressed. Both works exhibit a strong interest in ethics. The ethos of love-patriarchalism, as expressed in the household codes, has become more conservative than in the authentic epistles. The strong emphasis on the re-created universe under the authority of Christ, evident in the cosmological baptismal language, however, may be related to a plea for the subjection of wives to husbands, children to parents, and slaves to masters. The implications of baptism are articulated in terms of the Greco-Roman household. What is experienced in ritual both affects, and is affected by, the existing social structures.

4

BELIEF

The following section explores the relationship between the transformed Pauline symbolic universe visible in Colossians and Ephesians and the changed social situation reflected in these writings. Instead of simply noting the differences between Colossians and Ephesians and the authentic letters, it relates the historical circumstances, providing possible catalysts to change, to the cosmological symbolism evident in these deutero-Pauline writings. The connection between the social situation rendered by the death of the Apostle and the transformation of the belief system is of particular relevance.

4.1 Changing symbols

In light of Paul's place in the chronology of early church writings, it is not surprising that subsequent doctrinal developments, both in the New Testament and in later church writings to the present day, have often been measured according to Pauline standards. Unfortunately, this may have had an adverse effect on the investigation of development after Paul. Instead of relating relevant texts to their social situations in order to understand the significance of a changed belief system, scholars have been content simply to highlight differences. Deutero-Pauline writings have only rarely been considered as closely linked with the life of a movement. These writings have been held up as the first evidence of the dangers threatening the purity of the earliest days.[188] One may judge deutero-Pauline writings to be lacking in the kind of religious genius that characterizes the writings of the Apostle. However, this should not preclude consideration of deutero-Pauline writings in terms of their own communal situations.

Problems with existing approaches to analyzing development after Paul have been noted by L. E. Keck.[189] Keck points to the dialectical relationship existing between New Testament writers and the ethos of their communities — the practices and habits, assumptions, problems, values and hopes of community life. Doctrinal developments should be related as closely as possible to communal situations. This means more than connecting changes in belief patterns to a gnostic threat or to an attempt to deal with a delayed parousia; it means relating existing beliefs with every aspect of community life.[190]

Since Keck issued his remarks in 1974, little attempt has been made to study the development evident in Colossians and Ephesians in terms of communal contexts.[191] Valuable work has continued in the investigation of the historical background of gnostic influences. The nature of the Colossian heresy has been the subject of numerous historical studies. In addition, the negative value judgements of the 1950s and 1960s about development after Paul have receded. By and large, however, investigation of Colossians and Ephesians continues to be dominated by the history of ideas methodology which inevitably yields an incomplete picture of the situation underlying these deutero-Pauline writings. Koester's treatment of Colossians and Ephesians in his book, *Introduction to the New Testament*, is a case in point.[192]

It is significant that Koester considers Colossians and Ephesians under the title: 'The Transformation of Pauline Theology into Ecclesiastical Doctrine'. Doctrinal considerations are investigated almost exclusively. In his analysis of Colossians, for example, the teaching of the opponents is outlined. The opponents are described as '... Jewish-Christian syncretists who wanted to achieve a fresh interpretation of Jewish rites and rules of cultic purity in accord with the religious thinking of their time, thus adapting the worship of Christ to the general world-view of Hellenism'.[193] Koester illustrates that the author of Colossians shows affinity to Gnosticism, but also rejects certain gnostic ideas. He argues that the table of household duties was taken over from Stoic popular ethics; he points out that the normal ordering of society was not questioned on the basis of the theological considerations. Koester notes that in contrast to the doctrine of the opponents, the author of Colossians propounded a positive view of the world.

When one reads Koester's analysis, one gains the impression that careful historical work has been undertaken. However, his investigation leaves the question 'What is going on at the level of community life?' largely unanswered. The origin of Colossians is related exclusively to a desire to propound certain ideas. The struggle between the author and opponents takes place primarily in the arena of ideas. Theological presuppositions are said to determine straightforwardly the ethical position advocated. The social implications of teaching are given little consideration.

The failure to consider the social implications of the existence of deutero-Pauline writings is a major deficiency in present scholarship on Colossians and Ephesians. There is a requirement to consider exhortations in relation to the efforts of associates or disciples to make the authority of the Apostle a continuing reality in community life. Hesitation to discuss the social situation of the 'Pauline school' is, however, not without foundation. We know nothing about such an entity beyond the existence of deutero-Pauline writings. Moreover, the fact that Colossians and Ephesians contain so much apparently traditional material makes their study in terms of social setting much more difficult than Paul's authentic letters. In investigating deutero-Pauline writings, how is the investigator to know which elements point to the unique circumstance of underlying communities?[194] When the author of Ephesians imitates Colossians, for example, can this reveal something unique about the situation in the community or communities underlying Ephesians? Error is indeed a great possibility when speaking about the communal contexts of these writings, but without such an attempt, one is left with literary documents disconnected from any real base.

An investigation of deutero-Pauline writings is facilitated by analysis of the process of institutionalization. This brings the investigator in touch with the communal realities that come with growth and the passage of time. It leads one to consider the limits and possibilities encountered by an author who is part of a movement embraced by a fairly solidified symbolic universe; existing traditions act as guidelines for beliefs and actions. The fact that a movement is no longer in its earliest days of formation and can look back to the authority of the past, is a very important aspect of its social setting.

4.2 Enthronement in heaven and the community on earth

The difference between the theology of Colossians/Ephesians and the theology of the authentic epistles is often explained in terms of the influence of Gnosticism.[195] Certainly one can draw parallels between some of the ideas found in Colossians and Ephesians and the terminology of later gnostic systems. But, due to a lack of historical information, it is difficult to determine whether the authors of deutero-Pauline writings are in fact responding to specifically gnostic social entities or simply exhibiting contacts with a syncretistic environment.

While it is uncertain whether the opponents in Colossians may be called 'gnostics', they obviously represent a group whose teaching is attacked by the author. The philosophy at Colossae is often described by scholars under the label of Jewish gnosticism. Despite the considerable amount of information that is revealed about the content of this teaching, the nature of the false teaching escapes easy categorization.[196] This difficulty is heightened by the problem of determining how many of the author's statements are polemical and how much is shared in common between author and opponents.[197]

The author of Colossians criticizes the philosophy for being according to human traditions and the elements of the universe (τὰ στοιχεῖα τοῦ κόσμου) instead of being according to Christ (Col 2:8, 22).[198] In Gal 4:3 Paul describes the pre-Christian life as one of slavery to the elemental spirits of the universe. Similarly, in Col 2:20, the author speaks of the recipients of the letter as having died to the elements of the universe. The elements of the universe are evidently the powers and principalities described in Col 2:10, 15 and perhaps also the angelic powers mentioned in Col 2:18.[199] It appears that the opponents in Colossae sought to establish a proper relationship with these elements by means of appropriate ritual and ascetic acts; only then would it be possible to participate in divine fullness (πλήρωμα Col 2:9; cf. Col 1:19).[200] It is unclear, however, whether these powers were understood as representatives of this divine fullness or as evil principalities which could block access to divinity and allowed passage only when they had received due reverence.[201]

The opponents at Colossae sought to gain access to the divine fullness by participating in various rites. The reference to 'circumcision' in Col 2:11 may point to a rite of initiation. Instead of referring specifically to circumcision, it is possible that term was employed by the opponents in a figurative sense to describe a rite that dramatized the putting off of the body of flesh. The beginning of an ascetic departure from the world would then be proclaimed.[202] It is possible that two different understandings of the significance of baptism for life in the world are in dispute (Col 2:11–13). The author responds by stressing that baptism is the decisive point of entry. The body of flesh is removed (once and for all) through the circumcision of Christ (cf. Rom 6:6).

Participation in some kind of mystical rite is the object of concern in Col 2:18. The reference to humility (ταπεινοφροσύνη probably denoting fasting and related rigours), angel('s) worship (θρησκεία τῶν ἀγγέλων) and visions (ἃ ἑόρακεν ἐμβατεύων) points to a kind of ascetic/mystic rite.²⁰³ Participation in this rite would ensure a visionary ascent and entrance into heaven. It is probable that experiences of heavenly enthronement were related to such ascetic practices as fasting. It is also likely that the rite provided a locus for instruction concerning the ascetic practices that renewed the participants' departure from the world.²⁰⁴ The connection between the philosophy at Colossae and participation in an ascetic/mystic rite is further supported by the reference to 'would-be-worship' (ἐθελοθρησκεία), humility (ταπεινοφροσύνη) and severity of the body (ἀφειδία σώματος) in Col 2:23.²⁰⁵ The ascetic regulations for community life dictated by the false teaching include the observances of special days and seasons and the prohibition against certain foods and beverages (Col 2:16, 21).

The author of Colossians responds to the problems in Colossae in a manner that recalls Paul's remarks in Galatia against the Judaizers. The remarks made to the Colossians are harsh and unrelenting. They are faced with a choice: either they will live according to the elements of the universe or according to Christ (Col 2:8).²⁰⁶ This 'for or against Christ' option presented by the author is deceptively 'doctrinal'. It is much more likely that it is the life-style of his opponents which is at the heart of the author's rebuke. The author attacks a wrong understanding which is perceived to be the foundation of the opponents' behaviour. They are criticized for considering themselves to be superior to others (Col 2:8, 16, 18).

While the practical issue in Galatia is one concerning the entry of Gentiles into the sect, the problem in Colossae has to do with the continued existence of the sect. If one speculates about the social consequences of the opponents teaching at Colossae, the author's response becomes more readily comprehensible. A strongly ascetic world view accompanied by an interest in mystical experiences might accompany a strong desire to become detached from the world.²⁰⁷ It might even reinforce an introversionist type of response to the world rather than one which encourages continued interaction with the world. Time devoted to the acquisition of spiritual knowledge and insight through esoteric practices (Col 2:18, 23), takes time away from other matters, including such practical things as caring for one's household and involvement in one's daily tasks. Unconventional and insubordinate behaviour in the household might elicit suspicion and criticism from outsiders.

The author of Colossians stressed the importance of the ethos of love-patriarchalism for the life of the sect by means of the Haustafel.

Through the various ethical exhortations, guidelines were laid down for appropriate behaviour for life in the body. These guidelines were, according to the author, the fruition of the salvation that the members had experienced. With a concern for life-style in the community, the disciple reinforced the ethos that had played a significant role in Paul's instruction. Divisions based on claims of spiritual superiority were abhorred within the community; all individuals were to have the access to salvation. For the author of Colossians — the close associate of Paul who had perhaps been active on the mission route with him — behaviour that might thwart the carrying out of the universal vision of salvation could not be according to Christ.

Fred O. Francis has argued that the pre-eminence of Christ over all powers was the presupposition held in common by the writer, audience and opponents. He believes that, in contrast to the author, the opponents saw Christ as a pattern that had to be imitated. As Christ put off his body, so they too had to handle their own bodies with severity. As he took his place above all powers and principalities, so they too sought to enter heavenly realms.[208] Thus, in stating that by dying and rising with Christ, believers had been delivered once and for all, the author sought to illustrate the misguided nature of their activity (Col 2:9–15, 20).

It is evident that the beliefs expressed in Colossians are articulated with respect to a conflict in community life. The cosmological symbolism is clearly rooted in the baptismal experience. However, traditional baptismal material is employed in relation to the social situation. Decisions to highlight certain aspects of the belief system are made in terms of the author's attempt to restore harmony in community life. In order to bring the destructive activity in Colossae to an end, the author chooses to stress the present nature of salvation. The relationship between Christ and the community is outlined. Recipients are reminded that they have been raised with Christ and are instructed with respect to the life-style which is fitting to their present condition.

Although the notion of future coming is not completely missing from Colossians (Col 3:4, 6), it is often noted that statements have a more spatial orientation than a temporal-eschatological one.[209] In Paul's letters, hope might be described as an attitude which characterizes Christian existence and is rooted in the anticipation of a future consummation to be brought about through the coming of Christ. In Col 1:5, however, hope refers to the content of the message which the community has heard and accepted (cf. Col 1:23). It is described as that which is prepared already in the heavens. In other words, the hope of the community is directed toward the Lord who is enthroned at God's right hand (Col 3:1) and who is himself the 'hope of glory' (Col 1:27).[210] God has already made his own capable of participating in the heavenly inheritance (Col 1:12). When Christ appears, the Colossians will of course appear with him in glory. Nevertheless, in Colossians, this appearance is depicted as the revelation of a heavenly union that already exists in the present (Col 3:1−4).

Ephesians also depicts the present heavenly enthronement of believers (Eph 1:3; 2:6−7). This writing, however, exhibits a greater awareness of time than Colossians. Christ broke down the wall of hostility between Jews and Gentiles and this culminated in the construction of the household of God − a household built on the foundation of apostles and prophets (Eph 2:20). God is glorified in the church and in Christ Jesus throughout all generations for ever and ever (Eph 3:21). The Holy Spirit is a seal which guarantees inheritance until possession of it is acquired (Eph 1:13−14; cf. 4:30). Addressees are instructed to stand prepared for the evil day (Eph 6:13; cf. 5:16).

It is evident that the kind of imminent expectation discovered in Paul's letters is absent from Colossians and Ephesians. Are the communities underlying Colossians and Ephesians dealing with an awareness of the delay of the parousia, or have the realities of community life caused them to set their minds on other things? From the two short writings, it is impossible to draw comprehensive conclusions about the beliefs of recipients. It is reasonable to assume that aspects of the symbol system were highlighted or played down depending on the author's purposes. In Part 1, the many dimensions of eschatological language and the flexible use of this language by the Apostle to respond to various communal situations were noted.[211] The variety of uses of eschatological language by Paul himself makes it impossible to use the presence or absence of imminent expectation to measure development after Paul.[212] The apparent transformation of Pauline symbols to reach new cosmic dimensions must be analysed in terms of the realities of the communities that formed them. In the face of the death of important leaders, the entrance of rebellious newcomers, the dissent of once faithful members and the threat of false teachers, members needed to be reminded that they were indeed God's chosen ones. 'You are light in the Lord', they were told, 'Walk as children of Light' (Eph 5:8). If the parousia had been delayed, it was not their concern.

The present necessity was to maintain harmony in communities that believed that Christ held the universe together.

4.3 Cosmological symbols and life in the sect

If one compares the way the body of Christ symbol is employed in the authentic epistles with its usage in Colossians and Ephesians, it becomes evident that the symbol of the body has been both expanded and transformed in these deutero-Pauline writings. The body of Christ is equated explicitly with the church in Colossians and Ephesians (Col 1:18, 24; Eph 1:22–3; 5:23). Furthermore, the symbol has been augmented; Christ is now the head while the members of the communities make up his body (Col 1:18, 24; 2:10, 17, 19; Eph 1:22; 4:4, 15; 5:23). Christ is portrayed not only as the head of the church, however, but also as the head of every power and principality (Col 2:10; cf. Eph 1:21–3).

The theory about the relationship of the head to the body in Colossians and Ephesians clarifies the relationship between Christ and community. The exercise of authority in community life provides a possible social correlate for the head/body language in Colossians and Ephesians. Under the head, community members are to maintain the order and synchronization of a healthy body. The connection between harmony in community life and the recognition of the authority of Christ is especially visible in Col 2:19 and Eph 4:15. Here the notion of holding fast to the head (clinging to authority) to which the whole body is joined is linked with a depiction of the body's harmonious growth. Unity in the body is further encouraged by recalling that the members of the community were called into one body (Col 3:15; Eph 4:4). In Ephesians, this remembrance takes place within a masterful expression of unity in the ekklesia (Eph 4:1–7). Of particular significance is the connection between unity and authority in the body expressed in Eph 5:23. Here the authority of husband over wife is seen to reflect the authority of Christ over the church. It appears that the symbol of Christ as head of the church could be employed in an attempt to legitimate authority structures in the Christian household and in the church understood on the model of the household. In communities that may have been experiencing a crisis of governance, the symbol of Christ as head may have proved useful for stabilizing relations among members.

The authority of Christ is also expressed in the description of all things as being held together in him (Col 1:17), and the fullness of

God as being pleased to dwell in him (Col 1:19). Christ is the image of the invisible God, the first born of creation, and in fact, all things were created through him and for him (Col 1:15–16). All things were reconciled to himself in heaven and earth; peace was made by the blood of his cross (Col 1:20). The Colossians have been reconciled in his body of flesh by his death in order that they might be presented holy, blameless and irreproachable before him (Col 1:21–2). Similar ideas occur in Ephesians (Eph 1:3–14). The point of the language of cosmic reconciliation in these writings is clear: everyone and everything come under Christ's authority.

As the communities underlying Colossians and Ephesians engaged in the process of self-definition, they articulated the meaning of the Christ event in terms of a heavenly enthronement and exaltation in a manner that exceeded the constraints of the symbolism visible in Paul's letters. In light of their experiences in community life, they responded to the question, 'Who are we in relation to Christ?'. The continued existence of the sect required legitimation. The Pauline symbolic universe was expanded and transformed. In Colossians and Ephesians, the relationship between the church, here below, and Christ, exalted and enthroned up above, is explored. The cosmological symbols used to describe the relationship underline the immortality of the union. The communities are stabilized as they proclaim their eternal connection with the heavenly reality.[213]

It is possible to make cautious suggestions concerning the connection between cosmological symbols, with their stress on the present salvation of believers, and the social situation in the Pauline sect after the disappearance of the Apostle. The situation in the communities had changed. The issue concerning the means through which Gentiles enter the body of those being saved, characteristic of those early community-building days, had been resolved. In the predominantly Gentile church, the concern was now to harmonize relations between Gentile Christians and the Jewish Christian minority. In a growing movement that was becoming increasingly visible to outsiders, the relationship between the sect and the outside society may have been becoming more precarious. In particular, the difficult situation caused by membership in the household of God of subordinate members of unconverted Greco-Roman households may have been a source of suffering for community members. With the intake of new members, the threat of evil penetrating the sect was even greater than before. The absence of the Apostle had caused difficulties with respect to the governing of Pauline communities. The task fell to fellow workers.

But, without the guidance of their leader, they were faced with major difficulties. These Pauline associates chose to bring the authority of the Apostle to bear on community life by writing pseudonymous letters. The Apostle spoke about the authority of Christ over the church that was growing to embrace the world. Appealing to baptismal traditions, he assured them of their deliverance. He reminded them to live in a manner that was appropriate to their membership in the body of those who had risen with Christ. He spoke predominantly of the present salvation of believers in order to reinforce their common identity as God's chosen. He laid out definite guidelines for their life-styles in the form of household ethics. With his exhortations, he sought to stabilize community life.

4.4 Conclusion

It is essential to analyze the changes that have occurred in Colossians and Ephesians in terms of the social situation underlying these writings. Attempts to measure the value of these pseudonymous writings in terms of the presence or absence of certain beliefs, without considering the dialectical relationship between social setting and belief, will inevitably distort historical realities. It is useful to consider the development in the Pauline school after the death of the Apostle in terms of the process of institutionalization. Existing beliefs act as guidelines for the instructions given by deutero-Pauline authors. One must consider the relationship between beliefs expressed and the intent of fellow workers to make Paul's teaching speak to new situations.

Investigation of the conflict at Colossae disclosed a close relationship between the articulation of beliefs proclaiming salvation as a present reality and social situations. Moreover, the transformation of the body symbol in Colossians and Ephesians may be related to a need to underline the authority of Christ and to reinforce authority structures in community life. The articulation of cosmological symbols in these writings takes place in the context of an attempt to stabilize community life. The social experience of the communities is at the heart of the formulation of symbols. The symbols in turn act back upon the producers to shape their lives.

5

GENERAL CONCLUSION

The preceding study of development in the communities of Colossians and Ephesians was undertaken in order to trace the process of institutionalization in the Pauline movement which continued in the absence of the Apostle. It illustrated that communal norms, leadership structures, ritual forms, and beliefs were affected by the realities experienced in the sect on account of the death of its central leader. During Paul's lifetime, a symbolic universe had been forming. The disappearance of Paul did not mean the disappearance of the Pauline symbolic universe. Close associates believed in the Pauline mission and sought to continue the work of their teacher. Communities continued to depend on the authoritative voice of the Apostle. In the attempt to bring Pauline teaching to new situations, the Pauline symbolic universe was transformed. Beliefs became detached from their original settings and were made to fit their new social settings. The symbolic universe gained a new objectivity as it passed into the hands of a new generation. Some aspects of the symbolic universe, such as the faith in Christ/works of the law contrast, faded almost completely from view. Other aspects, such as the heavenly enthronement of Christ and the notion of the body of Christ, gained new relevance.

In the earliest days of community-building institutionalization, much ambiguity surrounded the question of how members should act and what they should believe. The authors of the deutero-Pauline writings of Colossians and Ephesians, however, were in possession of many traditions to guide their teaching. Institutionalization had become set on a more definite course than in the early days of the formation of the Pauline movement. Increased problems of management necessitated more definite guides for living, such as those expressed in the household codes.

Colossians and Ephesians exhibit characteristics of communities which continue to rely on the authority of the Apostle in his absence;

the stage of development they reflect is aptly described as 'community-stabilizing institutionalization'. The Pastoral Epistles point to the continuation of the Pauline movement into the second century. In the Pastoral Epistles, the authority of the Apostle is defended vigorously against false teaching. The following section traces the development in a community engaged in the process of 'community-protecting institutionalization'.

PART 3

THE PASTORAL EPISTLES: COMMUNITY-PROTECTING-INSTITUTIONALIZATION

1 Timothy, 2 Timothy, and Titus reflect the continuation of the Pauline movement into the second century. However, in these writings one discovers a very different style of religiosity from the type found in the authentic epistles or in Colossians and Ephesians. The Pauline symbolic universe has been transformed in relation to the changed social situation. The following study considers the historical circumstances that acted as catalysts to change.

Despite the great differences among the writings of the Pauline corpus, it is evident that some continuity exists. For example, the authority of the Apostle to the Gentiles is reinforced in the Pastoral Epistles and in the other letters. The ethos of love-patriarchalism continues to play a prominent role in the community life. Therefore, it is useful to consider the relationships between the Pastoral Epistles and the early Pauline writings in terms of the ongoing process of institutionalization.

Like the communities of Colossians and Ephesians, the community of the Pastorals is characterized by the changed situation that resulted from the death of the Apostle. However, the need to stabilize community life has reached crisis proportions in the community of the Pastorals, which is experiencing a severe conflict surrounding the problem of false teaching. Social mechanisms are brought into play in order to safeguard the church from destructive forces. The authority of official leaders as the protectors of sound teaching is emphasized. The following study of attitudes to the world/ethics, ministry, ritual and belief in 1 Timothy, 2 Timothy, and Titus, relates these aspects of community life to the activity of Pauline Christians engaged in the process of 'community-protecting institutionalization'.

1

ATTITUDES TO THE WORLD/ETHICS

The following study investigates the social setting of the Pastoral Epistles. On the one hand, it considers the influence of the structures of Greco-Roman society on the life of the church; on the other hand, it focuses on the community's relations with the outside world. The social tensions related to a strong desire to evangelize are studied. The implications of the ethos of love-patriarchalism for the community's dealings with the outside world are considered. The attitudes to women and wealth visible in the text are investigated in order to clarify the significance of this ethos for community life.

1.1 Studying contacts with the Greco-Roman world: problems of methodology

It is somewhat ironic that commentators consistently point to influences from Greco-Roman society evident in the Pastorals but only rarely speak of the implications of such influences for the life of the community behind these writings. Parallels are drawn with current philosophical thought. However, because connections are made on a purely literary level, almost nothing is revealed about their significance for understanding the situation underlying the Pastorals.[1] Furthermore, among scholars believing 1 Timothy, 2 Timothy, and Titus to be deutero-Pauline, there is a tendency to describe external influences as penetrating the Pauline world as quickly as a quotation from a contemporary philosopher might be mechanically inserted into a given text. This is not to suggest that influences from the Greco-Roman world are not more prevalent in the Pastoral Epistles than in other Pauline writings. Rather, it is to argue against the tendency to see complete discontinuity between the relation of the church to the world in the Pastoral Epistles and that visible in other Pauline works. For one who notes the significance of the household structure for the formation of the Pauline sect, for example, the dominance of household ethics in the Pastorals does not appear as an unexpected slide into Greco-Roman society, or for that matter, as some have argued, as an unexpected slide downhill. A few examples of how commentators have understood the relationship between the community underlying the Pastorals and Greco-Roman society should help to clarify the point.

Spicq, who argues for the authenticity of the Pastoral Epistles, believes that the writings represent the first expression of Christian religiosity and morality in Greco-formulations.[2] Spicq identifies not only a confrontation in the Pastorals between Christianity and Greco-Roman thought, but also discovers a reaction of Christian orthodoxy against various aspects of that thought:

> Les Pastorales représentent donc une mise au point de la confrontation du christianisme avec l'esprit grec, et une réaction de l'orthodoxie chrétienne contre l'éclectisme de la pensée grecque, juive, orientale et romaine.[3]

In addition, despite the presence of outside influences, Spicq is careful to point out the essentially Christian context of the composition of the Pastorals by the Apostle. Traditional formulations receive new Christian meanings.[4]

Spicq's description of the Pastorals as showing the influence of the Greco-Roman thought world, while at the same time depicting a conscious reaction to various aspects of that world, is problematic. His interpretation seems to suggest that traditional literary forms are adapted but always intentionally Christianized. In addition, his understanding of the struggle of orthodoxy against various outside thought world influences leads to a description of the Pastorals as a kind of battleground for ideas. By confining influences from the outside world to the literary realm, Spicq has succeeded in disconnecting 1 Timothy, 2 Timothy, and Titus, for the most part, from Greco-Roman society.

In contrast to Spicq, commentators who view the Pastorals to be deutero-Pauline often judge evidence of contact with Greco-Roman society negatively. Scott, for example, believes that, unlike Paul, the author of the Pastorals has not succeeded in fusing faith and ethics:

> The Pastoral Epistles are different from the undoubted writings of Paul, not because their interest is chiefly ethical, but because they teach an ethic which, in some respects, is not that of Paul. The distinction, to state it in the broadest

terms, is this. Paul's ethic is a purely Christian one; he insists that action must spring directly from the impulse of the Spirit, and otherwise loses all moral worth: 'Whatever is not of faith is sin' (Rom XIV.23).[5]

It is evident that Scott's comments reflect a 'downhill after Paul' position. What seems particularly objectionable about his judgement is that it is based on the idea that in Paul we find a purely Christian ethic. There is no doubt that Paul's ethical instructions grow out of life in Christ, but earlier discussion on Paul's teaching with respect to women and slaves, for instance, revealed his firm grounding in Greco-Roman society. It is simply invalid to set the ethic visible in the Pastorals, which shows affinities with the ethical position current in the society of the day, in opposition to a purely Christian ethic, as does Scott.

Even scholars who are not as blatantly negative as Scott tend to disconnect the Pastorals from the realities of Greco-Roman society. When one reads the popular Dibelius/Conzelmann commentary, one cannot help but be impressed by the numerous parallels noted with literature from both Jewish and Gentile sources in the Greco-Roman world. For an illustration of the methodology employed, consider the following comments on 1 Tim 3 where the duties of a bishop are listed. Parallels from the biographies of heroes, where virtues are mentioned in accordance with a fixed schema, lead to the following conclusion about the list in 1 Tim 3:

> Such a schema clearly underlies the teaching of duties in 1 Tim 3. This explains why so little is mentioned which would especially characterize a bishop or deacon. For this reason the specifically Christian element is missing. The popularization of such schematic doctrines of virtue was furthered not only by the philosophical definitions (e.g., the Platonic Ὅροι, the Aristotelian divisions and the like), but above all by the honorary inscriptions. By listing the virtues of the person being honored, their intention was to inspire posterity to similar accomplishment.[6]

Dibelius/Conzelmann do not examine the possibility that fixed schemas employed to describe virtues in the literature of the Greco-Roman world reflect real values prevalent in the society of the day. Furthermore, one must question how realistic it is to assume that traditional lists of duties were adopted by the author of the Pastorals without their content being relevant for the situation in the community. Why might it be important for a bishop to govern his own house well (1 Tim 3:4–5)? Why should a bishop have a good reputation among those on the outside (1 Tim 3:7)?[7] There is no doubt that Dibelius/Conzelmann see the Pastorals as somehow embedded within this world. In contrast to Paul, who lives in the tension between this world and God's world, we are told that the author of the Pastorals seeks to build the possibility of a life in this world. The ideal of good Christian citizenship becomes an expression of existence in this world; the clearest sign of a Christianization of the world is seen in a developing family ethic.[8] In the end, however, beyond the presence of numerous literary parallels, it is impossible to discover how Dibelius/Conzelmann perceive the relationship between the Pastorals and the Greco-Roman world.

1.2 Church or sect?

From the previous discussion it should be clear that scholars find evidence in the Pastoral Epistles for the development of Christianity as a world movement. For example, as has already been noted, at the heart of Dibelius/Conzelmann's thesis about the Pastorals, is the idea that they represent a Christianization of the world. Some scholars have made little attempt to hide their value-judgements as they contrast the world-accommodating standards of an emerging 'catholic' church detected in the Pastorals with the world-rejecting values of the communities underlying the genuine Pauline letters. The negative presuppositions characterizing von Campenhausen's association with the Pastorals with the development of canon law, Käsemann's identification of a rising monarchical episcopacy or Bultmann's conclusions about the presence of a picture of Christian bourgeois piety, come out clearly in their work.[9] It is evident that the Pastoral Epistles lack the mark of religious genius that characterize Paul's correspondence. But an acknowledgement of a decline in theological profundity should not prevent consideration of these writings in terms of their own communal context. Moreover, it is important to investigate whether the almost diametrical opposition between the situation reflected in the Pastorals and that seen in the authentic Pauline epistles described by these and other scholars, either implicitly or explicitly, is in fact justified.

The correctness of the insight that with the Pastorals we have discovered something 'new' should, however, be acknowledged.

When compared to the other Pauline and deutero-Pauline writings, the Pastorals demonstrate a remarkable change in orientation. This change is especially visible in the attitudes to the world and the internal structures of the church evident in these epistles. It is indisputable that we find a more established or institutionalized church in the Pastorals than can be traced in other Pauline or deutero-Pauline writings.

To say that in the Pastorals we find evidence of a more institutionalized church is to raise numerous questions, the most obvious being 'Why change?'. In short, we need to look for both external and internal factors impinging on community life that may have acted as catalysts to change. In the study of Pauline and deutero-Pauline writings found in Parts 1 and 2 of this book, Bryan Wilson's sectarian analysis was employed as a helpful means of understanding the communities' relations with the outside world. Wilson's work on sects is, in many ways, an elaboration of the study done by Ernst Troeltsch early in this century.[10] Troeltsch distinguishes between the church-type and the sect-type.[11] Some of the general characteristics of the church-type as described by Troeltsch include:

1.   an objective institutional character;
2.   individuals are born into it;
3.   control by hierarchy;
4.   the protection of tradition;
5.   impartation of grace through sacraments;
6.   compromise with the world; and
7.   universalism and education of the nations.

Major characteristics of the sect-type are:

1.   voluntary community;
2.   entry on the basis of a conscious conversion;
3.   control by laity;
4.   emphasis on personal service and co-operation;
5.   criticism of the sacramental idea;
6.   opposition to the world; and
7.   gathering of the elect.[12]

In Parts 1 and 2, Wilson's description of a conversionist sect-type was employed as a helpful aid for coming to terms with a Pauline sect which seeks to evangelize the world, while at the same time calling for world rejection. It is with caution that we raise the question of whether, in the Pastoral Epistles, we find the reflection of a church or a sect, remembering that the typology was constructed with events in mind that happened much later than the beginning of the second century. Typologies are useful to us only in as much as they provide categories against which to measure data in order to describe and compare historical situations more accurately. If Troeltsch's church–sect typology allows the something 'new' which is happening in the Pastoral Epistles in comparison to other Pauline and deutero-Pauline writings to stand out more sharply, it will have achieved its purpose.

As has been noted numerous times before, according to Wilson's analysis, it is conversionist type sects, characterized by a tension between world-rejection and mission to save the world, which show the greatest tendency towards 'denominalization' (a new level of institutionalization involving some accommodation to the standards of the world).[13] In terms of Troeltsch's typology, this would mean a movement away from the sect-type toward the church-type.[14] Do we find evidence for such a movement in the Pastorals? A good starting point for investigation is an examination of the text to discover any indication of a desire for separation from the world.

The lack of evidence for tendencies of world-rejection in 1 Timothy, 2 Timothy, and Titus is striking. Language of separation is connected for the most part with the problem of false teaching. The evil people that will appear during the last days will include those who make their way into households and capture weak women. Such people (presumably some type of Christian teachers) are simply to be avoided (2 Tim 3:1–9). False teachers must be silenced since they are upsetting entire families. They are contrasted with the pure for whom all things are pure, and associated with the defiled and un-believing whose minds and consciences are defiled (Tit 1:10–16).[15]

There can be no doubt that the Pastorals exhibit evidence of norms determining what is appropriate for those inside the Christian community. The pure Christian community is set apart from the corruption of the outside world. In a church apparently burdened by a problem with widows, one who does not provide for relatives, and especially for the members of one's own family, is accused of being worse than an unbeliever (1 Tim 5:8). As for those who are factious, after having admonished them once or twice, community members are to have nothing more to do with them (Tit 3:10). However, beyond instruction to avoid false teachers, as well as all those who cause division within the community and who are understood as embodying the values of the unbelieving world, the encouragement for separation from past associations and patterns of life, clearly visible in other Pauline and deutero-Pauline writings, is virtually absent.

An exception to the above generalization might be Tit 3:3–8. Here we find language of transference. The recipients of the letter are reminded of the pre-conversion life characterized by a variety of evils and of the saving event which put an end to this life. According to his mercy, God saved them through the washing of regeneration and renewal of the Holy Spirit which he poured out on them richly through Jesus Christ their Saviour. What is especially remarkable about this passage, underlining the separation of the community from the outside world, is that it appears to function in legitimating a certain kind of behaviour which is demanded with respect to outsiders and which suggests relative openness. In the preceding passage, Tit 3:1–2, Christians are instructed to be subject to rulers and authorities, to be obedient and to be ready for every good work. They are to speak evil of no one, to avoid quarrelling, to be gentle and to show meekness. The presence of the conjunction 'γάρ' in Tit 3:3 links the description of appropriate behaviour required of Christians in their dealings with the outside world with a passage pointing to the purifying significance of the Christ event.

It is clear that the community of the Pastoral Epistles does consider itself to be set apart from society at large. They constitute God's elect (Tit 1:1; 2 Tim 2:10; cf. 2 Tim 1: 9–10; 2:19). Yet, the emphasis on distinction from outsiders which underlies Paul's depiction of transference into a community gathered in Christ, and which is reinforced by the elaboration of the body symbol by the authors of Colossians and Ephesians, is rarely apparent. It is true that a lack of evidence for a strong desire for world-rejection in the text cannot by itself reveal a great deal about the attitudes to the world exhibited by the community underlying the Pastorals. If the focus of a writing is on dealing with internal matters, such as the division caused by certain teachers or the necessity of ensuring appropriate leadership, for example, important aspects of a community's self-understanding may be left unexpressed. If, however, the tendencies thus far observed in the Pastorals are confirmed by our study of passages dealing more directly with how the community understands its relations with outsiders, we will be in a better position for determining whether the community best fits the church-type or the sect-type.

1.3 Dealing with outsiders

Commentators in general give little consideration to passages in the Pastorals which explicitly mention the community's interaction with outsiders. One such passage is 1 Tim 3:7. Here we read that the bishop must be well thought of by outsiders (ἀπὸ τῶ ἔξωθεν) or he may fall into reproach and 'παγίδα τοῦ διαβόλου'. Noting the double mention in verses 6 and 7 of the word 'διάβολος', Dibelius/Conzelmann argue that it cannot refer to a slanderous person, for then verse 7 would add nothing new to verse 6. They therefore insist that in both verses the translation 'devil' should be assumed. Furthermore, they argue that a reference to a human slanderer is excluded by 2 Tim 2:26.

Dibelius/Conzelmann may be too hasty in their dismissal of the possibility of the translation 'slanderer'. The idea of the newly converted bishop being in danger of falling into the judgement of the slanderer expressed in verse 6, and the connection made between the good reputation of the bishop and the danger of falling into the snare of the slanderer in verse 7, do not lead to unnecessary repetition. In fact, the notion of a human slanderer may give a clearer indication of the situation community members are facing.[16] Although Dibelius/Conzelmann are undoubtedly correct to prefer the meaning 'devil' for 2 Tim 2:26, they appear to have neglected the appearance of the word 'διάβολος' in the nearby passage of 1 Tim 3:11 where the sense of a human slanderer is obviously preferable. The limits of modern translation may stand in the way of understanding a more fluid relationship between the devil and a human slanderer. Whatever translation we choose for 'διάβολος', the link between the good reputation of the bishop and the prevention of disaster is clearly expressed in 1 Tim 3:7. A bishop is apparently viewed by the author as being in a position to improve or damage the church's image in the eyes of the general public, based on his personal standing.[17]

The presence of the word 'adversary' (ἀντικείμενος) in 1 Tim 5:14 suggests that we are dealing with some form of outsider although it is much less clear than in 1 Tim 3:7 (where the actual word 'outsiders' is employed) whether these outsiders are Christian or non-Christian. Although Dibelius/Conzelmann equate the adversary simply with the devil, it would seem that more attention needs to be drawn to the human context of this instruction.[18] In 1 Tim 5:13–15 we read that there are young widows who, while remaining unmarried, are learning to be idle and are going from house to house. These women are worse than idle; they are gossips and busybodies who speak of things that are improper. They are instructed to marry, to bear children and to rule their households in order that the adversary might have no occasion to revile them. We are told that some already have strayed after Satan. There are apparently opponents who are slandering the church on account of the activity of women.[19]

It will be illustrated below that the kind of behaviour exhibited by these young widows is related to the false teaching against which the author argues (cf. 1 Tim 4:3; 2 Tim 3:6; Tit 1:11). The false teachers who encourage the emancipated behaviour of women should be distinguished from opponents who criticize the community on the basis of such behaviour. The kind of conduct which gives the adversary no occasion to revile them is the kind of behaviour that is encouraged throughout the Pastoral Epistles – behaviour which is honourable in the Greco-Roman household. Members of the community underlying the Pastorals may be experiencing criticism from members of other Christian circles, but the use of a strong word such as adversary, makes non-Christian criticism more likely (cf. 1 Tim 5:7).

In 1 Tim 6:1–2 and Tit 2:9–10, slaves are instructed with a view to the impression of outsiders. Barrett is largely correct when he points out that the decisive motive of 1 Tim 6:1–2 is missionary.[20] In 1 Tim 6:1, it is argued that slaves should be good servants 'in order that the name of God and the teaching not be blasphemed'. In Tit 2:10 the same rationale appears except this time it is stated in more positive terms: '... in order that they may adorn the doctrine of God our savior in all things'. As Verner indicates, obedient servanthood is portrayed here as Christian witness.[21] The connection of a desire to evangelize with a plea for respect for the institutions of society reminds one of the link between mission and social respectability. That Christian teaching be well thought of by outsiders is of crucial significance for the identity and, indeed, for the very existence of the group.

Even the instruction in 1 Tim 6:2 concerning the relations between a Christian slave and master may have been made with a view to outsiders. Severe departure from traditional slave – master relationships would be a visible violation of the house relationships fundamental to the society embracing the Christian community and would most certainly provide a stumbling block for the evangelization of that society. There may have been a tendency among the slaves of Christian masters to overstep the traditional boundaries of slave – master relationships on the grounds that Christians were 'brothers and sisters'. In fact, such slaves could find justification for their actions if they read Paul's letter to Philemon. The author of the Pastorals, however, views the slaves among the congregation from the perspective of the slave-owner. The concern is that Christian slaves in general not damage the church's public image by insubordination. Of course, as Verner points out, insubordination among slaves would damage the church's image primarily, if not exclusively, among the slave-owning class.[22]

In addition to Tit 2:9–10, other passages in Titus point to the author's anxiety concerning the good reputation of the Christian community. In Tit 2:3 older women are exhorted not to be slanderers or slaves of drink (cf. 1 Tim 3:11). Although these instructions reflect an apparently popular stereotype of old women in Greco-Roman society, it is nevertheless worth noting that the kind of behaviour condemned in this society is repeated by the author as inappropriate for Christians.[23] In Tit 2:4–5 the older women are told to teach the younger women to love their husbands and children. The younger women are to be sensible, chaste, domestic, kind, and submissive to their husbands in order that the word of God not be blasphemed (1 Tim 6:1). Beyond the appeal for the 'model' behaviour of younger men in Tit 2:6–7, it is their teaching which is of particular concern to the author. Sound speech which cannot be censured is demanded in order that an opponent (ὁ ἐξ ἐναντίας) might be put to shame and have nothing evil to say about them (Tit 2:8; cf. 1 Tim 5:14).

Although Tit 3:1–2 contains exhortation of a general nature evidently including much traditional language, it can nevertheless reveal something of the general attitude of Christians toward the outside society.[24] The reminder to be subject to rulers and authorities (cf. 1 Tim 2:1–4) recalls the appeal for submission in the household (cf. 1 Pet 2:13–3:7). The verb 'ὑποτάσσεσθαι', which is employed to describe the relationship of the members of the community to the rulers and authorities, also characterizes the dealings of husbands with wives and slaves with masters (Tit 2:5, 9; cf. 1 Tim 2:11; 3:4). The qualities encouraged in Tit 3:1–2, including being ready for every good work (cf. Tit 3:8), to speak evil of no one (cf. 2 Tim 2:24) and to show meekness towards all men, point to a general attitude of openness with respect to outsiders. This openness is particularly well brought out by Tit 2:11–15 which might be understood as a summary of the community's self-understanding (cf. 1 Tim 2:1–7). Salvation is for all (v. 11). The members of the community are being trained to renounce worldly passions, and to live sober, upright, and godly lives in this world (v. 12). Yet they await their great God and Saviour

Jesus Christ who gave himself to them to redeem them from all iniquity and to purify for himself a people of his own who are zealous for good works (v. 13–14). They are to speak these things, exhort and reprove with all authority. They are to let no one disregard them (v. 15). The attitude towards outsiders exhibited by the Pastoral Epistles is inseparably linked to the vision of universal salvation which is at the heart of the community's identity.[25]

To summarize, the study of passages which reveal something of the relationship between the community underlying the Pastorals and the outside society allows one to draw the following conclusions:

1. the author believed that it was important that the bishop be well thought of by outsiders;
2. the members of the community were being criticized for departing from values which, as we shall see, were highly esteemed by the members of Greco-Roman society; and
3. there is a clear relationship in the Pastorals between desire for social respectability and desire for evangelization.

For a community with a universal vision of salvation, not only was a certain amount of openness to outsiders inevitable, but the approval of outsiders was essential for its continued existence. The following section explores the connection between an appeal for sound speech and a desire for evangelization in 1 Timothy, 2 Timothy, and Titus.

1.4 Gospel or deceitful speech?

A church with a universal vision of salvation seeks to grow. In a world which recognizes a variety of gods, it struggles in a field of competition.[26] Paul's defence against the accusation that 'his speech is of no account' (2 Cor 10:10; cf. 11:6) suggests that rhetorical skill was a powerful tool employed by some teachers to win adherents. It is difficult to discern how much of Paul's distrust of skilled speech is due to his own lack of skill in speaking (2 Cor 11:6), but it is clear from the Pastorals that speech continued to pose problems for the early church. Here, however, the contrast is set up not between the true signs of the apostle and skill at speaking, but between wholesome and unwholesome speech.[27]

In 2 Tim 4:2, Timothy is admonished to '... preach the word, be urgent in season and out of season [εὐκαίρως ἀκαίρως], convince, rebuke and exhort, be unfailing in patience and in teaching'. Abraham J. Malherbe indicates that the concern with the appropriate or inappropriate occasion on which to speak and how to speak stretches back to the fourth century B.C.E., and asserts that an awareness of the discussions of the subject may help us to place 2 Tim 4:2 in a new light.[28] He notes that the use of 'kairos' and its cognates became commonplace and gives a sampling of a wide range of material to illustrate the point.[29] According to Malherbe, the philosophical moralists from the first and second centuries of the Empire disclose a general concern for opportune speech as it relates to their own efforts. The emotions and moral conditions of those persons they sought to benefit deserved serious consideration.[30]

The use of the oxymoron 'εὐκαίρως ἀκαίρως' in 2 Tim 4:2, implies that the author wishes to draw special attention to this part of the admonition.[31] In light of the current concern with the opportune time for speech, the command to Timothy to preach 'in season and out of season' is extraordinary.[32] Why does the author come out so strongly against the cautious attitude recommended by contemporary philosophers when many of the instructions throughout the Pastorals would lead us to believe that the author would be in sympathy with such an attitude (e.g. Tit 3:2)?[33] Leaving 2 Tim 4:2 for further investigation below, it is useful to consider other passages in the Pastorals where the author refers to speech in order to gain greater understanding of this defiance of conventional principles.

In the polemic against false teachers, the author of the Pastorals makes use of conventional categories. These teachers abuse speech. In 1 Tim 6:3−4 we are told that the teacher who does not agree with the wholesome words (ὑγιαίνουσιν λόγοις) of the Lord is puffed up with conceit. Such a teacher knows nothing and has a morbid craving for controversy and for disputes about words which produce envy, dissension, slander, base suspicions, and wrangling among individuals who are depraved in mind and bereft of the truth, imagining that godliness is a means of gain (cf. 2 Tim 3:1−9, 12−13; Tit 1:10−11). They are like undiscriminating Cynics who trap their audiences. There are certain persons who have wandered away into vain discussion (1 Tim 1:6). Godless chatter is to be avoided (1 Tim 6:20; 2 Tim 2:16). As a means of setting themselves apart from the misbehaving heretics, the audience is encouraged to exhibit qualities characteristic of the discerning philosopher. Members are advised to be gentle, patient and discriminating in their speech and their relations with all people (e.g. 1 Tim 4:12; 6:11; 2 Tim 2:24−6; Tit 3:2).

The medical language frequently found in philosophical discussions of opportune and inopportune speech is echoed in the Pastorals.

This is particularly evident in 2 Tim 2:17 where the speech of the heretics is said to eat away like gangrene. The language of sickness is also present in 2 Tim 4:3, where we are told that the time is coming when people will not endure wholesome teaching (τῆς ὑγιαινούσης διδασκαλίας), but having itchy ears, they will accumulate for themselves teachers to suit their own tastes. Malherbe argues, however, that despite the presence of such condemnation of unhealthy speech, it is not surprising that the author of the Pastorals did not define a method for appropriate speech.[34] Elaboration of techniques for instruction, including indications of when certain types of teaching were appropriate and when they were not, would undoubtedly cause more problems than it would solve in a community where members are being lured into vain discussions. Disputes about words would surely follow (1 Tim 6:4). Instead, empty talkers and deceivers must be silenced (Tit 1:10–11).

Yet, Malherbe may have overstated his case when he discusses the lack of evidence in the Pastorals for the fact that the speaker will bring about health in his opponents by applying sound words.[35] It is true that such a conclusion can only be inferred from Tit 1:13 since neither the expressions 'sound teaching' nor 'sound words' occur. However, it is nevertheless stated that opponents should be rebuked sharply in order that they be sound in faith (ὑγιαίνωσιν ἐν τῇ πίστει). The use of sound teaching as a tool against opponents is encouraged in Tit 1:9. The bishop must hold firm to the sure word as taught, that he may be able both to exhort by sound teaching and to confute the objectors. Although, as Malherbe points out, it is never explicitly said that the morally or religiously ill person will actually be cured by the sound of healthy words, the possibility of this happening is surely implied by 2 Tim 2:24–6. Here God's servant is instructed not to be quarrelsome but kindly to everyone, an apt teacher, forbearing, correcting his opponents with gentleness. God may perhaps grant that they will repent and come to know the truth and that they may escape from the snare of the devil after being captured by him to do his will. Thus, despite the harshness of the author's description of the opponents, the possibility of repentance is not dismissed and, indeed, repentance is connected with orthodox teaching (cf. Tit 3:10).

The interest in 'sound words' (literally translated 'healthy or wholesome words' – 1 Tim 6:3; 2 Tim 1:13; Tit 2:8) and 'sound teaching' (1 Tim 1:10; 2 Tim 4:3; Tit 1:9; Tit 2:1; cf. Tit 1:13) in the Pastoral Epistles points to an effort to maintain the health of the community. These terms which characterize Christian preaching do not occur anywhere else in the New Testament. The discussion of this language by Dibelius/Conzelmann illustrates how widespread these expressions were in the philosophical terminology of the day.[36] It is not, however, the contact of this language with contemporary thought that has been of primary interest to commentators, but the apparent change it reflects in the nature of Pauline thought. Seeking to defend the authenticity of the Pastorals, J.N.D. Kelly connects the transformation with the ageing of the Apostle.[37] A diametrically opposite position to that of Kelly is adopted by Dibelius/Conzelmann. They identify in 'sound teaching' a certain rationality which provides a strong argument in favour of the Pastorals' pseudonimity. According to Dibelius/Conzelmann, Paul's Christianity is pneumatic throughout.[38]

In devoting their energies to measuring this language according to the standards of Paul's letters in an effort to determine authorship, these scholars have neglected to consider the relationship of this language to community life. Dibelius/Conzelmann are justified in attending to changes in Pauline thought that make Pauline authorship unlikely despite arguments by Kelly and others who defend authenticity on the basis of an ageing apostle.[39] However, while acknowledging an element of rationality in the Pastorals, can one not do more than draw a contrast with the true Paul? It is essential always to keep in mind that the Pastorals are written from the perspective of an author who understands the community to be plagued by a kind of false teaching and seeks to ensure that its health will be maintained through the adherence to sound teaching. The rationality or, perhaps more accurately, the objectivity, expressed in the concern for sound teaching must be understood in terms of a struggle against heresy.[40] The identification of heresy leads to self-definition and to the formulation of objective pronouncements. Readers are instructed, 'Here are words you may trust' (1 Tim 1:15; 3:1; 4:9; 2 Tim 2:11; Tit 3:8). In a world that had long been accustomed to discussing the soundness of the teaching of various philosophers, it must have seemed very natural to adopt similar terminology to distinguish between unhealthy and healthy teaching when problems arose in the Christian community.

Thus we find in the Pastorals an attempt to set healthy words and healthy teaching apart from unhealthy speech. Yet, in 2 Tim 4:2, Timothy is commanded to speak 'out of season' — precisely what one might imagine that the propounders of the unhealthy speech were doing. How are we to explain the flying in the face of convention expressed in 2 Tim 4:2 when in other respects the Pastorals show affinities with the values expressed in philosophical literature? Malherbe believes that this verse must be understood in light of the Pastorals' perspective. He argues that the persons whom the author has in mind are not well-meaning individuals who have gone astray and are open to reason and persuasion which would effect a return to truth. In an extreme situation, Timothy is directed to preach without giving consideration to whether it is opportune or inopportune to do so. The attitude is that of the pessimistic Cynic who flays his deluded audience.[41]

The prediction of a time (undoubtedly already arrived) when people will not endure sound teaching, but having itchy ears will accumulate for themselves teachers to suit their own likings and will turn away from listening to the truth and wander into myths in 2 Tim 4:3–4, certainly supports Malherbe's interpretation. There can be no doubt that the style of preaching that Timothy is instructed to adopt is related to the extreme conditions caused by those who have gone astray. However, other passages discussed above, such as 2 Tim 2:25, imply that the possibilities of opponents returning to truth are not understood to be as bleak as Malherbe suggests. In addition, 2 Tim 4:5, where Timothy is instructed always to be steady, to endure suffering, to do the work of an evangelist and to fulfill his ministry, suggests that what is reflected is not primarily the pessimistic attitude of a teacher who struggles with the obstinence of those who have gone astray. Rather, the mission to preach is encouraged despite the existence of such problems. When it comes to the preaching of the word, traditional conventions may be pushed aside. Timothy is to be urgent in opportune and inopportune time.

The mission to evangelize expressed in 2 Tim 4:2 is at the heart of the community's identity. 2 Timothy as a whole is particularly interesting in this regard. Dibelius/Conzelmann understand its purpose to be to portray Paul as the model of patient endurance in suffering, and thereby of the Christian life in general.[42] In 2 Tim 1:8, Timothy is instructed not to be ashamed of testimony of the Lord nor of Paul. He is to share in suffering for the gospel in the power of God. Timothy's mission is to be in imitation of Paul's mission. For the gospel, Paul was appointed preacher, apostle and teacher, and it is because of the gospel that he suffers as he does. But Paul is not ashamed, for he knows whom he has believed (2 Tim 1:11–12).

The community's vision of universal salvation is explicit throughout the Pastorals. That salvation is for all people is emphasized on numerous occasions (e.g. 1 Tim 2:1–7, 8; 1 Tim 4:10; Tit 2:11). In 1 Tim 2:7 and in 2 Tim 1:11, Paul is described not only as an apostle and a teacher, but also as a preacher. The word preacher (κήρυξ) undoubtedly lays stress on the evangelical aspects of the apostolic office.[43] In the hymnic passage which sets forth the 'mystery of our religion' we read: 'He was preached among the nations and believed in throughout the world' (1 Tim 3:16). But do these passages with missionary colouring refer to any organized effort to evangelize within the community underlying the Pastorals? Or are they reminiscences associated with the authority of Paul, Timothy, and Titus which act as an expression of community identity without being directly related to evangelization activity? It is impossible to be sure. A connection with a real situation in the community is implied, however, by 1 Tim 5:17, where we hear that some elders labour in preaching and teaching. Similarly, in 2 Tim 2:2, Timothy is told that what he has heard from Paul before many witnesses he is to entrust to faithful men who will be able to teach others also. These passages may refer mainly to ministry directed within the community, but where a need for teaching and teachers is expressed, it is likely that expansion is occurring.

If evangelization of outsiders is taking place, where and how is it happening? In his book *Christianizing the Roman Empire*, Ramsay MacMullen discusses this question at length. Acknowledging his puzzlement at the rapid growth of the Christian movement between 100 and 400 C.E., he notes the decline of reference to missionary effort from the turn of the second-century.[44] When attempting to identify where believers could make contact with unbelievers to win them over, he points to the driving-out of demons and to the obscure settings surrounding life in the household and at work.[45] With respect to public appearances, on the whole Christians were cautious.[46]

According to Malherbe, nowhere in the Pastorals is there an interest in private or individual instruction as there is in such passages as 1 Thess 2:11–12 or Acts 20:20, 31. On the contrary, he tells us, Timothy's duties are always portrayed as out in the public for all to see (e.g. 1 Tim 4:12–15; 5:19–21, 24–5; 2 Tim 2:2; cf. Tit 2:7–8).[47] This is indeed a remarkable fact in the light of MacMullen's observations. Malherbe is most likely correct when he connects this emphasis on the public nature of Timothy's ministry with the tactics of heretics who sneak into the household upsetting the faith (2 Tim 3:6; Tit 1:11). It is necessary for Timothy to distinguish himself from his opponents in his method of teaching as well as in its content.[48] But would not the adoption of a kind of public pastoral method increase the potential threat to Christians from hostile outsiders?

In 1 Tim 4:13, Timothy is instructed to attend to the (public) reading of scripture, preaching and teaching. It is important that Timothy practice these duties so that his progress may be clear to all (1 Tim 4:15). He is to continue in his teaching for, in doing so, he will save both himself and his hearers. The primary emphasis here, and throughout the Pastorals, is not on the successful evangelization of outsiders, but on ensuring that community members adhere to healthy teaching. However, the language in 1 Tim 4:15–16 prevents one from drawing sharp boundaries between teaching intended for the evangelization of unbelievers and teaching directed to the already-converted. Here the author undoubtedly has in mind the winning of adherents. The idea of visible progress implies competition. For an author determined that healthy teaching must be distinguished from sick teaching, ensuring that community members adhere to healthy teaching and making such teaching available to the world are both expressions of a universal vision of salvation: '... God our savior, who desires all men to be saved and to come to the knowledge of the truth' (1 Tim 2:3–4).

1.5 Women and false teaching in the household

In this section, it will be argued that the 'suspicious' behaviour of women in the community of the Pastorals is related to the false teaching so fervently condemned throughout the epistles. Underlying 1 Timothy, 2 Timothy, and Titus, one discovers an effort to suppress the activity of teachers who are understood as threatening the conventional male–female roles in the household of God. In order to clarify the implications of their activity, it will be necessary to place the women we hear about in the Pastorals within their social world – a world shaped by the realities of the Greco-Roman household.

That women in the community of the Pastorals may have sought to procure their freedom from traditional household roles, to become teachers and to live the kind of celibate life in anticipation of the kingdom that Paul himself recommends in 1 Corinthians 7, is not incompatible with what we know of women more generally in Greco-Roman society.[49] Women were visible in public as holders of sacred and secular offices; they were the donors and protectors of the cultic associations so popular in antiquity. Women were active in business transactions, owned property, and were influential in the politics that make the world go round. The activity of one woman who lived in a city renowned among students of the New Testament for housing problematic women illustrates the point. In the large city of Corinth, which served as a provincial capital, Junia Theodora opened her household to merchants, envoys and travellers from all over Lycia. She received their thanks later in the form of senatorial decrees for having 'rendered sympathetic to the province most of the authorities, helping to promote a friendly disposition toward us among all the leading people', and 'contributing to all the affairs that mattered most to all Lycians'.[50] This wealthy woman obviously did not limit her public activity to formal appearances on balconies and the like.

Emancipated behaviour was not only characteristic of the elite, although it is of such women that there is most evidence. The ruins of Pompeii reveal the existence of a woman named Eumachia. She made her money through brick-manufacturing concerns. Eumachia paid for one of the major buildings and donated it to a workmen's association; her name and office (*sacerdos publica*) are there advertised.[51] Freedwomen were often upwardly mobile in Greco-Roman society. Their wealth can be observed from the burial places they were able to build for themselves and sometimes for their own slaves and freedmen.[52] Pomeroy speaks of Lyde, the freedwoman of the Empress Lyvia, who owned at least four slaves. She notes, however, that most freedwomen were not extremely wealthy and comprised a large part of the Roman working class. They served as shopkeepers, artisans or continued in the domestic service for which they had been trained as slaves.[53] Nevertheless, women, according to Pomeroy, were active in textile manufacture throughout classical antiquity. Freedwomen from the eastern provinces traded in luxury goods including purple dye and perfumes.[54]

Lydia, who is mentioned in Acts 16:14ff, is perhaps such a freedwoman. Paul encounters her in Philippi among a group of women who have come together. The author of Acts describes her as a dealer in purple dyed garments of the city of Thyatira. Her encounter with Paul leads to her becoming baptized along with all of her household. She strongly urges Paul to come to her house and stay. Paul does visit the house of Lydia which apparently becomes the site for the exhortation of the brethren (Acts 16:40). Although the historical reliability of Acts is questionable, that a woman could have been depicted so clearly in a position of authority in her household is significant from the perspective of the role of women in the author's own community.

Side by side with values that made emancipated behaviour possible in Greco-Roman society, there existed traditional values that had a stronghold in the philosophical thought of the day. As noted in the previous discussion of the household codes in Colossians and Ephesians, the teaching of Aristotle, which understood the individual household as a microcosm of the city state, remained at home in the philosophical teaching and morals of the Empire.[55] A woman's religious practices were generally seen as indicative of the stability of the household, and indeed, of society as a whole. Plutarch, for example, insists that the wife should not only share her husband's friends, but also his gods. The wife must '... shut the front door tight upon all queer rituals and outlandish superstitions. For with no god do stealthy and secret rites performed by a woman find any favour' (140d).[56] This naturally raises questions about how women who were converted to early Christianity, Judaism or other religions understood as threatening, such as the cult of Isis, were perceived in Greco-Roman society.[57]

The main goal of the preceding historical discussion has been to place the women we hear about in the Pastorals in a particular social context. An awareness of the social tensions surrounding a woman's role in the Greco-Roman household provides the starting point for consideration of relevant passages in 1 Timothy, 2 Timothy, and Titus. Connections can now be drawn between the nature of the false teaching condemned by the author and references to women's activity.

We cannot be sure from the author's argument whether the false teachers have come from within the Christian community or whether they belong to a movement embracing a variety of elements external to the church. We do know of wandering teachers active in the early church and it is plausible that such teachers were receiving hospitality from members of the community and were gaining adherents in various households (e.g. 2 Tim 3:6). Whatever the origin of this false teaching, we can be sure that it was a real internal problem of the community underlying the Pastorals, causing division in the House-hold of God.[58]

Study of the doctrine at the heart of this false teaching will not be undertaken here for the simple reason that the text reveals so little. Barrett rightly points out that the author of 1 Timothy, 2 Timothy, and Titus was more concerned to combat the evil moral effect of his opponents' teaching and to note their own moral deficiencies than to analyse their beliefs.[59] It may be that the author shared many of the beliefs of the false teachers, but the disruption they were causing in the community led to a sharp and relentless attack against them. The teaching of the opponents is most often discussed under the label of Jewish gnosticism.[60] Myths, genealogies and interpretations of the law play a part (1 Tim 1:4; 4:7; Tit 1:14; 3:9). A higher knowledge is claimed (1 Tim 6:20; Tit 1:16) and ascetic demands are made, such as abstinence from marriage and from the consumption of certain foods (1 Tim 4:3; 5:23; Tit 1:14−16). The resurrection is said to have already happened (2 Tim 2:18).[61] We can by no means equate this teaching with that of later gnostic systems, but affinities nevertheless exist between the two. The most obvious connection is that the heresy is explicitly identified as what is falsely called gnosis (1 Tim 6:20).[62]

The passage in the Pastorals which sets out most clearly the behaviour recommended by the false teachers is 1 Tim 4:3. We are told that the opponents forbid marriage and enjoin abstinence from foods which God created to be received with thanksgiving by those who believe and know the truth. The response of the author is to stress the goodness of creation (1 Tim 4:4−5; cf. 1 Tim 4:8; Tit 1:13ff). The false teaching is understood as devaluing the created order, rejecting the earthly and the bodily in favour of spiritual falsehood and giving heed to deceitful spirits and to the doctrine of demons (1 Tim 4:1). The possibility of women teaching and having authority over men is viewed as being a violation of the created order and of the natural distinction between the sexes (1 Tim 2:11−15). It is clear from this and other passages that the author of the Pastorals opposes any emancipation of women. This is in keeping with a concern for the preservation of the order of society and a general opposition to emancipation from the structures of the household in any form (e.g. 1 Tim 6:1f; Tit 2:9f, 15; 1 Tim 2:1ff; Tit 3:1f; 1 Tim 3:4f; Tit 2:1−10). 1 Tim 2:12 suggests that women in the church of the Pastorals were involved in public teaching, or at least were exerting strong pressure to be allowed to do so. It is also possible that the author knew of communities (perhaps connected with the false teachers) where women played a major role in leadership (cf. Rev 2:20ff).[63]

The passage that enables one to make a firm connection between women and the false teaching is 2 Tim 3:6. No other social group in the church is explicitly named by the author as being attracted by the false teaching.[64] The false teachers are condemned for creeping into houses and capturing silly women. The picture presented is one of the clandestine attack on households. These women are vulnerable. Having been burdened by sin, they are being led by various lusts. The author here shares a popular belief that women are susceptible to bizarre religious impulses.[65] Recall, for example, the words of Plutarch cited earlier about the importance of women keeping the doors of the house shut to these impulses. The statement in 2 Tim 3:7 about women always learning and never being able to come to the full knowledge of the truth has a sarcastic tone. The repudiation of women who are eager to learn and ask questions in 1 Cor 14:35 comes to mind as does the author's adamant rejection of women as teachers in the church in 1 Tim 2:11ff. The conviction with which the author argues the case about women not teaching and not having authority over men, as well as the general reference to 'silly women', suggests that all women are viewed as being incapable of 'knowledge of the truth' on the same level as men.[66]

What appeal did this false teaching have for women? In attempting to answer this question, the passage that first comes to mind is 1 Tim 4:3 with its explicit expression of the content of the teaching. The prohibition against marriage stands out sharply in a society where marriage is, for the most part, understood as being for the rearing of children and necessary for all women.[67] It seems likely that the young widows, whom the author describes as causing problems in the church, have taken this prohibition against marriage seriously (1 Tim 5:11–15). Furthermore, the sexual asceticism recommended by the opponents finds support in the teaching of Paul and in the Jesus traditions (e.g. Mark 12:18–27 [Matt 22:23ff; Luke 20:27ff]; Matt 19:12; Luke 23:29; Mark 10:28–31 [Matt 19:27ff; Luke 18:28ff]). It is difficult to imagine the Paul of 1 Corinthians 7 making a general pronouncement about the marriage of all young widows as in 1 Tim 5:14 or declaring that a woman will be saved through her bearing of children as in 1 Tim 2:15. It is difficult to imagine him being so concerned to relate leadership in the church to marriage and fatherhood as in 1 Tim 3:1–5. One could argue that 1 Corinthians 7 and the passages cited above from the synoptic gospels are connected with an imminent expectation of the kingdom and that the Pastorals reflect the changed situation of the church settling down for a long stay in the world. However, the persistence of ascetic tendencies in some circles into the second-century and beyond prevents us from making a simple appeal to the popular delay of the parousia solution. It is possible that the church of the Pastorals is threatened by a controversy surrounding Paul's 'gospel' read in terms of practice. The Paul of the Pastorals stands to challenge any radically ascetic interpretations of his teaching.[68]

1.6 The Pastoral Epistles and the Acts of Paul and Thecla

The prohibition against marriage by the opponents in the Pastoral Epistles (1 Tim 4:3) brings to mind the asceticism visible in the second-century Acts of Paul.[69] The influential church thinker Tertullian writes in *De baptismo* 17 (approx. 200 C.E.):

> If those who read the writings that falsely bear the name of Paul adduce the example of Thecla to maintain the right of women to teach and to baptize, let them know that the presbyter in Asia who produced this document, as if he could of himself add anything to the prestige of Paul, was removed from his office after he had been convicted and had confessed that he did it out of love for Paul.[70]

Thecla, a woman who would certainly not have been popular with the author of the Pastorals, figures prominently in a section of the apocryphal Acts of Paul known as the Acts of Paul and Thecla. The Pastorals may represent a response to the kind of development visible in the Acts of Paul and Thecla. Both of these writings probably have their origin in Asia Minor. While dating is uncertain for each, it is not unreasonable to think that they were written as little as a generation apart.[71]

According to the Acts of Paul and Thecla, Paul is accused of corrupting women. Thecla, a woman betrothed to Thamyris, becomes enchanted by 'the word of the virgin life' spoken by Paul. Her mother, worried about the consequences of this attachment, speaks to Thamyris: '... for all the women and young people go to him. "You must" he says, "fear one single God only, and live chastely." And my daughter also, like a spider at the window bound by his words, is dominated by a new desire and a fearful passion; for the maiden hangs upon the things he says, and is taken captive. But go thou to her and speak to her, for she is betrothed to thee' (3:9). Paul preaches against marriage on the grounds that in order to participate in the resurrection, one must remain chaste and not defile the flesh, but keep it pure (3:12). Thecla renounces her role as wife and is sentenced to death for her behaviour. Her mother cries: 'Burn the lawless one! Burn her that is no bride in the midst of the theatre, that all the women who have been taught by this man will be afraid!' (3:20)(!) Thecla miraculously escapes from the flames that were to burn her alive and the beasts that were to devour her. She baptizes herself during the confrontation with the wild beasts (3:34). She sets off to find Paul and, when she eventually locates him, he appoints her to be a teacher of the word (3:41).

When Thecla rejects marriage, she is, in fact, staging a rebellion against the traditionally subordinate role of women in Greco-Roman society. When she rejects her determined role in society, the reaction of her household is one of sorrow: 'And those who were in the house wept bitterly, Thamyris for the loss of a wife, Theocleia for that of a daughter, the maidservants for that of a mistress' (3:10). That Thecla's actions are supported by many other women is clear from the reaction of the crowd of women who are spectators as Thecla is brought before beasts (3:32–5). Thecla can be a teacher like Paul. She is emancipated and independent. She will cut her hair off short and follow him wherever he goes (3:25). After enlightening many with the word of God, we are told that she slept a noble sleep.

In light of the accusation against the false teachers in 2 Tim 3:6 about making their way into households and capturing weak women, the frequency of movement in and out of houses in the Acts of Paul and Thecla is indeed remarkable. Paul is received into the house of Onesiphorus (3:2) and speaks in the midst of the assembly in this house (3:7). Later, we are told that Onesiphorus has left the things of the world and followed Paul with all his house (3:23).[72] Thecla goes with Tryphaena and rests in her house for eight days, instructing her in the word of the Lord. We are told that the majority of the maid-servants also believed and that there was great joy in the house (3:39). The kind of 'in-house' teaching we find here may be contrasted with the stress on public teaching in the Pastorals noted earlier.

The network of households we hear of in the Acts of Paul and Thecla are characterized by substantial wealth. If Thecla were to marry Thamyris, she would be a mistress with many maidservants (3:10). When Thamyris encounters Demas and Hermogenes, he attempts to bribe them in order to gain information about Paul: 'I promise now to give much money if you will tell me about him; for I am the first man of this city' (3:11). From what we know about the marriage practices of the day, it is not surprising that the picture we find of Thecla is of a woman of the same social background as Thamyris. In order that she may visit Paul in prison, the resourceful Thecla takes off her bracelets and gives them to the door-keeper; to the gaoler, she gives a silver mirror (3:18). It is a rich woman, Tryphaena, who takes Thecla under her protection. Tryphaena, whose own daughter has died and who adopts Thecla as her second child, is a widow (3:30). Tryphaena's fainting at the side of the arena where Thecla is to be devoured by beasts causes great alarm, for this woman has connections in very high places (3:36). In order for Thecla to carry out her ministry, Tryphaena sends her clothing and gold for the service of the poor (3:41).

Noting the story-like quality of the Acts of Paul and Thecla, Dennis Ronald MacDonald has argued that it represents the efforts of a collector to gather oral legends about Paul.[73] In describing the social situation underlying the work, he points to the story telling of celibate women who took Paul's recommendations about remaining un-married in the advent of the Lord very seriously.[74] During his own lifetime and beyond, Paul's teaching seems to have been a source of controversy.[75] The conflicts echoed at various points in Paul's letters imply that his apostolic methods and teachings were by no means universally accepted. That legends circulated about Paul after his death is evident from various New Testament writings. Commentators often note the disparity between the Paul of the epistles and the Paul of Acts. The Paul of the Pastoral Epistles also stands at some distance from the Paul of the authentic letters. That conflicts took place over which teachings belonged to the true Paul is evident from the com-ments found in the second-century writing, 2 Peter, about the unlearned and unstable twisting aspects of Paul's teaching to their own destruction (2 Pet 3:15ff). The Acts of Paul and Thecla come as a reminder that the Pastoral Epistles do not represent the inevitable outcome of the Pauline tradition in the second century, but reflect only one option in competition with others − although it was the Pastoral Epistles that were canonized.[76] The Pastorals may have been written to counter the image of Paul as given in stories told by women. The battle against stories is implied by the recommendation found in 1 Tim 4:7 to have nothing to do with profane and old-womanish tales.[77]

The picture of the wealthy, independent Thecla who renounces marriage to become a teacher of the word is not inconsistent with the knowledge we have of the activity of women from the historical sources discussed earlier. Neither is the reaction to Thecla's behaviour inconsistent with what would be expected, considering current values. It is important to note that it is not for Christianity that Thecla was sentenced to death, but for her refusal to marry Thamyris.[78] But, is it such women as Thecla or the wealthy widow Tryphaena who are causing problems for the author of the Pastorals? Did they, like Thecla, wish to enlighten many with the word of God (3:43)?

1.7 Service in the household as service in the household of God

1 Tim 5:3–16 suggests that widows had a special place in the leadership of the church. This passage, however, contains many ambiguities. It is not clear how these women served the Christian community or even whether they constituted an office of widows. For the sake of clarity, this passage will be considered in terms of three questions:

1.   Who were the real widows?
2.   What was the significance of the fact that certain widows were enrolled? and
3.   Why were young widows being encouraged to remarry?

Who were the real widows? The demand to honour widows who are real widows (τὰς ὄντως χήρας) in 1 Tim 5:3 might be thought of as evidence for the existence of an office, since 'honour' could mean 'pay'. This interpretation is supported by the fact that in 1 Tim 5:17 'honour' apparently refers to the financial compensation of elders. However, the word 'τιμή' and its cognates are employed in the Pastorals in a variety of ways. In 1 Tim 6:1f for example, the reference cannot possibly refer to a payment of any kind. Here slaves are exhorted to consider their masters 'worthy of all honour'. Verner is correct when he points out that the best means of determining the meaning of 'honour' in 1 Tim 5:3 is by relating it to its immediate context in 1 Tim 5:3–16 where we find a concern for the practical help of needy women.[79] That the problem at hand is a matter of practical support is evident from 1 Tim 5:4, 8 and 16.

1 Tim 5:4 urges that the children and grandchildren of widows should support them. Dibelius/Conzelmann believe the passage could be paraphrased as follows: 'If a widow has a family, then she has no need of such honours by the church.'[80] Such respect for elders is acceptable before God. 1 Tim 5:8 resumes the point of 1 Tim 5:4 but this time suggesting that some community members have indeed neglected some of their own (widows). The strong statement against those who neglect their own, who are accused of denying their faith and being worse than unbelievers, implies that the author is concerned about a threatening problem in the church of the Pastorals.[81]

The connection between need and the 'real widows' is also evident from 1 Tim 5:16. Here the author instructs any believing woman 'τις πιστή' to assist relatives who are widows. The church should not be burdened (financially?) so that it may be able to assist real widows (i.e. those who are alone).[82] It appears from 1 Tim 5:16 that the women who 'have widows' are of high social status. The picture of real widows as widows alone and in need is confirmed by 1 Tim 5:5–7. The real widow is one who is left alone, who has set her hope on God and continues in supplications and prayers day and night. She is contrasted with the widow who is self-indulgent. This kind of woman is probably living a luxurious life-style which the author considers worthless.[83] Having access to wealth and using it for her own pleasure, she is not a real widow. That the community of the Pastorals was being criticized for the behaviour of such women is suggested by 1 Tim 5:7, where Timothy is told to instruct the widows in order that they may be without reproach.[84]

The recommendation to believing women to assist relatives who are real widows brings to mind the role of Tabitha in Acts 9:36ff. When Tabitha, a woman noted for good works and acts of charity, has died, widows gather around her and display clothes she apparently had made for them when she was alive. When Tabitha is revived, the widows are a special group which must be informed; Tabitha is apparently their benefactor.[85] It is most likely women like Tabitha whom the author addresses in 1 Tim 5:16. Perhaps some of these women are widows themselves. We can easily imagine the widow Tryphaena, who takes Thecla into her house, being able to render such a service. Wealthy widows could exert considerable influence in the Greco-Roman world. The praise given to the wealthy widow Cornelia, who lived in the second century B.C.E., is a case in point. Having turned down an offer of remarriage, not only did this woman continue to manage her household, but she also exerted considerable influence in Roman politics.[86]

The above discussion reveals that 'real widows' probably desig-nates, not a group of official widows, but simply widows who were alone with no family members or wealthy believing women to look after them.[87] Does this mean that we have no evidence for the existence of an office of widows in the Pastorals? This brings us to our next question: What was the significance of the fact that certain widows were enrolled? The act of enrolling (καταλέγω) mentioned in 1 Tim 5:9 does not necessarily mean we have evidence for an office of widows for it could refer to nothing more than the writing of names down on a list.[88] However, since the church keeps such a list and membership is limited in terms of certain characteristics, the existence of an office seems likely. The requirements for the enrollment of widows resemble the requirements for the offices of bishop, elder, and deacon (1 Tim 3:1–13; Tit 1:6ff).[89] The somewhat peculiar expectation that a male office holder be the husband of one wife (μιᾶς γυναικὸς ἄνδρες) takes on a female expression in the statement that an enrolled widow be 'ἑνὸς ἀνδρὸς γυνή' (1 Tim 5:9). Moreover, the virtues of hospitality (1 Tim 5:10; 1 Tim 3:2; Tit 1:8) and the proper care of children (1 Tim 5:10; 1 Tim 3:4; Tit 1:6) are demanded of the widows as well as of male leaders in the church.[90] Despite the uncertainty as to what exactly were the duties of these enrolled widows, there is no reason to suppose that we have no evidence for the existence of an office. As Verner points out, the Pastorals offer no information about the office of deacon either, but they certainly presuppose the existence of such an office.[91]

Another argument in favour of the existence of an office of enrolled widows is the rejection of the younger widows for enrollment in 1 Tim 5:11ff. Thus Verner is most likely correct when he seeks to distinguish vv. 9ff, which speak about an office of widows, from vv. 3–8, 16, which are concerned with the church's social responsibility for widows.[92] Real widows are poor widows who must depend on the church for support and are not necessarily identical with enrolled widows. For example, if a fifty-five year old widow is left without family or financial resources to support herself, she would certainly be considered a real widow in terms of the author's description, but the declaration that only widows who are sixty years of age or over be enrolled would make her ineligible for the office. Nevertheless, since we would expect that the problems of being left alone would be particularly grave for those of sixty or over, it is not unrealistic to assume that the office of enrolled widows included many real widows who were dependent on the church for support. Tit 2:4 indicates that the author of the Pastorals particularly valued the example of older women.

We now arrive at our third question: Why were young widows being encouraged to remarry? Younger widows are explicitly prohibited from being enrolled and are encouraged to remarry (1 Tim 5:11). The author gives various reasons for this. When young official widows desire to be married, they stand condemned for having set aside their first pledge.[93] Here we discover more indirect evidence for an office of widows. It is likely that this pledge was an óath of celibacy taken on the occasion of their enrollment.[94] Some young widows had apparently violated this pledge. It is probable that, at one time, young widows were enrolled. In fact, such enrolled young widows probably played an active role in community life. But, by setting the age of

eligibility at sixty years of age or over, the author is preventing any
new young widows from participating in the office. As is the case in
his definition of real widows, the author appears to be limiting
participation in and reliance on the church on the part of widows to
a minimum.

A second reason given by the author for refusal of enrollment is
found in 1 Tim 5:13 where we hear of young widows going from house
to house, being idlers, gossips, busybodies, and saying things that they
should not. Despite the possible ministerial intent of such visits, the
negative tone indicates that the author understood them to be in no
way pastoral. The language used to describe the activity of these
women calls to mind the description of false teachers in 2 Tim 3:6
where they are said to make their way into households and capture
weak women. In both instances (which are probably related) the
author is concerned with putting to an end activity which is considered
to be disruptive to community life.[95] These young widows who can
afford to be idle are perhaps financially independent. At any rate,
in the face of probable instances of violation of a celibacy pledge and,
perhaps more seriously, engagement in activity which represents a
misuse of the freedom connected with widowhood, the author
commands that they should marry, bear children, and rule the
household (1 Tim 5:14). The author of the Pastorals is inviting the
widows to become matrons of traditional well-to-do households.[96]
Hence, the author recommends that young widows take on the roles
that are rejected fervently by Thecla. They are to be wives, subject
to their husbands, respectful of their mothers. They are to be the
rearers of children and the mistresses of slaves. In Tit 2:4–5 the author
instructs the older women in the community to teach the younger
women to love their husbands and children, to be sensible, pure,
domestic, kind, and submissive to their husbands. The author's
position comes out clearly throughout the epistles: it is as wives and
mothers that women are to serve the household of God.

1.8 Widows or wives: a conflict in community life

The epistles to Timothy and Titus present a more unified understanding of the role of women in the household and, indeed, in the
household of God than is perhaps first apparent. The problem of false
teaching in the Pastorals is inseparably linked with the activity of
women in the community. The opponents are depicted as going into
the household and capturing weak women. Women, especially young

women, were apparently the most susceptible group in the church to this teaching. Perhaps some women propagated this teaching themselves as the description of young widows going from house to house implies. Its appeal was probably connected to the ascetic prohibition against marriage which would make emancipated behaviour more possible in a world where marriage involved a variety of social obligations and restrictions. The strong warnings against women teaching or having authority over men in 1 Tim 2:11ff suggest that some women in the community of the Pastorals were interested in leadership roles that the author believed should be reserved for men. There is no evidence to suggest that women were either elders or bishops in the community. They may have been deacons, but this is far from certain. The reference in 1 Tim 3:11 may be either to wives of deacons or female deacons. If women were involved in such a ministry, of which the Pastorals reveal so little, their tasks were probably similar to that of Phoebe (Rom 16:1–2) – the practice of hospitality and the general care of the needy. Similar responsibilities may have been given to those women belonging to the office of widows.

The activity of widows seems to have been of great concern to the author. The descriptions of the issues at hand reveal that the community included women from various social strata. The real widows are needy women who, finding themselves alone, are dependent on the church for subsistence. We also hear of the existence of wealthy believing women who are able to relieve widows and are recommended to do so in order that the church not be unnecessarily burdened. The author's instructions concerning the remarriage of young widows and those directed to young women in general reflect a respect for the matronly virtues highly valued by the society of the day. It is likely that some women in the community were the wives of wealthy householders and, as such, were encouraged to comply with social responsibilities involving the rearing of children, subjection to their husband and the general management of the household. The actions of idle young widows going from house to house implies a certain financial independence which may be related to emancipated behaviour. As a whole, the author's instruction concerning widows is designed to limit the church's responsibility and, indeed, their own activity as much as possible.

In insisting that real widows are only those who are alone and really needy and in encouraging families and wealthy patrons to look after widows, the author is placing as many under the auspices of the household as possible. A similar intent underlies instructions to younger widows to remarry. The author obviously respects older widows and older women in general, understanding their service to be particularly valuable in the teaching of younger women who are susceptible to being led astray. The author is, however, suspicious of younger widows. In the praise of older widows, the instructions to younger widows, and all the exhortations concerning women, the author's belief comes out clearly: it is as wives and mothers that women are to serve the household of God.

Why is the author so insistent that women continue in the traditional roles associated with the patriarchal household? The discussion of the Ephesian household code in Part 2 illustrated that the activity of women in the Pauline sect was considered as a special reflection of the purity of the sect. In the Pastoral Epistles, the activity of women is seen as corrupting community life. A crucial part of maintaining the boundaries surrounding the sacred space of the community involves the stabilizing of relations with those on the outside. Historical investigation has revealed that the Aristotelian belief in the individual household as a paradigm of the state was widely held in Greco-Roman society. The behaviour of a woman who neglected household responsibilities was considered subversive. Numerous passages, including many concerned with the behaviour of women, which were cited in previous sections indicated the likelihood that Christians were receiving criticism from outsiders. Behind the author's recommendation of quiet behaviour, modest dress, and submission as virtues becoming a woman probably lies the hope that their behaviour will disprove slanderous accusations against Christians.[97] But what might these outsiders have been saying? We should listen to the non-Christian Celsus' second-century description of Christians to gain a greater understanding of the author of the Pastorals' attitude to women:

> In private houses also we see wool-workers, cobblers, laundry-workers, and the most illiterate and bucolic yokels, who would not dare to say anything at all in front of their elders and more intelligent masters. But whenever they get hold of children in private and some stupid women with them, they let out some astounding statements as, for example, that they must not pay any attention to their father and school-teacher ...[98]

1.9 A stratified society

'The love of money is the root of all evils' (1 Tim 6:10). Why did the author of the Pastorals appeal to this popular maxim in his instructions to the church community? What kind of attitude to riches does it reflect? The wealthy are not advised to give all to the poor; there is no demand for a redistribution of wealth. Warning the rich not to be haughty nor to set their hopes on anything but God, the author recommends only that they do good, be rich in good deeds, be willing to give and be generous (1 Tim 6:18). What kind of attitude to the rich does this exhortation exhibit? In a modern world where economic policies are often divided in terms of left and right, the author's position may appear contradictory. A strong condemnation of the accumulation of wealth (1 Tim 6:6–10) does not accompany censure of the rich or the desire for the revamping of social structures.

The attitude to wealth is not a topic usually discussed in detail by New Testament scholars for the simple reason that the text contains so little which is directly concerned with this topic. It will be argued here, however, that what little is said directly about wealth and what can be reasonably inferred from statements in the text is of paramount importance for understanding the ethos of love-patriarchalism shaping community life.

If one were to visit the cities of Corinth, Ephesus or Rome at the end of the first century, one would undoubtedly notice rigid social segregation. The lives of the urban non-elite were not untouched by those who lived in the·other quarter of the city however. Bruce Malina has argued that perhaps the most important role of the elite was that they were the bearers of the culture's 'Great Tradition' (the norms and values which gave continuity and substance to the ideals of society). He indicates that to find the ideal forms of social norms governing marriage, religion, education and government, one would need to look at the urban literate elite, since they were best able to fulfil exacting requirements.[99]

The previous study of women in the Pastorals pointed to the probable membership in the community of the relatively well-to-do. It is impossible to determine how wealthy these members were or even whether they might be classified as the elite. It has also been noted that these well-to-do women belonged to a community which included slaves and needy widows. As this study will demonstrate, however, it is the values and norms of the well-to-do which are dominant in the Pastorals, even though such members may have been greatly in the minority. The author's conservative tendencies expressed in the desire to confine women to the household may be more readily understood in terms of Malina's description. The upper-class priestess who presides in public most likely comes from the world found in the other quarter of the city. The author may be once-removed from 'where it is at'. Nevertheless, the world found in the other quarter of the city exerts a tremendous influence on the world of the Pastorals. The culture revealed by the author's statements may be a simplified and outdated expression of the norms and values that are shaped by the city elite. The author of the Pastorals may not have personally read Aristotle, but instructions concerning behaviour in the household bear witness to a culture where Aristotelian thought was prevalent.

The influence of literary culture can also be found in classical allusions and quotations in the Pastorals. Commentators often point out that when, in Tit 1:12, the citation 'Cretans are always liars, evil beasts, lazy gluttons' is attributed to 'a prophet of their own', the author may have had Epimenides, who was a Cretan, in mind. Although this appears to be a direct quotation from the work of the religious teacher and wonder-worker of the sixth century B.C.E., Malherbe warns against making hasty conclusions. This statement had become proverbial by the end of the first-century; hence, it provides insufficient evidence of a first hand knowledge of the work of Epimenides.[100] A second proverbial statement quoted at the beginning of this section, 'The love of money is the root of all evils' (1 Tim 6:10), also alludes to the Greek authors. One of the many examples given by Dibelius/Conzelmann of its appearances in contemporary literature is found in Stobaeus (Ecl. 3) who writes, 'Bion the Sophist used to say that the love of money is the mother-city of all evil.'[101]

Malherbe argues that the presence of classical allusions and quotations in the New Testament reveals a certain level of literary culture. He points out that the writings of the Hellenistic authors, especially those of the moral philosophers, abound with quotations of this type. Writers were not always read in their entirety, but instead schools collected selections from classical works which were often arranged according to moral topics. The work of Stobaeus in fact provides a very good example of this.[102] According to Malherbe, the moral philosophers who attempted to reform the masses used these statements because they believed the poets were the authorities on the masses and best represented the common wisdom.[103]

The author of the Pastorals, like the moral philosophers who attempted to reform the masses, probably cited the proverbial statements because of the belief that they reflected common wisdom – wisdom that was understood to be appropriate in the context. It is likely that many whom the author addressed recognized the statements as common wisdom as well. Perhaps the author had access to the kind of handbook used in the upper levels of secondary education which contained such statements, or perhaps had often heard them cited by various philosophers. Whatever the case, what is especially interesting from the perspective of Malina's study is that the writings discussed in the highest literary circles made their way into an address directed to a community where many probably had little education. But this is not extraordinary considering the practices of the day. The Greek authors cherished and discussed by the most literary people could be heard in the proverbial statements that were part of the language of more common folk. In a similar fashion, values that were cherished by the elite made their way into the lower classes. The picture of the Roman matron who rules her house well, who rears her children, obeys her husband and is a mistress to slaves appears to have been held up as an ideal by the author of the Pastorals, but how many of the women addressed were in a position to fulfil this ideal? Cultural norms and values appear to move from the top down.[104]

Malina has argued that the perception of limited good is characteristic of Greco-Roman society – a society polarized in terms of an elite minority and a non-elite majority. His description proves helpful for understanding the attitude to wealth visible in the Pastorals. The members of Greco-Roman society understood their existence as being limited by the natural and social resources of their environment.[105] The insight that there is simply not enough to go around is accompanied by a belief that there is no way directly within a person's power to increase the available quantities. The result is that any major improvement in an individual's status is perceived as threatening, not only to other single individuals and families, but in fact to all individuals and families in the community. In light of this perception of limited goods, the strong condemnation of the accumulation of wealth (1 Tim 6:6–10; cf. 1 Tim 3:3, 8; 6:5, 6; 2 Tim 3:2; Tit 1:7, 11), which is accompanied by a favourable attitude towards the established rich, is more easily understood (1 Tim 6:17–19; cf. 1 Tim 2:2; Tit 3:1). The author of the Pastorals appears fully to support the preservation of inherited status. Community harmony and stability becomes inextricably linked to maintenance of existing arrangements of statuses.[106]

1.10 Attitudes to wealth in the Shepherd of Hermas

Before turning to the text of the Pastorals, it is useful to consider another writing which exhibits similar attitudes to wealth, the Shepherd of Hermas. Written probably before the middle of the second century, the Shepherd presents a good description of the problems that can occur in community life surrounding the accumulation of wealth; hence, it provides suggestions as to the social setting of the exhortations against the amassing of capital we find in the Pastorals.[107]

In 1927, Donald Riddle observed that the reason for the general failure to understand the Shepherd of Hermas is to be found in the method of study.[108] He noted that with hardly any exception (and indeed hardly an exception since 1927) work on the Shepherd of Hermas has been approached from the perspective of abstracting from its teaching some point of doctrine or evidence of some feature of an institution. Riddle rejected methodologies which encourage the extraction of such passages as Mand 4 from their contexts and lead to the conclusion that the central message of the writing is the treatment of sin after baptism. He argued that the Shepherd should be studied for what it can reveal about the ways in which the early Christian community met the problems encountered with respect to the social forces at work in Greco-Roman society.[109]

Riddle draws attention to the condition referred to by Hermas as 'double-mindedness' or 'doubt' (διψυχία and cognates, cf. Vis 4:2:4; Mand 9; Sim 8:8:3; Sim 9:21:1–4). He argues that its various aspects are directly related to the lack of unanimity and unity which is the danger in any social group.[110] The result is a breakdown of the Christian community and the formation of schisms (Sim 8:7:2; Sim 8:7:5; Sim 8:7:6).[111] According to Riddle, the offer of repentance acts as an inducement to return to obedience in the Shepherd of Hermas (Sim 8:8:5; Sim 8:9:4; Sim 9:31:4).[112]

Riddle points to the influence of business and wealth as the social force most directly operative in the breakup of the unity of the social group.[113] Carolyn Osiek has recently arrived at similar conclusions with respect to the problems characterizing the community life of the Shepherd of Hermas. She argues that this writing is not a dreary treatise on penitential discipline, but in fact has much to offer toward understanding second-century Christianity as it struggled to maintain its integrity in the Greco-Roman environment.[114] This is indeed a problem to which Hermas continuously returns. Hermas' vision of the building of the church reveals that wealth and involvement in business affairs are related to denial when persecution comes (Vis 3:6). The parable in which various sticks are the figures makes the same point (Sim 8:8:1−2). Business affairs involve lies (Mand 3:1:5). Every luxury is foolish and futile for the slaves of God (Mand 12:2). Those who live in luxury and pleasure are tormented for the same length of time as they spend in luxury and pleasure (Sim 6:4). Preoccupation with wealth and business, as well as involvement in heathen friendships, means that Christians are drawn aside from their true purpose and lose all understanding of righteousness (Mand 10:1:4−5). Connections with wealth and business tend to break down social solidarity (Sim 9:20:1−3).

Riddle believes that it is against the background of the tensions associated with the rise of freedpersons that the teaching of Hermas concerning wealth and business should be understood. Riddle argues that it is hardly to be expected that, in such a changing world, the constituency of the churches would be unaffected.[115] Riddle's analysis gains support from the study conducted by Meeks on the ambiguous social position occupied by freedpersons in the Empire.[116]

In a limited goods society, involvement in business transactions means exposure to the temptations to accumulate wealth. The information in Vis 1:1 and Vis 3:6 suggests that Hermas was a freedman who had fallen into this temptation. As a rich man Hermas was useless. It is against the historical situation described by Riddle and Meeks that one must understand such passages as Sim 1:1−11. It recalls the tensions and uncertainties surrounding the life of the freedperson in the Greco-Roman city. Pointing out that the lives of the slaves of God are subject to those above them, the shepherd warns of the futility of the accumulation of wealth (Sim 1:1:4−6). The shepherd underlines the impermanence of upward mobility. Underlying this parable is the fear that members of the Christian community are losing their allegiance to ideal values (Mand 10:1:4; Sim 8:9:1−4).[117]

A connection between social disruption and wealth is also visible in the New Testament epistle of James.[118] The rich are condemned in no uncertain terms in James; they are oppressors (James 2:6; 5:1−6). Like Hermas, the author of James warns of the impermanence of wealth (James 1:9–11; 4:14–16; 5:1–6). The demand for the equality between rich and poor in community life (James 2:1–7) stands out sharply against the values of the day and recalls some of the radical statements of the synoptic tradition (Mark 10:25 [Matt 19:24; Luke 18:25]; Matt 6:19–21 [Luke 12:33–4]; Luke 6:24ff; 16:1ff). Like the community of the Shepherd of Hermas, the community of James suffers from division caused by the desire and the ambition of some of its members (James 1:14; 3:13–18; 4:1–10). The ambition of the trader (James 4:13) is said to be foolish in terms of the uncertainties of life in this world (James 4:14–16). The condition that plagued the church of the Shepherd of Hermas apparently also causes strife here. The members of the community are double-minded (cf. James 1:8; 4:8); they are doubters, like waves in the sea, driven and tossed by the wind (James 1:6).[119] It seems clear from the closing exhortation of the letter that the author of James is struggling with problems of deviant behaviour similar to those encountered by Hermas. The author of James seeks to consolidate the community and to bring back those who have gone astray. The brethren are informed that if anyone among them wanders from the truth and someone brings the person back, the one bringing the sinner from the error of his ways is to be informed that his soul will be saved from death and he will hide a multitude of sins (James 5:19–20).

It is hardly surprising that the members of the early Christian community were subject to tensions with respect to their involvement in the business of the Empire. As the epistle of James illustrates, the Christians were called to set themselves apart from the ways and associations of the outside world, yet their work brought them in constant contact with that world. Life in city churches required participation in trade and commerce for the sake of subsistence. The Christians did not form self-sustaining communities separated from the outside society by virtually impenetrable barriers. Rather, they lived side by side with their pagan neighbours and indeed required the co-operation of these neighbours for existence. They depended on the household, including the household church, to provide boundaries separating them from outsiders. But, for a sect with a vision of universal salvation, the door of the household was always open to some degree.

Immersed in the life of the Greco-Roman city, how could Christians deal with tensions that threatened community unity? If daily involvement in the business of the Empire was a necessity, how could values which were associated with such involvement, but which were considered incompatible with the ethos of community life, be kept outside? Riddle argues that Hermas' teaching discloses a desire to exercise control in community life.[120] For example, in Sim 4:5–7, the shepherd instructs that much business should be avoided for it leads to sin. However, if a man works at a single business, he can serve the Lord also. A recommendation as to the kind of life-style that is appropriate for the slave of God is being made in this passage. It is not suggested that business as a whole should be abandoned. Such work is undoubtedly good and necessary. It is excess of ambition, which leads to an inability to serve the Lord, that is being warned against. The involvement of Christians in business activities has evidently led to a breakdown of the unity of the group.[121]

The temptations of wealth and luxury associated with business transactions are connected to the problems of deviant behaviour in the Shepherd of Hermas. Discipline is forcefully demanded. The exercise of charity appears to be an important aspect of church discipline (Vis 3:9:4–5; Sim 9:30:4–5; Sim 9:31:2).[122] This raises a central question: What were church members who had been successful in business instructed to do with their wealth? Hermas points to an imbalance of wealth in the church. Some, by eating too much, bring on bodily sickness and injure their bodies, while the bodies of those who have nothing to eat are injured because they do not have enough food (Vis 3:9:3). This lack of solidarity is harmful to those who do not share with the needy (Vis 3:9:4; cf. Mand 2). The elderly woman warns of the judgement to come on those who pride themselves on their wealth. Those who are well-to-do in the church are to use their wealth to look after the needs of the poor while they still have the opportunity to do so (Vis 3:5–6).

Does sharing with those who are in want mean that the rich should become poor? Hermas answers this question for us as well. The round bright stones of the tower (the church) are representative of the rich in the community. Although their riches have hidden them a little from the truth, they have never departed from God. Consequently, the Lord commanded that their wealth be cut down, but not wholly taken away from them, in order that they might be able to do good with what is left. With some minor reshaping, these stones can be made to fit the tower (Sim 9:30:4–5). It is not the mere possession of wealth that is condemned, but the selfish amassing of, and preoccupation with, riches. One who puts his wealth to the service of the church is praised (cf. Sim 5:2:5–11).

The Shepherd of Hermas implies that there is a place for both rich and poor in the church, but their relationship must be one of love-patriarchalism: the social divisions are maintained but the rich have a responsibility to care for the poor. The rich may be able to play the role of patron and provider, but the poor also have a special role in the church:

> Therefore the two together [the rich and poor] complete the work, for the poor works in the intercession in which he is rich, which he received from the Lord: this he pays to the Lord who helps him. And the rich man likewise provides the poor, without hesitating, with the wealth which he received from the Lord; and this work is great and acceptable with God, because he has understanding in his wealth and has wrought for the poor man from the gifts of the Lord, and fulfilled his ministry rightly. (Sim 2.7)

1.11 Attitudes to wealth in the Pastorals

A study of the Shepherd of Hermas helps us in our understanding of the situation underlying the Pastorals; although these writings exhibit similar attitudes to wealth, the Shepherd of Hermas deals with problems arising in community life in much more detail than do the Pastoral Epistles. We cannot assume that the problems faced by the church of the Shepherd of Hermas were identical to those experienced by the church of the Pastorals, but study of the Shepherd enables one to make more plausible suggestions as to the tensions at work in the community underlying 1 Timothy, 2 Timothy, and Titus. There are two passages in the Pastorals where wealth and the wealthy are discussed specifically and in some detail, 1 Tim 6:6−10 and 1 Tim 6:17−19; other passages, however, make brief and indirect references to wealth.

1 Tim 6:6−10 follows a section where false teachers are attacked (1 Tim 6:1−3). The theme of greed connects the passages. In 1 Tim 6:5 we are told that the false teachers imagine godliness to be a means of profit. Perhaps they are charging for the instruction they give to their adherents. However, this in itself would not be outrageous, since the author appears to encourage the payment of church officials engaged in teaching (1 Tim 5:17f; cf. 2 Tim 2:6). Once again it seems to be the amassing of wealth which is condemned. Elsewhere the author describes these teachers as being lovers of money (2 Tim 3:2) and of teaching things they should not for the sake of base gain

(Tit 1:11). In contrast to the false teachers, church officials should not engage in this kind of dishonourable behaviour. Bishops and Deacons are instructed not to be greedy for gain (1 Tim 3:3, 8; Tit 1:7).

Robert J. Karris has pointed out that greed was a common criticism of sophists in antiquity.[123] In the Shepherd of Hermas, the false prophet is identified as one who lives in great luxury and accepts rewards for his prophecy (Mand 11:12). However, the fact that the polemic against false teachers in the Pastorals draws on many traditional elements does not mean that the exhortations have no connections to real situations. The author of the Pastorals, grounded in the Greco-Roman world, may well have understood the false teachers as exhibiting qualities that were traditionally condemned by the society at large.

In 1 Tim 6:6−10 the author seems to move beyond the specific example of the behaviour of false teachers to more general exhortations directed toward the whole community. He indicates that there is in fact a sense in which godliness (ἐυσέβεια) leads to gain, namely the way of self-sufficiency or contentment (αὐτάρκεια, v. 6). Once again we find contacts with the value system of the Greco-Roman world. Dibelius/Conzelmann point out that the virtue 'αὐτάρκεια' was a favourite amongst Stoics and Cynics. They draw our attention to the apothegm in Stobaeus: 'Self-sufficiency is nature's wealth' (Ecl 3).[124] The point of this statement is that despite a person's outward situation, contentment is in itself great gain. The same sense appears in Phil 4:11 where the cognate adjective occurs (αὐτάρκης). Paul has learned to be content in all circumstances, including hunger and abundance, for he can do all things in the one who strengthens him (Phil 4:11−13).[125] In 1 Tim 6:7−8 we find a justification for this aiming for contentment. The futility of wealth, a theme we saw forcefully underlined in the Shepherd of Hermas, is emphasized here as well. The reminder of the nakedness of birth and death, coupled with the observation that contentment requires no more than food and covering, also finds parallels in Greek literature and especially in Stoic thought.[126]

In 1 Tim 6:9−10, the author speaks out against those who desire to become rich. Their aspirations are very dangerous; they lead them into temptation and ultimately into ruin and destruction (v. 9). It is here that the author quotes the proverbial statement: 'The love of money is the root of all evils.' The connection of this strong condemnation of the accumulation of wealth with Malina's observations about the perception of limited good needs no elaboration. It is not the already rich that are condemned. It is through a craving for wealth that some have wandered away from the faith (v. 10).

Such an emphatic condemnation suggests that the author considered the attitude described above as a serious problem in the community which he addressed.[127] In light of the depiction of false teachers as lovers of money, it is interesting that the desire to amass wealth is related to the wandering away from faith. We can be certain that the author held these teachers responsible for the deviation of community members. There may well be a connection between a desire to accumulate wealth and adherence to false teaching. Perhaps some of the adherents and, indeed, teachers were ambitious, upwardly-mobile freedpersons and slaves who found the content of this teaching more supportive of their ambition in the household of God than the sound words endorsed by the author. Despite the reasonableness of this proposal, it is necessary to exercise caution, for the text itself provides no direct evidence to support it.

In the case of the relationship between wealth and false teaching, we are on somewhat firmer ground when we consider certain passages dealing with women. In our earlier work we connected the passage where women are firmly forbidden to teach or have authority over any man (1 Tim 2:11–15) with the apparent tendency of women to become adherents of the false teaching (2 Tim 3:6). Women were probably spreading words which the author considered destructive to community life. It is interesting to note that the passage where women are explicitly forbidden to teach follows immediately after the exhortation that women should adorn themselves in seemly apparel, with modesty and sobriety, and not with braided hair, gold, pearls or costly attire − attributes of wealth (1 Tim 2:9). It may well have been wealthy independent women who were primarily guilty of engaging in behaviour which the author understood as being dishonourable in the household of God. The teaching activity of women is also suggested by 1 Tim 5:13 where young widows are accused of going from house to house. As noted earlier, the activity of such widows may be related to the possession of wealth which would make such independent behaviour more possible.

In 1 Tim 6:17–19 the author speaks of a different group from those who aspire for riches, namely, those who are already wealthy. The rich are exhorted not to become haughty and not to place their hopes in fleeting material possessions. They are instead to place their hope in God 'who furnishes us richly with all things for enjoyment' (v. 17). The impermanence of wealth as contrasted with the certainty of God also finds expression in the synoptic gospels. For example, in Luke 12:33, Jesus' followers are instructed to sell their possessions and give alms, and in so doing, to provide themselves with an unfailing treasure in the heavens where neither thief can come near nor moth can destroy (cf. Matt 6:19–21). As Verner indicates, the possibility of the righteous maintenance of wealth is not envisioned here.[128] It is not a matter of simply developing the right kind of attitude to wealth; radical action is forcefully called for.

A much more moderate attitude to wealth is exhibited by 1 Timothy. The wealthy are not exhorted to sell their possessions but rather to be rich in good works, ready to share, and generous. In this way they will be able to store up for themselves a good foundation for the future, so that they may be able to take hold of the life which is really life. The use of the term rich ($\pi\lambda o\acute{u}\sigma\iota o\varsigma$), and its cognates, occurring four times in 1 Tim 6:17–19, underlines the fact that the author is not instructing the wealthy to divest themselves of their riches, but is exhorting them on how to be rich. It is very much a question of attitude. As in the Shepherd of Hermas, we encounter the ethos of love-patrarchalism: the social distinctions between rich and poor are maintained, but the rich have a responsibility to care for the poor.

As in the Shepherd of Hermas, the presence of the ethos of love-patriarchalism in the Pastoral Epistles is tied to a need for control. The balance of authority and subordination implicit in this ethos makes for an ordered community life. The ethos of love-patriarchalism seeks to maintain the social differences between rich and poor, while calling on the rich to fulfil their responsibility to the poor. This ethos is not confined to the arena of wealth, however, but stretches to encompass other factors determining social status. The distinctions between the traditional roles of males and females, slaves and free, children and parents are to be maintained. The author of the Pastorals expresses a concern that subordinate groups do not overstep the bounds of their stations in the social order.[129]

1.12 Conclusion

Is the community of the Pastorals best described in terms of the church-type or the sect-type, as defined by Troeltsch? With respect to Greco-Roman society as a whole, it is clear that the community of the Pastorals constitutes a sect. When one compares the community of the Pastorals with the communities that emerge from the authentic epistles and Colossians and Ephesians, however, it is possible to speak of a movement away from the sect-type, towards the church-type. Investigation of the attitudes to the world/ethics in 1 Timothy, 2 Timothy, and Titus has revealed a concern for social respectability coupled with a strong belief in universal salvation. Such elements are present in the other letters of the Pauline corpus, but gain new significance in the Pastoral Epistles. The impression made on outsiders is an important concern reflected in the text. The movement toward the church-type is indicated especially in the author's willingness to adopt the values of Greco-Roman society as appropriate for the household of God. This is particularly evident in the author's description of the qualities essential for leadership roles which will be discussed in the subsequent section on ministry.

Throughout the Pastorals, the author adopts the perspective of the householder – the husband, father, and master of slaves. The kind of stress on mutual obligation and respect one finds in the Colossian and Ephesian Haustafeln (which also call for subordination in household relationships) is impossible to discover. The author of the Pastorals' attitude to subordinate groups is more conservative than that of the authors of these writings. The position of slaves and women in particular seems to have worsened. It is important to note, however, that in encouraging the ethos of love-patriarchalism, the author may have had the church's relations with outsiders in mind. As has been already noted, there is a concern in the text that Christian women and slaves not give occasion for the Christian faith to be slandered by outsiders. The office of bishop must be filled by a man who possesses a good reputation in the society at large. Such considerations are related to a desire to stabilize community life, to reduce tension in dealings with the outside society, and to the church's universal vision of salvation.

In this section passages on wealth have been related to the social realities of the stratified Greco-Roman society. Some of the tensions experienced by community members as they sought to distinguish themselves from the life-styles of their pagan neighbours, while at the same time being brought into daily contact with them as they participated in the business of the Empire, have been identified. A study of the attitudes to wealth visible in the Pastorals has been useful in order to clarify the ethos shaping community life. A condemnation of the accumulation of wealth, coupled with an acceptance of already established wealth on the condition that the wealthy recognize their responsibility to the poor, is characteristic of love-patriarchalism:

social distinctions are maintained with those in authority demanding the obedience of subordinate groups while ensuring their care and protection.

Work on Paul in Part 1 revealed that an ethos of love-patriarchalism is evident in his instructions concerning women and slaves and in his attitude to the social stratification at Corinth. Work on Colossians and Ephesians in Part 2 revealed this same ethos as reflected in the Haustafeln. When Bultmann asserts that the paraenesis of the Pastoral Epistles offers as its norm a picture of Christian bourgeois piety, he implies that the ethical stance visible here is remarkably different from that found in Paul.[130] It is true that the connection between community ethics and eschatological hope surrounding life in Christ is more difficult to discover than in Paul and there is more emphasis on propriety in the Pastorals. Furthermore, the ethical teaching found in the Pastorals is more conservative than that found either in Paul or in Colossians and Ephesians. Nevertheless, one must be careful not to overlook the thread of love-patriarchalism providing continuity between all these Pauline and deutero-Pauline writings. The ethos of love-patriarchalism which was born in the Pauline communities stretched far beyond the Apostle's own lifetime to shape the life of the second-century church.

2

MINISTRY

The following study analyzes authority structures in the community of the Pastorals. It investigates how the pseudonymity of the epistles functions in an attempt to exercise control in community life. The importance of the Greco-Roman household as a model for ministerial organization is considered. The connection between criteria for leadership positions and the attempt to protect the household of God against divisive forces is illustrated.

2.1 The Paul of the Pastorals

Throughout this study the process of cumulative institutionalization, involving the construction, solidification, and transformation of the Pauline symbolic universe, has been considered. Three stages of the institutionalization process have been delineated. Paul's letters have been studied in terms of the process of 'community-building institutionalization'. In these early days of the Pauline movement the process of institutionalization was relatively open − it could proceed in many different directions.

Colossians and Ephesians have been seen to reflect the process of 'community-stabilizing institutionalization'. This level of institutionalization is associated with the disappearance of Paul. Paul's work was being carried out by a circle of his associates to whom it seemed natural to write in the name of their inspiring leader. At the level of 'community-stabilizing institutionalization', the Pauline communities were in possession of a fairly solidified symbolic universe shaped under Paul's influence. Future institutionalization would be guided by a corporate tradition which included the major contributions made by Paul. For the authors of Colossians and Ephesians, creativity was no longer possible in the same way it was for Paul, nor was it in the same sense necessary. Despite the fact that the solidification and transformation of the symbolic universe continued, it was the process of maintaining the Pauline symbolic universe which gained particular significance.

Universe maintenance – surely in no Pauline or deutero-Pauline writing is the need for this process more visible than in 1 Timothy, 2 Timothy, and Titus. Is it legitimate to speak of a new level of institutionalization with respect to the Pastorals? The dating of the Pastorals to some point between the end of the first century and the first half of the second century suggests that the community they represent was as much as one generation farther removed from the events that brought the sect into being than the communities of Colossians and Ephesians. Unlike Colossians and Ephesians which are addressed directly to church communities, the Pastorals are addressed to the intermediaries, Timothy and Titus – perhaps reflecting the distance in time and lack of personal contact with the Apostle. The greater presence of traditional lists and regulation-like statements than in the earlier deutero-Pauline writings implies that institutionalization is even less free to proceed in various directions.

As in Colossians and Ephesians, community stability is of central importance in the epistles to Timothy and Titus. But in contrast to the earlier works, stability is not encouraged through an elaboration of Paul's body symbol, nor primarily through remembrance of the kind of transformation that takes place at baptism, but rather through an effort to ensure that competent and honourable officials protect the household of God against false teachers. The author of the Pastorals seeks to exercise control in the face of a communal crisis involving what is perceived to be deviant behaviour. Universe maintenance has become even more crucial than in the communities underlying Colossians and Ephesians. In light of these considerations, it is helpful to speak of the Pastoral Epistles in terms of a third level of institutionalization – 'community-protecting institutionalization'.

The way in which the Paul of the Pastorals asserts his authority is inextricably linked to the communal situation beneath these writings. The Pastorals are much less like the authentic Pauline letters than are Colossians and Ephesians.[131] This might be explained by the fact that they were written later, about the beginning of the second century. It is perhaps useful to consider the Pastorals as twice-removed from the real Paul. They may have been written by a fellow worker of one of Paul's fellow workers. As the Pauline movement and its teachings were transmitted to a new generation, ideas were transformed because they stood in relation to new social situations. It is probable that the recipients of the Pastorals knew that Paul had died long ago. Perhaps the writings were presented as previously unknown private letters, providing pertinent instruction with respect to their own communal conflict. As the existence of the Pastorals indicates, however, the teaching of the Apostle remained authoritative in community life long after his disappearance.

The authority of Paul is accentuated more forcefully in the Pastorals than in either Colossians or Ephesians. The Paul of the Pastorals is the Apostle *par excellence* — no others are necessary. According to the author of the Pastorals, not only is Paul an apostle but he is also preacher and teacher (1 Tim 2:7; 2 Tim 1:11) of the Gentiles in faith and truth (1 Tim 2:7; Tit 1:1). That Paul is willing to suffer in order that the gospel might penetrate the whole world is expressed in 2 Timothy — an epistle which is particularly devoted to encouraging community members to endure suffering (2 Tim 1:8–12; 4:16–17). Paul is held up as the model who suffers for the sake of evangelization. As seen earlier, it is likely that the members of the community of the Pastorals were subject to hostility and slander from outsiders, but belief that salvation is for all required that the door into Greco-Roman society be kept open. The image of Paul as the apostle to Gentiles who suffers for the sake of his mission breathes encouragement in the midst of a tense community.

The Pastorals reveal a vivid picture of Paul as a redeemed persecutor. The obvious point of the 'autobiographical' material of 1 Tim 1:12–17, where this image appears, is to underline his authority: Paul received the grace of the Lord so that he might become an example to all those who believe in him. However, this passage may have a direct relation to the struggle in the community against false teaching. The accusation against false teachers in 1 Tim 1:7, concerning their desire to be teachers of the law, triggers a discussion about the function of the law. The author of the Pastorals asserts that the law is good if anyone uses it lawfully (1 Tim 1:8). The law is not laid down for the just, but for the lawless and disobedient, and whatever else is contrary to sound doctrine. Sound doctrine is in accordance with the glorious gospel of the blessed God with which Paul was entrusted (1 Tim 1:9–11).[132] The authority of Paul here is being set up against the false teachers who probably make legalistic ascetic demands on their adherents (1 Tim 4:3).[133] Paul's life is presented as the prototype of the Christian life where law is not necessary. This is the point of the then / now contrast of 1 Tim 1:12–17. In 1 Tim 1:12–15 we are told of Paul's earlier life as persecutor of the church, but because he acted in ignorance and unbelief he received mercy.[134] Paul received the grace of the Lord. The traditional statement 'here are words you may trust' (πιστὸς ὁ λόγος), which is used elsewhere in the Pastorals (1 Tim 1:15; 3:1; 4:9; 2 Tim 2:11; Tit 3:8) and which precedes the statement 'Christ Jesus comes into the world to save sinners' stresses the importance of the transformation which led to the appointment of Paul to the Lord's service.

The same theme is repeated in 1 Tim 1:15b−17 where the importance of Paul's example in the church is emphasized. We are told that Paul obtained mercy so that, in him, as the foremost of sinners, Jesus Christ might display all long-suffering as an example to those who were to believe in him to eternal life. The weight of the proclamation is expressed by the doxology of 1 Tim 1:17 where we hear of the all-encompassing reign of God. That 1 Tim 1:12−17 is constructed with the problem of false teaching in mind is supported by the instructions given to Timothy in 1 Tim 1:18−20 concerning the deviation from the truth which has occurred in the community.

That the Paul of the Pastorals is an authoritative teacher is an obvious point that requires little elaboration (e.g. 1 Tim 2:7; 2 Tim 1:11). The description of Paul as the Apostle to the Gentiles who suffers in order to carry out his mission (2 Tim 1:8−12a) moves into a statement which emphasizes the authority of Paul's teaching (2 Tim 1:12b−14). Paul is confident that Christ Jesus is able to guard that which has been entrusted to him (or the deposit) until that day.[135] Paul instructs his audience to follow the pattern of sound words which they have heard from him in faith and love which are in Christ Jesus. They are to guard the truth which has been entrusted to them (or the good deposit). The word 'παραθήκη' (deposit) occurs three times in the Pastorals (2 Tim 1:12, 14; 1 Tim 6:20). In each of these passages the word is accompanied by the verb 'φυλάσσω' (to guard). In 1 Tim 6:20 and 2 Tim 1:14 it is Timothy who must guard, but in 2 Tim 1:12 the author is confident that God will do so.[136]

The translation of 2 Tim 1:12b−14 is difficult and the exact sense is impossible to determine. Yet, it is possible to set out the general argument: Paul has received the 'deposit' from divine sources and it will remain protected until the end. Paul is the authoritative teacher to the church bearing witness to this 'deposit'. The members of the community are to follow the pattern of sound words which they have received from Paul. This will result in a healthy community life. Timothy is to guard the truth or the good 'deposit' which has been entrusted to him by the Holy Spirit. The 'deposit' entrusted to Paul is related to this good 'deposit' entrusted to his beloved child Timothy and protected by Pauline authority against false teaching (cf. 1 Tim 6:20).

The pseudonymity of the Pastorals allows the authority of Paul to be communicated to an audience faced with different problems than those encountered by the young communities the Apostle addressed. The fact that the epistles are not addressed to the church as a whole, but to Timothy and Titus, is especially interesting for it implies that Paul's authority need not be communicated directly by him (he soon will be dead, cf. 2 Tim 4:6−8), but may be communicated through a fellow worker − another member of the Pauline school. Although to describe Timothy and Titus as prototypes of the monarchical bishop is to go beyond the constraints of the evidence, they do in fact have an important leadership role in the church (cf. 1 Tim 4:14; 2 Tim 1:6).[137] As Paul's special assistants, their role is the transmission of healthy teaching (1 Tim 4:11−13; 5:1−2; 6:2; Tit 2:1) and the protection against false teaching (1 Tim 4:1ff; 6:20; Tit 3:8ff). Timothy and Titus are expected to be examples to the whole community in their conduct (1 Tim 4:12; Tit 2:7).

2.2 The household roles and offices in the household of God

In 1 Tim 3:14−15 the Paul of the Pastorals tells his audience that he is writing these things to them so that they may know how to behave in the household of God. The greatness of the social entity is proclaimed through the description of the household as the church of the living God and pillar and bulwark of truth. The author's statement of purpose is reinforced by the Christ-hymn in 1 Tim 3:16. When the 'mystery of our religion' is presented in a hymn-like fashion, familiar doctrinal material is cited in order to make a connection with the appeal for appropriate conduct in the household of God.[138]

The use of the architectural imagery of the pillar and bulwark of truth to describe the nature of the Christian community points to the close connection in the text between the church modelled on the household and the necessity of protection against heretical tendencies. The church as household provides structures that assist the community in keeping undesirables on the outside. Within the Haustafel material of 1 Tim 2:1−6:1 we find a strong condemnation of false teaching in 1 Tim 4:1−10 (including the house-related injunction against marriage). The connection between behaviour in the household of

God and the struggle to preserve truth expressed in 1 Tim 3:14–16 appears to be fundamental to the author's purpose.

The author's apparent desire to reduce tension in the community is especially visible in his instructions to the various house-related groups in the community. Part 2 illustrated that the household codes of Colossians and Ephesians reflect authority structures in community life. Power is being placed more firmly in the hands of householders – the husbands, fathers, and slave owners in the community. In the Pastoral Epistles, the connection between the household code and leadership is even more strongly evident than in Colossians and Ephesians. One's position in the household and one's behaviour with respect to that position occupy a central place in the list of requirements determining who is eligible for the various offices.

As in Colossians and Ephesians, the husbands–wives, parents–children and masters–slaves relationships continue to be considered in various contexts. But, there are two major differences between the household codes of Colossians and Ephesians and the similar material in the Pastoral Epistles. In the first place, the emphasis on mutual responsibility one discovers in the earlier deutero-Pauline writings is absent from the Pastorals. In the epistles to Timothy and Titus, husbands are not exhorted to love their wives. Fathers are not commanded not to provoke their children. Masters are not told to treat their slaves justly. The second major difference involves the flexible use of the Haustafel material in the Pastorals. The pure form of the station code schema visible in Colossians and Ephesians disappears. Exhortations for subordinate groups to be subject to groups in authority disclose a departure from an exclusive focus on relationships in the individual household. The relationships between groups in the community as a whole are considered. The importance of household behaviour for leadership in the church is urged.

In Tit 2:1–10, one discovers the most straightforward use of the station code schema. Here various groups are exhorted, including older men and women, younger women and men, and slaves. On the one hand, the instructions to younger women and slaves reveal the kind of concern for household relationships that one discovers in Colossians and Ephesians. On the other hand, the exhortations directed to the older and younger men, and to older women exhibit an awareness of their responsibility to the community as a whole in terms of their personal example and teaching.[139] In the Pastorals, one discovers the spelling-out of the implications of roles in the patriarchal household for roles in the church understood on the model of the household.

A similar shift of emphasis occurs in 1 Tim 2:1–6:1. Once again the sphere of vision includes, but stretches beyond, the boundaries of the household. The section on slaves addresses the household concern of the master–slave relationship (1 Tim 6:1–2). The section on widows (1 Tim 5:3–16), however, focuses on both the individual household and the interests of the larger community. The household responsibilities of widows are outlined (1 Tim 5:4). The behaviour and responsibilities of widows in the larger community are also given considerable attention. The qualifications by which one meets the community's definition of real widowhood and fills the requirements to be enrolled are presented (1 Tim 5:4–7, 9–15; cf. Pol. Phil 4:3). Moreover, the whole community is exhorted with respect to its responsibilities to real widows (1 Tim 5:3, 8, 16; cf. Ign. Pol 4:1).[140] Finally, the sections on bishops and deacons reveal an interest in both the community as a whole and in the individual household. Qualifications for community leaders are concerned with household relationships (1 Tim 3:2, 4–5; 3:11–12; Tit 1:6). The focus here is on the prerequisite for office rather than on the duties of office.[141]

The household-related exhortations concerning various groups in the community of the Pastorals may be divided into three types, all of which exhibit authority structures. Some instructions concern the behaviour of members within the individual household. The slave–master exhortations may be placed in this category. These instructions resemble the household codes of Colossians and Ephesians. They are primarily concerned with relationships within the individual household, but carry implications for the way in which power is distributed within the community as a whole. The slave who is instructed to be subject to his or her master is being provided with a pattern for lifestyle in the household which impinges on how the slave will relate to master-members of the household of God (1 Tim 6:1–2; Tit 2:9–10).

Some exhortations, however, are concerned with the interaction of household groups within the community as a whole – behaviour which is related to the roles played in the individual household. The older women in the community are instructed to teach and provide examples for the younger women in the community. The value of their instruction is understood as being the encouragement of young women to be model wives and mothers. This type of exhortation carries even more explicit implications for the way in which power is distributed within the community. The encouragement of older and younger women to adopt these roles may be related to an attempt to eliminate women from leadership positions (Tit 2:3–5).

Finally, exhortations concerning church leaders demonstrate the close connection between one's position in the household, one's behaviour with respect to that position, and eligibility for office. The role of bishop is closed to those who are not model householders (1 Tim 3:4–5). It is in the house-related instructions concerning church offices that one discovers the strongest evidence for the claim that the patriarchal household provided a model for the organization of the community. Household relationships and practices seem to have important factors in the formation of the offices one discovers in the Pastoral Epistles.

By listing qualities for office, the author of the Pastorals is actually setting forth a means of social control for access to office. The passage describing the qualities for the office of bishop opens in 1 Tim 3:1 with a faithful saying: 'If anyone aspires to the office of bishop he desires a good work.'[142] There is evidently a connection between this exhortation and the general understanding of aspiration to municipal office in Greco-Roman society: office holding is public service undertaken by the relatively well-to-do.[143] The main point of this passage appears to be that by performing a good work, the bishop renders a vital service to the community. Throughout the Pastorals, the doing of good works is associated with service to the less privileged (cf. 1 Tim 2:10; 5:10, 16; 6:18; Tit 3:14). The carrying out of good works is listed as the major responsibility of the wealthy (1 Tim 6:18). The exhortation to bishops apparently reflects the ethos of love-patriarchalism.

In the previous discussion of the community's dealings with outsiders, the importance of the role of the bishop in stabilizing relations with outsiders was noted (cf. 1 Tim 3:7). An interest in the relations of the community with outsiders may also be disclosed in the demand that a bishop be 'without reproach' in 1 Tim 3:2.[144] It is remarkable how little attention commentators have given to this quality for office since either the term 'ἀνεπίληπτος' or the synonym 'ἀνέγκλητος' appear in every passage where qualities are given for the offices of bishop, elder and deacon (cf. 1 Tim 3:2; 1 Tim 3:10; Tit 1:6, 7).[145]

1 Tim 3:10 states that deacons are to be irreproachable (ἀνέγκλητοι). If the exhortation to 'γυναῖκας' in 1 Tim 3:11 is to be understood as an address to deacons' wives not to be slanderers, the instruction that deacons be irreproachable has a special significance. It was argued earlier that the activity of women in the community of the Pastorals may have resulted in slanderous accusations against the community. That a deacon, as an office-bearer, be above the disdain of a critical

society seems to have been important to the author. That his wife not contribute to the slander of the community was crucial. 1 Tim 5:14 adds support to the argument that the danger of 'reproach' was at the heart of the community's struggles. In connection with the discussion of appropriate behaviour for widows, the author recommends that younger women marry, bear children, and become the mistresses of houses in order to give no occasion to the one opposing (τῷ ἀντικειμένῳ) on account of reproach (λοιδορίας, 1 Tim 5:14).

Both in Tit 1:6 and in Tit 1:7 the term irreproachable (ἀνέγκλητος) occurs in connection with church leadership. Leaving aside the question of the interchangeability of the titles bishop (ἐπίσκοπος) and elder (πρεσβύτερος), it is remarkable that the author employed the word apparently describing the virtues of the elder and in the very next passage to describe the virtues of the bishop. The repetition of the quality indicates that it was probably viewed as a fundamental requirement for leadership in the church.

In the light of the probability that the members of the community of the Pastorals were being criticized by outsiders, the author's insistance that leaders be without reproach may have been an attempt to reduce the tension between the Christian community and society at large, and to increase social respectability (an important prospect in a church with a mission to save the world). The absence of explanation as to why it might be important for the bishop to be well thought of by outsiders in 1 Tim 3:7 indicates the probability that the necessity of such a high profile was taken for granted by the author and the audience, or at least that it would meet with fairly wide agreement.

The author of the Pastorals demands that male office-holders in the community of the Pastorals be the husband of one wife (cf. 1 Tim 3:2, 12; Tit 1:6). A similar instruction with respect to enrolled widows occurs in 1 Tim 5:9. The interpretation which involves the most straightforward reading of the text is that these exhortations were intended to limit eligibility for church offices to those who had been married only once.[146] That the exhortation is intended specifically for office-holders and not for the congregation as a whole, is supported by the fact that the author urges young widows to remarry in 1 Tim 5:14. It is evident that the author is disqualifying young widows from the office of enrolled widows. This apparent inconsistency is clarified, however, in light of the author's desire to ensure that as many women as possible are under the auspices of an individual household. On account of the crisis in community life, the author may feel obliged to adopt this position.

The author desires church leaders to be those who are worthy household managers (1 Tim 3:4, 12). The bishop must govern his own household well and keep his children submissive (1 Tim 3:4). The notion of the bishop's dignity as head of the household brings to mind the need for social respectability. A similar instruction in 1 Tim 3:12 demands that deacons be men who govern their children and their households well. Verner argues that this phrase clearly indicates that the author is thinking of households that include slaves as well as wives and children; otherwise, the addition of 'τῶν ἰδίων οἴκων' would be superfluous.[147] In Tit 1:6 the question of managing children once again figures prominently. The elders are required to have believing children who are not open to the charge of being profligate or unruly. The notion of believing children fits both with the author's general concern for stability in the household of God/ household and with the belief in Greco-Roman society that the religion of the head of the household determined the religion of the whole family. The threats of insubordination and of lack of respect for the householder's religion are clearly related here. The elders are being held accountable for the religious training of their children.[148]

A final house-related quality found only as a requirement for the office of bishop is that he be hospitable (1 Tim 3:2; Tit 1:8). The fact that the bishop is expected to be hospitable presupposes that he possesses the means to perform such a function for the church (i.e. he owns a large enough house and perhaps possesses authority in a household church to be able to accept or reject travelers; cf. 3 John).[149]

There is probably a connection between the importance given to the community leaders' role as household managers and the need to protect the community against false teaching. The embracing of household structures as a means to organize the community provides a pattern for the stabilizing of communal relations. If women who seek to remain unmarried and become community leaders are the main propounders of the false teaching, the value of the patriarchal household as a model for the church, in the eyes of the author, becomes more readily understandable. The dignified behaviour of the householder/leader might also appease the criticism the community is receiving from outsiders, perhaps largely attributed to the activity of female members.

The exhortations concerning the roles of leaders as protectors of the community are closely related to exhortations concerning their roles as household managers. The author of the Pastorals insists that the bishop not be a new convert (νεόφυτον) in 1 Tim 3:6. The hazard described by the author is that a new convert, acting as a bishop, may become puffed up (τυφόω) and fall under the judgement of the devil. The author apparently fears that the newly-converted bishop will be more susceptible to false teaching; false teachers are described as puffed up in both 1 Tim 6:4 and 2 Tim 3:4.[150] As noted earlier, there is probably a connection between the fear that the bishop will fall under the judgement of the devil, and the danger of slander.

The emphasis on the reliability of the bishop in the instruction that he not be a recent convert is related to the demand in 1 Tim 3:9 that deacons hold the mystery of faith with a clear conscience. In other words, they must be thoroughly grounded in apostolic faith – unswerving in their beliefs.[151] A similar requirement is made of the bishop in Tit 1:9; he must hold firm to the sure word as taught (cf. 1 Tim 3:2; 5:17). Only then will he be able to give instruction in sound doctrine and confute those who contradict it. A thorough education in healthy teaching must precede the teaching of others.

1 Tim 3:10 indicates that deacons must be tested (δοκιμάζω); they must be found irreproachable before they are allowed to serve. The kind of testing envisioned here is uncertain. The mention of testing, however, suggests a procedure for selection and highlights the official nature of the office.[152] Furthermore, it underlines the connection made by the author between leadership and maintenance of control in community life. Barrett links the act of testing with the importance of the candidates' public reputation implicit in the requirement that the deacon be without reproach.[153] The importance of the leader's reputation in the community of the Pastorals is stressed in 1 Tim 3:13. Here the author observes that deacons who minister well will gain a good standing for themselves and confidence in the faith which is in Jesus Christ. Most commentators reject the notion that what the author has in mind is the promotion of the deacon to the office of elder or bishop. Rather, the most straightforward reading of the text leads to the conclusion that the author is thinking simply of the influence gained in the esteem of the Christian community, which is apparently related to standing in the sight of God.[154] The author appears to be legitimating the high standing of the relatively well-to-do deacons in the community. Serving well would probably entail making one's resources available to community members and winning their respect. The ethos of love-patriarchalism is reinforced.

Thus the criteria for office given by the author of the Pastorals exhibit a general interest in stabilizing community life in the face of the threat of the false teaching on the one hand, and in reducing the tension experienced by members of the community due to the criticism from outsiders on the other hand. The great openness to the values of Greco-Roman society visible in the text can be related to the concern for social respectability. Upholding values cherished by Greco-Roman society in connection with the household becomes an important means of stabilizing relations with that society and protecting the vision of universal salvation. The role of leaders as relatively well-to-do householders who act as masters of their wives, children, and slaves is inseparably linked with their authority in the church. The reinforcement of their patriarchal roles serves to reduce the internal-external tension characterizing community life. A tightly knit household organization and accompanying social norms provide useful structures in the struggle against the false teachers. The activity of the false teachers is related to the criticism the community receives from outsiders. Limiting leadership in the church to householders ensures that women who are perceived as being easily influenced by false teaching and visible representatives of the respectability of the community do not acquire any dangerous authority.

2.3 The organization of the community of the Pastorals

The Pastoral Epistles stand out sharply in the Pauline corpus on account of their witness to the existence of the offices of bishop, elder and deacon. The question of the origin of these offices has long interested scholars. H. von Campenhausen, for example, looks to Judaism to provide an explanation for the development of Christian elders. He comments:

> There had for a long time been elders at the head of every Jewish congregation, especially in Palestine, and the idea of organising themselves in a similar way must have suggested itself to the Jewish Christian community. The system of elders is therefore probably of Judaeo-Christian origin (using that term without any particular theological emphasis), just as bishops and deacons were at first at home only in Gentile Christian congregations. The designations and the types of organisation, it is true, quickly mingled and interpenetrated; but in the early days their separate existences were equally clearly marked. Just as Paul and the sources dependent on him know nothing of elders, so conversely Acts, 1 Peter,

James and Revelation mention only elders but neither bishops nor deacons. In these latter documents we may attempt to grasp the distinctive character of the concept of authority in the setting of the new 'patriarchal' overall vision of the Church.[155]

Von Campenhausen argues that the Pastorals reflect an attempt by the author to incorporate earlier traditions. He suggests that they provide evidence for the fusion of the Pauline-episcopal tradition with the traditions of the system of elders. He points out that the offices of bishop, elder, and deacon, are, for the most part, not mentioned in the same breath: where the bishop and deacons occur, the presbyters are commonly missing, and where presbyters are discussed, there is no mention of the bishop and deacons. Von Campenhausen describes Tit 1:5ff as 'a clumsy attempt to combine the two groups' and believes it to be an instance where the author of the epistles is himself acting as 'redactor'.[156] Von Campenhausen believes that the simplest explanation for the fact that the bishop is always spoken of in the singular in the Pastorals is that the monarchical episcopacy is not the prevailing system. Even if his position is not merely so strongly emphasized as in Ignatius, the bishop is clearly the head of the presbytery.[157]

There are several problems with von Campenhausen's proposal. In the first place, he connects the formation of the council of Christian elders with what he believes to be an organizational model characteristic of Jewish synagogues. Basing his assertion on the picture of the Jerusalem church one discovers in Acts, he believes that there were elders there from the beginning.[158] A study of the revised version of *The History of the Jewish People in the Age of Jesus Christ* by Emil Schürer reveals that there is much less certainty about the organization of first-century Judaism than von Campenhausen's analysis permits.[159] For example, in predominantly Jewish areas the separation of political and religious communities would have been most unnatural. There would have been no urgent reason for forming a council of elders for each separate synagogue, although the meagreness of the evidence obliges one to concede that this may have been the case.[160] There is simply not enough concrete evidence to support the assertion that early Christian communities adopted a Jewish form of organization in their formation of church offices.[161] The problems of investigation are heightened by the fact that in both Jewish and Christian sources the two meanings of 'πρεσβύτερος' as a designation for age and also as a title for office cannot be distinguished with any clarity.[162]

What is perhaps most open to objection about von Campenhausen's theory as to the origin of offices in the Pastorals, however, is the suggestion that the author intentionally fused the concept of ministry that grew up on Pauline soil with the concept of ministry reflected in the system of elders. If one considers the text in terms of an ongoing process of institutionalization, one soon discovers the artificiality of von Campenhausen's construction. In the first place, it is evident that the bishop/deacon and elder systems are not as independent as von Campenhausen suggests. This is especially visible in 1 Peter. In 1 Pet 5:1, Peter exhorts the elders, describing himself as a fellow elder (συμπρεσβύτερος), a witness of the sufferings of Christ, and a partaker in the glory that is to be revealed. The point is clearly to encourage the community in the face of suffering and to remind them of their solidarity with Peter. In addition, by calling Peter a fellow elder, the author underlines the authority of the elders as community leaders. In 1 Pet 5:5 those who are younger are instructed to be subject to their elders. The boundaries between the titular sense of 'πρεσβύτερος' and the more general sense of seniors in the community are indeed hazy (1 Pet 5:1 represents the former sense and 1 Pet 5:5 leans toward the latter). The instructions to the youngers–elders appear to be a type of continuation of the Haustafel material in 1 Pet 2:13–3:7. Here one discovers evidence that roles in the patriarchal household are inseparably linked to ministry roles in the community and to the formation of offices.

The term bishop (ἐπίσκοπος) does not appear in 1 Peter to refer to specific officials, but in 1 Pet 2:25 Christ is referred to as the shepherd (ποιμένα) and guardian (ἐπίσκοπον) of souls. In addition, some manuscripts include the verb 'exercising oversight' (ἐπισκοποῦντες) in the instruction to elders in 1 Pet 5:2. Thus, despite the fact that one discovers no evidence of bishops in the community of 1 Peter, the language that would later become associated with the episcopacy is employed to describe Christ's authority and, according to some authorities, to describe the ministerial action of elders.

Although the term bishop (ἐπίσκοπος) does not appear to be employed in a titular sense in Acts, it is clearly used in Acts 20:28 to describe the vocation of the elders; they are to be overseers of the Ephesian church. In addition, while the term 'deacon' (διάκονος) does not occur in Acts, cognates appear in Acts 6:1ff to describe the task of the seven. It is evident that the seven are understood as holding some kind of office (cf. Acts 6:3); they are commissioned by the apostles (Acts 6:6). It seems entirely reasonable to assume the story of the appointment of the seven is told by Luke to legitimate the existence of a service-ministry in his own community by rooting it in apostolic authority.

In Phil 1:1 Paul refers to 'ἐπίσκοποι' and 'διάκονοι'. Although this is best translated as 'overseers and ministers' rather than 'bishops and deacons', it is clear that these designations point to particular leaders and that the language employed is identical to that used to describe more firmly-established leadership structures. A similar argument might be made for the description of Phoebe as a 'διάκονος' in Rom 16:1.

The term 'πρεσβύτερος' is not employed in Paul's letters. Nevertheless, Paul recognizes the importance of the connection between seniority of faith and leadership. He instructs the Corinthians to be subject to the household of Stephanas who were the first converts of Achaia and who devoted themselves to ministry (διακονίαν) to the saints (1 Cor 16:15–16). In Part 1, it was argued that owning a house that could be made available to the church and offering the service of hospitality to travelling Christians may have been of determinative significance for emerging leadership roles in the Pauline movement. That Paul is concerned with the role of Stephanas as head of the household (hence a senior in more than faith) is suggested by the fact that he singles him out for mention with both Fortunatus and Achaicus. In 1 Cor 16:18 Paul praises these men for the hospitality they have offered and recommends that the Corinthians recognize such people. In Paul's recommendations concerning Stephanas, one discovers concerns similar to those that shaped the later instructions about elders in 1 Peter except that no fixed title is employed.

Thus, it is clear that von Campenhausen is incorrect when he makes hard divisions between the kind of ministry one discovers in Paul's churches and the kind visible in 1 Peter and Acts. In fact, similar development can be seen in these writings, regardless of the presence or absence of certain titles. Rather than envisioning the author of the Pastorals as representative of an effort to combine two distinct patterns of ministry, it is perhaps more useful to consider the organization as the product of institutionalization. In Paul's letters one discovers the presence of language to describe ministry roles that would later be employed as fixed titles and traces of the values that would later become normative for determining who would possess authority. Acts and 1 Peter disclose more highly institutionalized roles than Paul's letters. Like Colossians and Ephesians, they stand somewhere between the development visible in Paul's letters and that seen in the epistles to Timothy and Titus.

Despite the existence of fixed titles, however, the actual organization of the community of the Pastorals is more ambiguous than von Campenhausen allows for. The relationship between the various offices is especially difficult to understand since the author nowhere gives a straightforward presentation. That the Pastorals reflect the monarchical episcopacy is suggested by the fact that in both passages where the term 'ἐπίσκοπος' occurs (1 Tim 3:2; Tit 1:7), it is in the singular, while the passages dealing with deacons (1 Tim 3:8ff) and elders (1 Tim 5:17ff; Tit 1:5f) refer to these officials in the plural.[163]

A clear division between offices on the basis of plural and singular usages is prevented by various considerations. First, it is possible that the singular employed in connection with the bishop is generic. Dibelius/Conzelmann favour this interpretation, arguing that one would assume that the bishops were members of the presbytery whether or not they were elders in their own right. Bishops would either have come from the college of elders or would become members of the presbytery after their appointment as bishops. Pointing to analogies for a combination of administrative and patriarchal organization in Greco-Roman society, Dibelius/Conzelmann interpret the phrase 'προεστῶτες πρεσβύτεροι' in 1 Tim 5:17 as 'presiding presbyters', referring to presbyters who, in addition to the patriarchal position which they held, also exercised the function of 'bishop'. Hence, they distinguish between two groups of presbyters, 'presiding presbyters' and those who never became bishops.[164]

It is in the light of the existence of these two groups of presbyters that Dibelius/Conzelmann interpret the apparent equation of the offices of bishop and elder found in Tit 1:5f. Here the problem is that, while in Tit 1:5−6 elders are discussed, v. 7 turns unexpectedly to bishops in a manner which makes it seem that the author is describing the same office. Furthermore, connection between Tit 1:5−6 and Tit 1:7−9 is suggested by the presence of the conjunction 'γάρ' in v. 7. Dibelius/Conzelmann argue that the sudden reference to the bishop in vv. 7ff means that every presbyter must also be qualified to take over the office of bishop. The strange exchange of presbyter and bishop could then be explained by the thesis that Tit 1:7, like 1 Tim 3:2, came from a traditional list of regulations which spoke only of the bishop.[165]

Dibelius/Conzelmann's theory is supported by the fact that the Pastorals assume a council of elders (1 Tim 4:14; cf. Tit 1:5). The official nature of the elders' leadership roles is highlighted by 1 Tim 5:19 where the author expresses his fear that the elder will be deposed without due cause. The text indicates that among the group of elders there was a smaller group with particular leadership responsibilities that included, in some cases, preaching and teaching (1 Tim 5:17). The author demands that this group receive additional financial compensation which is implied by the phrase 'double honour'.[166] It is not necessary, however, to understand these governing elders as bishops. In fact, the very existence of Tit 1:7ff and 1 Tim 3:2ff tell against such an interpretation. Dibelius/Conzelmann's hypothesis about these passages being incorporated as lists of traditional regulations that spoke only of bishops cannot be tested. One might argue, for example, that in the community there was a bishop presiding over a council of elders from which he was chosen. The major problem with Dibelius/Conzelmann's theory about Tit 1:5–7, however, is that there is no explicit equation between the titles 'bishop' and 'elder'.[167]

The alternate hypothesis suggested by von Campenhausen, that Tit 1:5–7 represents an interpolation to make the text fit a conception of the monarchical episcopacy, is also unsatisfactory. The solution that the author is bringing together traditional material to fit a conception of the monarchical episcopacy is not only impossible to test, but also does little to explain why the two terms appear so closely related in Tit 1:5–7. The argument that because the bishop/deacons and elders are not discussed in the same breath, they represent two different strains of tradition that the author seeks to harmonize, has been brought into question by the foregoing analysis.[168]

In the end, the Pastorals leave us with many puzzles with respect to the organization of the community. This problem of interpretation may, however, be related to the author's purpose. The author does not seem to be especially interested in promoting a particular type of ecclesiastical organization in the way that Ignatius of Antioch, for example, seems to be. It is evident from Ignatius' statements that the threefold ministry (bishop, elders, deacons) is in place in the communities known to him. The authority of one bishop was apparently recognized (Trall 3:1). It is possible, however, that Ignatius gave greater weight to episcopal authority than many of the others who moved in the same circle (Magn 4). Throughout his correspondence he seems to reinforce the authority of the ministry and the authority of the bishop in particular (cf. Eph 3:2; 5:3; 6:1; Magn 3:1; 6:1;

Philad 1:1; Smyrn 9:1).[169] In contrast to Ignatius, the author of the Pastorals does not aim to defend a particular style of ministry, but attempts to ensure that appropriate candidates are chosen for office.

2.4 Conclusion

The Paul of the Pastorals seeks to exercise control in community life. This attempt is revealed especially by the statement of purpose in 1 Tim 3:14–15. Here the addressees are told that Paul is writing these things in order that they might know how to behave in the household of God. The Pastorals exhibit a strong interest both in the life of the individual household and in the church understood on the model of the household.

No simple solutions can be given with respect to the origin of offices in the Pastoral Epistles. The need to protect the community against the destructive forces of false teaching seems to have been the major factor providing impetus for the institutionalization process. Exhortations concerning leadership roles in the Pastorals provide evidence of a prevailing domestic ideal which apparently acts as an important means of stabilizing community life. The strong interest in the household evident in the qualities required of officers and the partriarchal authority structures which appear to be operating in community life suggest that the Greco-Roman household provided important leadership patterns for the organization of the community.

3

RITUAL

The Pastoral Epistles appear to have been written in order to ensure appropriate behaviour in the household of God. The aim of this section is to discover any connections between ritual and the concern for control in community life.

3.1 Worship and order

An appreciation for the powerful effects of the community gathering for worship underlies various passages in the Pastorals. That the author is aware of the dangerous consequences of false teaching is obvious. The importance which the author gives to the community gathering for teaching is less obvious but, nevertheless, deserves attention. In 1 Tim 4:16, Timothy is warned to take heed to himself and to his teaching, for in doing so he will save both himself and his hearers. Correct teaching is linked to the offer of salvation itself. Words carry the power to save. The instruction to Timothy in 2 Tim 2:14 makes it clear that words can also destroy. He is told to charge the community before the Lord to avoid disputing about words, which does no good but only ruins the hearers. Timothy is bestowed with the authority to determine what kind of teaching may be heard in the community. He is called upon to exercise control in the arena of worship. It is probable that the authority entrusted to Timothy acts to legitimate the authority of the community leaders.

The same kind of link between the authority given to Timothy and that given to the leaders of the community is found in passages which contain probable allusions to ordination. The laying on of hands serves as a final empowering of members to lead – a legitimation of their authority and an initiation into their new roles. In 1 Tim 4:14, Timothy is instructed not to be neglectful of the gift which was given to him by means of prophecy with the laying on of hands of the body of elders. The divine dispensation is apparently recognized by the community through the laying on of hands of the presbytery. It seems to be elder ordination which is envisioned here, with Timothy himself presented as the prototype of the elder.[170]

With the acceptance of the gift comes a certain responsibility. An emphasis on responsibility is found in 2 Tim 1:6 where ordination is probably also in view. In the context of this most personal of the Pastoral Epistles, it is the authority of Paul and the connection between Timothy and Paul that are given stress – not specifically the organization of the community underlying the Pastorals. Timothy is reminded to rekindle the gift of God which is within him through the laying on of Paul's hands. The connection between the laying on of hands and the Spirit mentioned in the following verse underlines the link between divine dispensation and authority in community life.

The allusion to ordination in 1 Tim 5:22 is the most uncertain of the passages where such an allusion is a possibility. Here Timothy is instructed not to be hasty in the laying on of hands, nor to participate in another man's sins, but to keep himself pure. Later sources reveal that the laying on of hands was also practised in connection with the restoration of sinners to the early church. In light of the place of the exhortation within the context of 1 Tim 5:17ff which contains instructions pertaining to the leadership of elders, most commentators believe that the allusion is to ordination.[171] The instruction not to be hasty in ordination is probably shaped by an awareness of the power within the communally witnessed rite. Moreover, it is possible that the good confession made in the presence of many witnesses by Timothy, which we hear about in 1 Tim 6:12, refers to his ordination.[172] The confession made in the presence of the whole community solidifies the authority that has been bestowed on the leader. However, in the face of the crisis wrought by false teaching, discernment is demanded.

The author of the Pastorals seeks to ensure the stability of the community by encouraging ritual activity which is considered to be healthy for community life. Prayer is understood to be of great value (1 Tim 2:1–2, 8; 4:5; 5:5; 2 Tim 1:3). That teaching plays a primary role in the worship of the community is implied by the instructions to Timothy in 1 Tim 4:11–13 where, having been warned of the importance of the example he sets for the community, he is exhorted to attend to the public reading of scripture, to preaching and to teaching. Similarly, in 2 Tim 4:2, he is exhorted to preach the word in the face of all circumstances and to employ every available method. The activity of the worshipping community is apparently linked with the carrying out of its universal vision of salvation. The importance of grounding the community in apostolic faith by means of healthy teaching is evident throughout the Pastorals. The teaching and exposition of scripture (2 Tim 3:16) to which Timothy has been exposed from childhood, symbolizes the process of maturing which occurs in order that the man of God may be complete (2 Tim 3: 14–17).[173]

Although teaching in the worshipping community can lead to communal harmony, it can also lead to incalculable conflict. That the gathering of the community for worship has become an arena for conflict is evident from 1 Tim 2:9–15. The elaborate argumentation made by the author here, complete with scriptural support from Genesis, suggests that women were indeed teaching during the public worship of the community and that a crisis had arisen because of their activity. The warning against extravagant appearances in worship probably means that well-to-do women are the object of concern. Yet the dress of women appears to have been only a symptom of a far greater concern in relation to community life.

The author tells little about what constitutes appropriate behaviour for women in 1 Tim 2:9–15. The reference to 'good works' in 1 Tim 2:10 is ambiguous; but, from the domestic ideal exhibited in v. 15 and in other exhortations concerning women, it is likely that good works in the household are being recommended. The author is more specific as to what the women are not allowed to do. Silence and submission are demanded. No woman is to teach or have authority over any man (1 Tim 2:11–12). The author is clearly banning women from a teaching role when the community gathers for worship. Such activity on the part of women is viewed as a reversal of the natural order of men having authority over women.[174] The fact that Adam was formed first means that he stands first in the order of creation and that he is to have authority over woman (cf. 1 Cor 11:8ff). The prohibition of v. 12 is further supported by the reason that it was the woman and not the man who was deceived.[175] Child-bearing becomes a kind of expiation for the crime committed by woman (1 Tim 2:15). The woman's subordination to man and her confinement to household roles are thereby, in the author's opinion, divinely ordained. The male leadership of the church is legitimated.

The argument given by the author with respect to the activity of women in the community is surely rooted in serious conflict. This passage, perhaps more than any other, points to the nucleus of the problem with respect to women in community life. With an awareness of the importance of ritual for the articulation of the beliefs and practices of the community, the author's forceful reply is more easily understood. The woman standing in the midst of the gathered community possesses a certain authority by the very fact that she teaches. Truth is expected to be revealed in the exposition of scripture and teaching witnessed in the community. The teacher can move the community. If well adorned women (perhaps wealthy widows) stood in the midst of the assembly prohibiting marriage, conflict would surely have arisen with those members of the community (especially male householders) who believed that the domestic ideal was not only compatible, but also integral, to Christian life. Those who sought the conversion of outside neighbours, or who were perhaps experiencing pressure from outsiders because of practices and general life-style, may have strongly objected to exhortation favouring a Christian emancipation. It might be understood as a conflict between tendencies toward 'church' and tendencies toward 'sect'. For those who sought to win the whole world, accommodation to the standards of the world was to a certain extent inevitable and social respectability was crucial. If the church was to embrace the whole of the Roman Empire, the order of the Greco-Roman household had to be preserved. Yet, the author's instruction must have provided a devastating blow to the women who sought to teach, and perhaps for a long time had been teaching, in the early Christian community. The author's response takes its place within a more general effort to limit leadership in the worship of the church to a select few which occurred in the late first century and early second century (e.g. 1 Clem 40:1–41:1).

3.2 Conclusion

The predominant concern evident in passages related to the ritual context of the community of the Pastorals is a need for control. This is particularly evident in the passage concerning the activity of women during worship (1 Tim 2:9ff). The author's exhortations concerning public teaching are marked by an awareness of the powerful influence of such activity on community life. Teaching can have the power to restore health or to encourage conflict in community life. The author desires to ensure proper leadership during community worship and recommends caution with respect to ordination.

4

BELIEF

A grave concern to protect the church from false teaching is evident throughout the Pastorals. In this section the relationship between the struggle against false teaching and the doctrinal stance in the text will be explored.

4.1 Orthodoxy or heresy?

The classical understanding of heresy is based on the notion that during the first period the church was able to remain untainted. This pure age was followed by an invasion of heresy from outside the church. Yet, the church was able to stage a victorious battle against heresy.

In his influential study entitled *Orthodoxy and Heresy in Earliest Christianity*, Walter Bauer stood this traditional view on its head.[176] The great strength of Bauer's thesis is that it enables the reader to confront the diversity and conflict that were part of the life of the church from the very beginning. His work illustrates the impossibility of determining which points of view were the most authentic on historical grounds. Statements such as the following exhibit Bauer's interest in an honest presentation of the historical situation:

> Both orthodox and heretics alike, seek by means of literature of all kinds, by letters and collections of letters, and of course also by personal contacts, to extend their influence at home and abroad and to obstruct the path of their opponents wherever they meet. So also, both parties make use of the sermon and the homily, delivered orally as well as circulated in writing; both produce religious poetry, psalms, odes, and other songs; or by means of the apocryphal acts, both introduce an abundance of the popular works so as to win the masses.[177]

Bauer's work is of special interest for this study in that it seeks to relate various forms of Christianity to their particular social contexts. Bauer describes the many types of Christianity and acknowledges their social settings without, however, attempting to discover specific connections between the social settings and the belief systems. His historical method enables him to affirm the existence of a different kind of Christianity in Asia Minor from that discovered in Egypt, for example, but does not allow him to draw conclusions about how beliefs originated and why beliefs differed in terms of social settings beyond an appeal to the solution that different understandings of Christianity developed in different locations. Bauer adopts a history of ideas approach: ideas act in a straightforward fashion to shape social realities. He continuously looks for the idea behind the development. For example, in his description of the origin of offices, Bauer speaks of an 'ecclesiastically orientated faith' which is the motivating force behind the writing of the Pastorals. The conflict exhibited in these writings is a conflict between this kind of faith and another understanding of faith:

> For us, it suffices to observe that the Pastorals also deal with a situation in which there existed the antithesis between ecclesiastically oriented faith of some sort and the many headed heresy (Titus 1.10, 'polloi') in one form or another.[178]

There is no doubt that the struggle against false teaching is of primary interest to the author of the Pastorals. In addition, a conflict with respect to teaching does imply a concern with belief. However, in dividing opponents solely in terms of beliefs, Bauer simplifies the situation too much. A complexity of social factors appears to have been related to the divisions that occurred in the community of the Pastorals. The probability that women in particular were susceptible to the influence of false teaching, for example, is related not only to the doctrinal content of this teaching, but also to their social situation as subordinate members of the household. In fact, it does not appear to be primarily the doctrinal content of the false teaching which is of concern to the author of the Pastorals, but its implications for lifestyle. Of the three clear references to the content of the false teaching in the Pastorals, only one deals with purely doctrinal matters.

In 2 Tim 2:18 we hear that some have swerved from the truth, holding that the resurrection is already past. The false teachers may have been teaching that the Christians had been made divine and were already immortal on account of a mystical dying and rising again experienced at baptism.[179] They would certainly have found support for their position if they had read Colossians and Ephesians. Unlike the authors of Colossians and Ephesians, however, the false teachers may have seen a connection between this type of doctrinal stance and the emancipation of women and slaves. This is implied by the weight given by the author to the connection between church leadership and the preservation of the order of the patriarchal household. At any rate, it is clearly the outcome of the false teacher's apparent exclusion of the future resurrection that worries the author. Hymenaeus and Philetus are named as deviants who have swerved from the truth (2 Tim 2:17).

The other clear statements of the content of the false teaching have to do with life-style rather than doctrinal stance. They are both found in 1 Tim 4:3. Much time has already been spent on discussion of the forbidding of marriage and it appears to have been this aspect of the false teaching which caused havoc in the community of the Pastorals. Both the forbidding of marriage and the recommendation of abstinence from foods may have been understood as a means of reinstating the perfection that Christians received through baptism. The exhortation not to drink only water but to drink a little wine for medicinal purposes may also be related to the activity of these teachers (1 Tim 5:23).

Although it is possible that the false teachers held a very different doctrinal position from that of the author, the lack of evidence for disagreement makes it more likely that, with respect to purely doctrinal notions, there was very little difference between the author and the opponents. The conflict seems to have arisen over the implications of belief for life-style. The setting of the gathering of the community for teaching and the exposition of scripture comes to mind. The ethical exhortations of some teachers were coming under question. If this reconstruction is correct, it is not surprising that the author would be content to appeal to traditional beliefs to legitimate a demand for the kind of behaviour understood as appropriate for the household of God. Doctrinal matters were not the area of major dispute.

It is clear, however, that doctrinal statements played an important role in the author's attempt to rebuke the behaviour of deviants. The goodness of God's creation is proclaimed in response to ascetic behaviour. An emphasis on universal salvation is perhaps made in relation to what the author believes is an unhealthy disregard for the impression made on outsiders. In addition, the vehemence with which the author comes out against the unhealthy consequences of the false teaching for community life suggests that this 'heresy' is truly a closely felt threat. The presence of a deviant in the community requires members to identify more clearly the consequences of their faith. The author presents his audience with prescriptions concerning both sexes and all age groups in the church.

Sociological thinking provides a new way for New Testament students to consider the old question of orthodoxy and heresy.[180] As noted in the introduction, Berger and Luckmann argue that because socialization in any human group is always imperfect, deviation from any given symbolic universe is inevitable.[181] Rival definitions of reality pose a dangerous threat to the stability of the symbolic universe and to the lives it embraces. Conflict results in the deviants being set apart from the others. Individuals of the symbolic universe will be required to establish mechanisms for the maintenance of the existing symbolic universe (e.g. tighter leadership structures; a more narrowly-defined idea of sound doctrine). The mechanisms for the maintenance of the symbolic universe will require legitimations (i.e. they will need to be explained and justified). Such legitimations will lead to the growth and the transformation of the symbolic universe which itself legitimates the transformed social reality. The conflict with false teaching in the Pastorals appears to have provided the impetus for a further level of institutionalization described as community-protecting institutionalization. Firmer boundaries were created to protect the universe from unwanted intrusion.[182]

From the way in which the author of the Pastorals argues the case against false teachers, it seems that the very existence of the group is at stake. This kind of conviction points to the importance of the preservation of the symbolic universe both for the community as a whole and for the individual standing under the canopy of the symbolic universe. Much is at stake for the individual who feels that the ordering of the universe is threatening to collapse. If the author of the Pastorals has come to understand the household structure as being an integral means of evangelization and of living a Christian life-style, women teachers who recommend abstinence from marriage will cause considerable alarm. If the author's leadership in the church is based on a personal role as male head of a Greco-Roman household, his desire to restrict the activity of such women will most likely increase.

The members of the community of the Pastorals were faced with a decision about which teaching was orthodox and which was heretical. Bauer's work has reminded us of the foggy lines separating the orthodox and the heretical in the early church and has warned us against making simple value judgements on the basis of later definitions. However, his work does not provide an adequate answer to the question: What factors contributed to the drawing of the lines between orthodox and heretical? In this section, and indeed throughout the study of the Pastorals, a description of the social setting of the community has been conducted to gain a clearer understanding of how and why such boundaries were drawn. Keeping in mind that in the Pastorals we hear the voice of one side of the conflict (although the Acts of Paul and Thecla may give us some indication of what the adherents of the false teaching might wish to tell us), we have discovered that the division between groups is not made purely on the basis of doctrinal positions, but on the basis of a complexity of social factors.

4.2 Beliefs in a social context

Although ordinarily little attention is given to the nature of the beliefs exhibited in the Pastorals, doctrinal explanations are usually stated to account for the kind of development (the something 'new') discovered in these writings. The hierarchical leadership, the notion of sound doctrine, and the dominance of ethical exhortations are all seen as arising from a need to combat false teaching and an awareness of the delayed parousia.[183] The problem with such explanations is that they are too simplistic. The previous section illustrated the inaccuracy that results from reducing the struggle against false teaching purely to a struggle against ideas. Similar distortion of the complex social situation underlying 1 Timothy, 2 Timothy, and Titus results from making a causal link between an awareness of the delayed parousia and the type of Christianity evident in these writings. E. Schweizer, for example, describes the church of the Pastorals as follows:

> Here too there is reflected the picture of a church that regards itself as living, not through a short interval, but through an extending history. While Paul himself still expected the parousia during his own lifetime, he is represented here, as in Acts 20, as taking thought for the period after his death, and even for the period after the death of those whom he will leave behind in the Church's service. It is a Church that has

established itself in the world and is taking over ordinary Hellenistic ethics.[184]

This investigation has illustrated that the kind of ethics visible in the Pastorals cannot be accounted for simply through an appeal to an aspect of the belief system, but must be studied in relation to the entire social world presupposed by the epistles. The hypothesis suggested by Schweizer is rendered especially problematic by the fact that there is no direct evidence of an awareness of the delayed parousia. It may be possible to speak of a general feeling in the community that the end is not necessarily imminent, but whether one can draw a direct connection between such a feeling and the organization of the community is questionable. Schweizer's remarks exhibit the kind of measuring according to the standards visible in Paul that has been criticized frequently throughout this study. Although comparison of deutero-Pauline writings with Paul's letters is essential for understanding the nature of the development in these writings, measuring in terms of the absence or presence of a particular element of the Pauline belief system can lead to a neglect of the Pastorals considered in terms of their own social situation.

In his recent book Roland Schwartz has reacted against the dismissal of the Pastoral Epistles as the reflection of a bourgeois piety.[185] Schwartz's investigation is to some extent in harmony with the interests of the present study. He notes the negative value-judgements associated with the description of the Pastorals in terms of bourgeois piety. In addition, he argues that if one insists on calling the Pastorals 'bourgeois', one must be willing to apply the same designation to much of Paul's work. However, employing a 'history of ideas' methodology, Schwartz does not consider the relation between the social realities of the community of the Pastorals and the development one finds there. Like the works criticized by him, his thesis is heavily dependent on comparing the doctrinal positions visible in the Pastorals with those visible in Paul.[186] Once again, one gains the impression that the Pastorals are not being considered enough on their own terms. How is the relationship of the community of the Pastorals with outsiders related to the kind of development one discovers in these writings? How are the realities of the Greco-Roman household connected to the recommendations one finds with respect to women? How does the fact that institutionalization has been progressing in the church bear upon the nature of community organization?

It is clear that the author of the Pastorals does not exhibit the same kind of theological creativity as the Apostle to the Gentiles. In light of the growing body of tradition, it is likely that creativity was no longer possible nor necessary in the same way as it was in the early days of community-building. Moreover, the appeal to traditional belief statements in the Pastorals may be indicative of an interest in matters other than the purely 'doctrinal'. If, however, one considers the doctrinal statements found in the Pastorals in terms of the communal context, the results are surprising. Statements that are often brushed aside as being theologically uninteresting can enrich one's understanding of the kind of Christianity attested to in these writings when they are considered in terms of the social setting of the community.

There are three major themes that recur in the doctrinal statements:

1. universal salvation;
2. future judgement; and
3. the purifying significance of the Christ event.

The Christ hymn of 1 Tim 3:16 is attached to the purpose statement of 1 Tim 3:14–15; hence it stands out as a key doctrinal statement in the Pastorals. Barrett suggests that the six verses might refer to:

1. the incarnation;
2. the resurrection;
3. the ascension;
4. the preaching of the Gospel;
5. the response to it; and
6. the final victory of Christ.[187]

Although such categorization is artificial and uncertain, there is no doubt that the centrality of the Christ event is being proclaimed here. As noted earlier, the connection of the doctrinal statement with the realities of community life is clear from its attachment to a demand for appropriate behaviour in the household of God and, indeed, from the fact that it is a hymn growing out of the ritual context of the community. A more subtle relationship with the social setting of the community, however, is discovered in the inclusion of the proclamation of Christ throughout the world as part of the Christ event. It has been suggested in this investigation that one of the dangers of the false teaching, and the resulting behaviour of women in the community who were attracted to this teaching, was a possible thwarting of the community's mission of universal salvation. The tensions experienced by the Christians in their relations with outsiders was probably one of the factors related to the author's stressing of proclamation as an integral part of God's plan of salvation – a plan they continued to carry out in the footsteps of Paul.

The universal vision of salvation is also expressed in 1 Tim 2:3–7, where doctrinal statements are presented as a justification of Paul's appointment as preacher, apostle and teacher to the Gentiles. It is explicitly stated here that God desires all to be saved and to come to the knowledge of the truth (1 Tim 2:4; 1 Tim 4:10). In Tit 2:11 the mention of the gift of salvation offered to all serves as an introduction to a demand in v. 12 to live in an appropriate fashion in the present age. The proclamations of the cosmic authority of God in the doxologies of 1 Tim 1:17, 1 Tim 6:15f and 2 Tim 4:18 appear also to be connected with a universal vision of salvation. God has authority in the world and this must be communicated. It is proclaimed in the ritual context of the community and is understood as transforming the life-styles of believers.

The purifying significance of the Christ event and the reality of his future coming are inseparably linked to the demand for appropriate behaviour in the household of God. In 1 Tim 2:5–6 Christ is described as the one mediator between God and humanity, who gave himself as a ransom for all. It is Christ who made a new situation possible for all. The formation of the 'pure' Christian community was the result of his actions. Having laid out the nature of the gift of salvation for which Paul was appointed to his mission to the Gentiles (v. 7), the author proceeds to make demands concerning the behaviour of men and women in worship (vv. 8ff). The stress on the goodness of God's creation that is found in 1 Tim 4:4–5 is also related to the purity that has been established through the gift of salvation. The forbidding of marriage and the abstinence from certain foods are rejected on the basis that everything that God created is good (the world is saved). Such ascetic behaviour, which aims to reinstate purity, is inappropriate for the members of the Christian community. The description of the goodness of God is unmistakably related to the struggles experienced in the community. The purifying significance of the Christ event is explicitly described in Tit 2:14. Jesus Christ is described as having given himself for the Christian community to redeem them from all iniquity and to purify for himself a people of his own who are zealous for good deeds. The behaviour of the Christian community is connected here with the purpose of Christ's saving actions. An appeal for virtuous behaviour in Tit 3:1–3 is legitimated by another description of the purifying Christ event which speaks of the washing of regeneration and the renewal of the Holy Spirit (Tit 3:4–5).

The connection between future salvation and the behaviour of the Christian community provides a valuable doctrinal base for the author's ethical exhortations. Instead of being captured by false teaching, the members of the community are instructed to train themselves in godliness (1 Tim 4:7). Godliness is understood as having promise for the present life, but also for the life to come (1 Tim 4:8; cf. 1 Tim 1:1). The authoritative nature of this statement is emphasised by the phrase, characteristic of the Pastorals, 'this saying is sure' (1 Tim 4:9). In 1 Tim 6:12, Christians are instructed to take hold of the eternal life to which they were called (cf. Tit 3:7). The importance of the ethical exhortation of 1 Tim 6:11–13 is stressed by the author's demand to keep the commandment unspotted, without reproach until the appearance of the Lord Jesus Christ (v. 14).

A reference to the parousia is probably made in the phrase 'that day' in 2 Tim 1:12, a passage where the guardianship of truth is related to the promise of future salvation (cf. vv. 13–14). The promise of future salvation is also implicit in the hymn or saying of 2 Tim 2:11–13 where an attitude of faithfulness is encouraged in the face of suffering. Once again, the doctrinal statement is given added weight by the introduction 'this saying is sure'.[188] The problem of deviation is probably envisioned here. Both suffering (vv. 8ff), discussed before the hymn, and disputing about words (vv. 14ff), mentioned after the hymn, are dangerous threats to the stability of the community. The link between suffering and future salvation is also found in 2 Tim 4:18, where God's heavenly kingdom is mentioned. The connection of the expectation of the parousia with the struggles of community life is also found in the prediction (undoubtedly a reality in the author's time) that, in the last days, grievous times will be at hand (2 Tim 3:1).

The ethical exhortation of Tit 2:12 (preceded by an exhortation about appropriate behaviour in the household), where Christians are instructed to behave correctly in this world, is augmented by a statement where hope for the appearance of the saviour Jesus Christ is expressed (v. 13). The statements concerning salvation in the Pastorals illustrate the interrelatedness of doctrinal and ethical pronouncements and the grounding of both of these in the realities of community life. While it is true that one does not discover the kind of imminent expectation in the Pastorals that one finds in Paul's writings, the notion of the parousia still holds an important place within the symbolic universe. In the light of the doctrinal statements found in the Pastorals, there is no reason to conclude that expectation and a sense of ongoing time are mutually exclusive. The community of the Pastorals seems to have held both together without any difficulty. In the end, it must be said that the delay of the parousia theory fails to account for the complexity of the situation in the early church.

4.3 Conclusion

The struggle against false teaching in the Pastorals is not purely doctrinal; it involves a complexity of social factors related to the position of the church in its Greco-Roman environment. In the Pastorals, it is the behaviour of the proponents of the false teaching that appears to be causing the greatest alarm. The conflict is related to the formation of structures to stabilize community life. The authority of officials is reinforced and the way one should act in community life is more clearly defined. The labelling of others as 'heretical' contributes to the process of self-definition. Development in the Pastorals cannot be attributed simply to a conflict of ideas or to an awareness of the delayed parousia.

The notion of universal salvation, the purifying significance of the Christ event, and the promise of future salvation are key elements of the belief system of the community of the Pastorals. Some connections have been drawn between these elements of the belief system and the realities of community life shaping them and being shaped by them. Doctrinal statements are, for the most part, expressed in traditional formulations in the Pastorals. They function mainly to legitimate ethical exhortations about appropriate behaviour in the household of God and not to expose a new understanding of what it means to be in Christ. In the Pastoral Epistles, the tools of the creative theologian are pushed aside and all attention turns to preservation and protection of existing beliefs.

CONCLUSION

The Pauline corpus provides a valuable locus for studying development in the early church, for it contains the earliest writings available to us (Paul's own letters), writings dating from about the beginning of the second century (the Pastoral Epistles) and writings which are characteristic of the ambiguous period following the disappearance of the earliest authorities (Colossians and Ephesians). The main aim of this book has been to trace the process of institutionalization in Pauline communities. The study has investigated the transformation of the early church from its loosely-organized, charismatic beginnings to its more tightly-structured nature in the second century.

Insights from the social sciences have been incorporated throughout the investigation in an effort to comprehend the relationship between the early church writings and their social worlds. Problems with methodologies which posit the shaping of development by the straightforward action of ideas have been highlighted. In order to understand the significance of the transformations in the early church, it is essential to describe the historical circumstances acting as catalysts to change as fully as possible. This means coming to terms with the complexity of social factors which characterize community life. The interplay between the ethos, ministry structures, ritual forms, and beliefs of a community within a Greco-Roman environment must be considered in an investigation of church development.

Understanding development in terms of an ongoing process of institutionalization which results in the construction of a symbolic universe gives an added dimension of realism to historical reconstruction. As time passes and groups grow, greater organization is required. Communal forms become increasingly 'solid'. As the body of tradition expands, the possibilities for innovation decrease. With the existence of a fairly solidified symbolic universe, creativity is no longer necessary, nor perhaps even possible, in the same way. This study has illustrated that the social situation in the earliest days of community-building was different from the social situation resulting from the death of Paul and the incorporation of a new generation. For his associates who wrote Colossians and Ephesians, the goal was not so much to legitimate the formation of a sect as to ensure its continued existence – to stabilize community life in the absence of the Apostle. Standing within the Pauline symbolic universe, they appealed to aspects of the symbol system which could remain relevant in light of new social situations. The symbolic universe simultaneously expanded and was transformed in relation to new circumstances.

The social situation underlying the Pastoral Epistles is marked by a strong desire to protect the community against false teachers. Deviation has become a problem in community life. The community that is far removed from the original events that brought the sect into being is characterized by a highly-transformed version of the symbolic universe. The appeal to traditional beliefs, the dominance of ethical exhortations, and the reinforcement of the authority of the Apostle are part of a response to a crisis in community life. The attempt to ensure that leadership is officially in the hands of male householders acts as a social mechanism to maintain the symbolic universe.

When comparing Pauline and deutero-Pauline writings, both differences and similarities must be considered. One of the major interests of this study has been to explore the lines of continuity connecting the writings. The ethos of love-patriarchalism, evident from Paul's letters, is given a more rigid expression in the Haustafeln of Colossians, Ephesians, and the Pastoral Epistles. The household codes provide a pattern for members to relate to one another in the communities, while at the same time acting as an effective means of stabilizing relations with outsiders.

The importance of the Greco-Roman household as a model for the formation of the ekklesia is especially visible in the ministry structures reflected by the Pauline and deutero-Pauline writings. From Paul's letters, it is clear that the ability to provide a house for community gatherings was probably an important criterion determining eligibility for leadership in the sect. The significance of position in the household for leadership is given more concrete expression in the household codes of Colossians and Ephesians. These ethical exhortations carry implications not only for distribution of power within the individual household, but also within the household church. In the Pastoral Epistles, one discovers an explicit link between position in the household and the development of church offices. Effective leadership in the household becomes an important criterion for leadership in the church.

The ritual context of community life shapes both the Pauline and deutero-Pauline writings. In Paul's letters, baptismal language is employed in relation to an attempt to legitimate the formation of a sect. This is especially evident in Gal 3:26−8 where Paul apparently believes that recalling the experience of baptism will reinforce his arguments concerning requirements for entry into the community. In Colossians and Ephesians baptism is recalled repeatedly in an effort to ensure that members behave appropriately. The strong argument against women teaching in the Pastorals points to the fact that the ritual context can become an arena for conflict. The author's comments act as a control measure in community life. With the increased threat of deviation that comes with growth and the passage of time, it is likely that guidelines determining what is appropriate during worship are becoming increasingly important. Paul's instructions in 1 Cor 14 make it plain that the institutionalization of ritual forms was progressing even in the earliest days of community-building.

A belief in universal salvation seems to have been of primary significance for the development of Pauline Christianity. This is especially evident in passages that disclose a desire to evangelize and/or a concern for the impression made on non-believers. In 1 Cor 14:23ff Paul expresses a concern that tongues may give the wrong impression to outsiders who might otherwise become converted. The recommendation that caution be exercised with respect to dealings with outsiders in Col 4:5−6 is probably shaped by a desire to evangelize. The household codes found in the deutero-Pauline writings may be partially shaped by an apologetic interest; they may have served to stabilize relations between a community (comprised of some subordinate members of households ruled by unconverted masters) and the outside world. 1 Tim 3:7 requires that a bishop be well thought of by outsiders. A desire for social respectability, coupled with a belief in universal salvation, seems to have strengthened as the Pauline movement became increasingly visible. In comparing the authentic epistles with the Pastoral Epistles, it is useful to envision a movement away from the sect-type toward the church-type. Colossians and Ephesians represent an intermediate step in the process.

Pauline Christianity is a complex phenomenon. The measurement of development in deutero-Pauline writings in terms of the presence or absence of certain aspects of a belief system associated with the real Paul has often prevented the consideration of the deutero-Pauline writings in terms of their own social situations. The transformation evident in these writings cannot simply be explained in terms of a delayed parousia or a struggle against gnosticism. A variety of social factors were involved in the establishment of offices, for example. The need to have individuals to protect sound doctrine was clearly an important factor. However, the struggle against false teaching was not confined to the arena of ideas. The desire to evangelize, the role of the Greco-Roman household as a model for the formation of the ekklesia and the tensions experienced in relations with outsiders were some of the social factors discussed with respect to the solidification of authority structures.

This study has been confined to the methods of socio-historical investigation; no specifically theological conclusions have been drawn. However, an approach to the study of the New Testament that seeks to describe the relationship between the writings and their social world has ramifications for those doing theology. The writings immediately gain new relevance when understood as directed toward concrete situations. Yet, some will undoubtedly find this methodology potentially threatening. Some might be frightened to observe that the power struggles that characterize society generally also make their way into the New Testament. A reader might be disheartened to discover that with the historical reconstruction ended, one finds oneself siding with the losers in the struggle for power – those clandestine false teachers that creep into households. But with the initial disappointment confronted, one might discover a theological challenge. As in the case of the female adherents to the false teaching in the Pastorals, one might need to rediscover the testimony of those who, for so long, have been silenced.

NOTES

Introduction

1 R. Bultmann, *Theology of the New Testament* (2 vols.; London: SCM, 1965) vol. 2, p. 97; Bultmann's remarks on church order take up the debate between Rudolf Sohm and Adolf Harnack (see Linton, *Das Problem der Urkirche in der neuren Forschung* [Uppsala Universitets Årsskrift, Uppsala: 1932], pp. 31–67). According to Sohm, ecclesiastical law stands in contradiction to the nature of the Ekklesia. Harnack, on the other hand, endeavours to show that from the very beginning, there were regulations in the early church which had the character of law and which necessarily developed into full regulations (Bultmann, *Theology* vol. 2, pp. 95–6). Bultmann finds himself basically in agreement with Sohm but insists that the working out of regulations does not necessarily go against the sway of the Spirit (Bultmann, *Theology* vol. 2, pp. 97–8). Bultmann appears to argue against the concept of a purely-pneumatic church. However, in speaking of the possibility of structures being solely the creation of the Spirit, he inevitably disconnects the early church from its societal base.

2 Bultmann, *Theology* vol. 2, p. 99.

3 Ibid, p. 95.

4 Ibid, p. 100.

5 H. von Campenhausen, *Ecclesiastical Authority and Spiritual Power in the Church of the First Three Centuries* (London: Adam and Charles Black, 1969), p. 79.

6 Schweizer, *Church Order in the New Testament* (London: SCM, 1961), p. 7.

7 Ibid, p. 99.

8 See E. Käsemann, 'Paul and Early Catholicism' in *New Testament Questions of Today* (London: SCM, 1969), pp. 236–7 and 'New Testament Questions of Today' in *New Testament Questions of Today*, pp. 20–1.

9 Käsemann, 'Paul and Early Catholicism', p. 246; for criticism of Käsemann on 'early catholicism', see J. H. Elliott, 'A Catholic Gospel: Reflections on "Early Catholicism" in the New Testament', CBQ 31 (1969), 213–23; D. J. Harrington, 'E. Käsemann on the Church in the New Testament', *Heythrop Journal* 12 (1971),

246–57; U. Luz, 'Erwägungen zur Enstehung des "Frühkatholizismus". Ein Skizze', ZNW 65 (1974), 88–111.

10 J. H. Schütz, *Paul and the Anatomy of Apostolic Authority* (Cambridge University Press, 1975); B. Holmberg, *Paul and Power* (Philadelphia: Fortress, 1980); W. Meeks, *The First Urban Christians* (New Haven and London: Yale University Press, 1983); N. Petersen, *Rediscovering Paul* (Philadelphia: Fortress, 1985).

11 G. Theissen, 'Social Stratification in the Corinthian Community' in *The Social Setting of Pauline Christianity* (Philadelphia: Fortress, 1982), pp. 69–119.

12 H. Conzelmann, *An Outline of the Theology of the New Testament* (London: SCM, 1969), pp. 267–8; see K. Kertelge, *Gemeinde und Amt im Neuen Testament* (München: Kosel, 1972), p. 114.

13 H. Koester, *Introduction to the New Testament* (2 vols.; Philadelphia: Fortress, 1982), vol. 2, pp. 304–5.

14 C. Rowland, *Christian Origins* (London: SPCK, 1985), pp. 258–9.

15 For a good example of the use of Berger and Luckmann's insights see W. Meeks, 'The Man from Heaven in Johannine Sectarianism', JBL 91 (1972), 44–72; see Petersen, *Rediscovering Paul*, pp. 200–86.

16 For criticism of Berger and Luckmann's work, see R. Gill, *Theology and Social Structure* (London and Oxford: Mowbrays, 1977), pp. 18–25. This criticism, which is concerned mainly with the epistemological aspects of Berger and Luckmann's work, does not affect the use of their insights as heuristic devices for this investigation of development in the church.

17 P. L. Berger and T. Luckmann, *The Social Construction of Reality* (Garden City, New York: Doubleday and Company Inc., 1966 [reprint by Penguin Books, 1981]), p. 78.

18 Ibid, p. 79.

19 Ibid, p. 114.

20 For use of Berger and Luckmann's thought to understand change in the modern Church, see J. A. Ecks, 'The Changing Church: Contributions from Sociology', *The American Benedictine Review* 23 (1972), 385–6.

21 Berger and Luckmann, *The Social Construction*, p. 72.

22 Ibid.

23 Ibid, pp. 76–7.

24 Holmberg, *Paul and Power*, pp. 175–6.

25 Ibid, p. 200.

26 S. N. Einsenstadt (ed.), *Max Weber on Charisma and Institution Building* (Chicago and London: The University of Chicago Press, 1968), p. 44.

27 Ibid, p. 48.

28 M. Weber, *Economy and Society* (3 vols.; ed. G. Roth and C. Wittich, New York: Bedminster, 1968), vol. 1, pp. 243–4.

29 Holmberg, *Paul and Power*, p. 162.

30 Einsenstadt (ed.), *Max Weber on Charisma*, p. 54.

31 Ibid.

32 Ibid, p. 58.
33 Ibid, p. 60.
34 Weber, *Economy and Society*, vol. 3, p. 1135.
35 Ibid, pp. 1146–7.
36 Einsenstadt (ed.), *Max Weber on Charisma*, p. 57.
37 Holmberg, *Paul and Power*, p. 166.
38 Ibid; see Holmberg for references to criticisms made by scholars of Weber's analysis and information concerning the ongoing debate among sociologists about 'charisma'.
39 Berger and Luckmann, *The Social Construction*, p. 79.
40 Ibid.
41 Ibid, pp. 102–3.
42 Ibid, p. 124.
43 Ibid, p. 125.
44 Holmberg, *Paul and Power*, pp. 172–3, 178–82.
45 See R. W. Funk, 'The Watershed of American Biblical Tradition: The Chicago School, First Phase 1892–1920', JBL 95 (1976), 4–22; L. E. Keck, 'On the Ethos of Early Christians', JAAR 42 (1974), 435–52.
46 On the 'Sitz im Leben', see R. Bultmann, *The History of the Synoptic Tradition* (Oxford: Basil Blackwell, 1972), p. 4.
47 O. Cullmann, 'Les récentes études sur la formation de la tradition évangélique', *Revue d'Histoire et de Philosophie religieuses* 5 (1925), 573.
48 See Meeks, *Urban Christians*, p. 3.
49 E. A. Judge, *The Social Pattern of Christian Groups in the First Century* (London: Tyndale, 1960), p. 7.
50 See R. Scroggs, 'The Sociological Interpretation of the New Testament: The Present State of Research', NTS 26 (1979–80), 165–6.
51 For detailed bibliography of socio-historical investigations, including discussion of the methodological implications of incorporating insights from the social sciences, cf. J. Z. Smith, 'The Social Description of Early Christianity', *Religious Studies Review* 1 (1975), 19–25; Scroggs, 'The Sociological Interpretation of the New Testament', 164–79; J. G. Gager, 'Shall We Marry Our Enemies: Sociology and the New Testament', Int. 36,3 (1982), 256–65; D. J. Harrington, 'Sociological Concepts and the Early Church: A Decade of Research', TS 41 (1980), 181–90; B. J. Malina, 'The Social Sciences and Biblical Interpretation', Int. 36,3 (1982), 229–42; C. S. Rodd, 'On applying a Sociological Theory to Biblical Studies', JSOT 19 (1981), 95–106; J. H. Elliott, 'Social-Scientific Criticism of the New Testament and its Social World: More on Method and Models', *Semeia* 35 (1986), 1–26.
52 Theissen, 'The Sociological Interpretation of Religious Traditions' in *The Social Setting*, pp. 176–7.
53 Theissen, 'Social Stratification in the Corinthian Community' in *The Social Setting*, pp. 69–119.
54 Theissen, 'The Sociological Interpretation of Religious Traditions', pp. 178–9.

55 Ibid, p. 194; see p. 192−4.
56 Ibid, p. 175.
57 J. G. Gager, *Kingdom and Community* (Englewood Cliffs, New Jersey: Prentice Hall, Inc., 1975), p. 13.
58 Scroggs, 'The Sociological Interpretation of the New Testament', p. 165.
59 Theissen, 'The Sociological Interpretation of Religious Traditions', p. 195.
60 See remarks of P. Brown on the promise of inter-disciplinary work in 'Sorcery, Demons, and the Rise of Christianity' in *Religion and Society in the Age of Saint Augustine* (London: Faber and Faber, 1972), p. 119.
61 See Malina, 'The Social Sciences and Biblical Interpretation', p. 233; Theissen, 'The Sociological Interpretation of Religious Traditions', p. 177; Elliott, *A Home for the Homeless* (London: SCM, 1982), p. 9.
62 On the relation between history and the social sciences, cf. Scroggs, 'The Sociological Interpretation of the New Testament', pp. 167−8; Malina, 'The Social Sciences and Biblical Interpretation', p. 233.
63 J. H. Elliott, *A Home for the Homeless*, p. 9.
64 Ibid, p. 4.
65 Ibid, p. 8; on the possibility of harmonizing literary and sociological modes of analyses, see especially Petersen, *Rediscovering Paul*.
66 Meeks, *Urban Christians*, p. 5; for examples of scholars who are suspicious about the use of social-scientific analysis for New Testament Interpretation, see Rodd, 'On Applying A Sociological Theory to Biblical Studies'; E. A. Judge, 'The Social Identity of the First Christians: A Question of Method in Religious History', *The Journal of Religious History* 11,2 (1980), 201−17.
67 Judge, 'The Social Identity of the First Christians', p. 202.
68 Ibid, p. 210.
69 Ibid, p. 213.
70 Meeks, *Urban Christians*, p. 5.
71 Ibid.
72 T. F. Carney, *The Shape of the Past* (Lawrence, Kansas: Coronado, 1975), p. 9.
73 Ibid, pp. 1−9 (pp. 1−43).
74 C. Geertz, 'Religion as a Cultural System' in *Anthropological Approaches to the Study of Religion* (ed. M. Banton, London: Tavistock, 1966), p. 5.
75 Ibid, p. 3.
76 Ibid, pp. 12−13.
77 P. Berger, *The Sacred Canopy* (Garden City, New York: Doubleday and Company Inc., 1967), p. 181.
78 The work of W. Meeks on the relationship between beliefs and social realities is of great importance for the present study. See *Urban Christians*, pp. 164−92, and 'The Social Context of Pauline Theology', Int. 36,3 (1982) 266−77.

Part 1

1 Rowland, *Christian Origins*, p. 224.
2 E. P. Sanders, *Paul, the Law, and the Jewish People* (Philadelphia: Fortress, 1983), p. 173; see discussion on the 'third race', pp. 171−9.
3 Ibid, p. 175.
4 Ibid, p. 173.
5 Ibid, p. 176; see Meeks, *Urban Christians*, p. 81.
6 See discussion in Sanders, *Paul, the Law*, pp. 176−8, where he responds in particular to W. D. Davies, 'Paul and the People of Israel', NTS 24 (1977), 4−39.
7 Sanders, *Paul, the Law*, pp. 176−7.
8 Ibid, p. 177.
9 Ibid.
10 Ibid, pp. 177−8.
11 See for example, Bultmann, *Theology*, vol. 1, p. 309.
12 Note that Rowland has recently employed the notion of sect with respect to the Pauline communities; see *Christian Origins*, pp. 194−7; pp. 222−4.
13 Elliott, *A Home*, pp. 73−8. A sectarian model for the study of New Testament texts is also employed by R. Scroggs, 'The Earliest Christian Communities as a Sectarian Movement' in *Christianity, Judaism and other Greco-Roman Cults*, part 2 (ed. J. Neusner, Leiden: E. J. Brill, 1975), pp. 1−23; and R. Markus, 'The Problem of Self-Definition: From Sect to Church' in *Jewish and Christian Self-Definition*, vol. 1 (ed. E. P. Sanders, London: SCM, 1980), pp. 1−15.
14 B. Wilson, *Sects and Society* (London: William Heinemann Ltd., 1961), p. 1; see Elliott, *A Home*, p. 75. For a more detailed definition of 'sect', see B. Wilson, 'The Sociology of Sects' in *Religion in a Sociological Perspective* (Oxford: At the University Press, 1982), pp. 89−120.
15 B. Wilson, *Magic and the Millenium* (London: Morrison and Gibb Ltd., 1973), pp. 22−3; see Wilson's description of other responses to the world in his seven part typology found in the same volume; see Elliott, *A Home*, p. 76.
16 See K. Stendahl, 'Call Rather than Conversion' in *Paul among Jews and Gentiles and Other Essays* (Philadelphia: Fortress, 1976), pp. 7−23.
17 E. Shils, 'The Concept and Function of Ideology' in IESS, vol. 7 (1968), 70; see Elliott, *A Home*, p. 104.
18 Shils, 'The Concept and Function of Ideology' p. 72; Elliott, *A Home*, pp. 104−5.
19 B. Wilson, *Religious Sects* (London: Weidenfield and Nicholson, 1970), p. 34.
20 For a description of the probable concerns of the members of the sect of 1 Peter, see Elliott, *A Home*, p. 105.
21 Meeks, *Urban Christians*, p. 85.

22 Ibid, p. 87; see his discussion of the similar language found in the literature of Judaism.

23 Ibid, p. 88; the notion of being 'in Christ' and the concept of the body of Christ also function as language of belonging, but will be considered in the section on beliefs.

24 See A. J. Malherbe, *Social Aspects of Early Christianity* (Philadelphia: Fortress, 1983), p. 66.

25 Meeks, *Urban Christians*, p. 94.

26 Wilson, *Magic and the Millenium*, pp. 23–4.

27 See for example, Bultmann, *Theology*, vol. 2, p. 95; Conzelmann, *Outline*, p. 257.

28 B. Wilson, 'An Analysis of Sect Development' in *Patterns of Sectarianism* (London: Morrison and Gibb Ltd., 1967), p. 36.

29 Ibid, p. 41; see Elliott, *A Home*, p. 103.

30 See Theissen, 'Social Stratification in the Corinthian Community' in *The Social Setting*, pp. 69–119.

31 Wilson, 'An Analysis of Sect Development' in *Patterns*, p. 39, pp. 44–5; on the development of other types of sects, see pp. 37–9; see Elliott, *A Home*, p. 104.

32 Wilson, 'An Analysis of Sect Development', pp. 37–8; see Elliott, *A Home*, p. 104.

33 See Meeks, *Urban Christians*, pp. 98–100; Theissen, 'The Strong and the Weak in Corinth: A Sociological Analysis of a Theological Quarrel' in *The Social Setting*, pp. 121–43.

34 Wilson, 'An Analysis of Sect Development', p. 41.

35 However, some believe that 1 Cor 14:33b–36 (34–5) is an interpolation; they argue that this passage contradicts the statements found in 1 Cor 11:2–16. For a summary of arguments and bibliography, see W. O. Walker Jr., '1 Corinthians 11:2–16 and Paul's Views Regarding Women', JBL 94 (1975), 95, note 6. In *The Legend and the Apostle* (Philadelphia: Westminster, 1983), pp. 87–9, D. R. MacDonald argues that the passage is an attempt to harmonize the text of 1 Corinthians with the Pastoral Epistles by a later interpolator; Meeks, on the other hand, takes the opposite view, noting the lack of manuscript evidence to support later interpolation; see *Urban Christians*, pp. 70–1 and especially note 108, p. 220.

36 V. P. Furnish, *Theology and Ethics in Paul* (Nashville and New York: Abingdon, 1968), p. 237; see Rowland, *Christian Origins*, pp. 232–5.

37 Theissen, 'Social Stratification in the Corinthian Community' in *The Social Setting*, p. 107; he derives the concept from E. Troeltsch, *The Social Teaching of the Christian Churches*, vol. 1 (New York: The MacMillan Company, 1931), pp. 69–89. Theissen finds examples of love-patriarchalism in the solutions given at the last supper and the conflict about food sacrificed to idols; see Theissen, 'Social Integration and Sacramental Activity: An Analysis of 1 Cor 11:17–34' in *The Social Setting*, pp. 145–74; Theissen, 'The Strong and the Weak in Corinth: A Sociological Analysis of a Theological Quarrel' in *The Social Setting*, pp. 121–43.

38 On Philemon, see P. Stuhlmacher, *Der Brief an Philemon* (Zurich: Einsiedeln, 1975); J. Gnilka, *Der Philemonbrief* (Freiburg: Herder, 1982). Both of these studies treat the letter in terms of the social realities of house churches. For a thorough study of Philemon which depends on insights from the social sciences, see Petersen, *Rediscovering Paul*.

39 Theissen, 'Social Stratification in the Corinthian Community' in *The Social Setting*, p. 108.

40 Schütz, *Paul and the Anatomy of Apostolic Authority*, p. 26; see Meeks, *Urban Christians*, p. 122.

41 See Meeks, *Urban Christians*, p. 122.

42 See Introduction of this book; Eisenstadt (ed.), *Max Weber on Charisma*, pp. 46–9; Rowland, 'Tradition and Charismatic Authority' in *Christian Origins*, pp. 266–71.

43 For a discussion of the identity of the apostles in the Pauline correspondence, see Meeks, *Urban Christians*, pp. 131–2.

44 For a discussion of the meaning of 1 Cor 9, see Theissen, 'Legitimation and Subsistence: An Essay on the Sociology of Early Christian Missionaries' in *The Social Setting*, pp. 27–67.

45 Rowland, *Christian Origins*, pp. 227–8; see 'The Problem of Authority', pp. 227–32.

46 See Introduction of this book.

47 On Paul's role in the early church, see von Campenhausen, *Ecclesiastical Authority*, p. 30; Holmberg, *Paul and Power*, pp. 27–8.

48 Rowland, *Christian Origins*, p. 230. The question of Paul's relationship with Jerusalem is too complex to be dealt with in detail here. See Rowland, pp. 227–31; Holmberg, *Paul and Power*, pp. 22–35.

49 The importance of the collection for the unity of the church, as Paul understands it, is discussed by von Campenhausen, *Ecclesiastical Authority*, pp. 33–4.

50 For a discussion on the identity of the poor that Paul and his churches were to remember, see Holmberg, *Paul and Power*, pp. 35–6.

51 Sanders, *Paul, the Law*, pp. 171, 179.

52 Holmberg, *Paul and Power*, pp. 40–3.

53 On the identity of the Corinthian opponents, see Holmberg, *Paul and Power*, pp. 44–50. There is disagreement among scholars as to the unity of 2 Corinthians. The crucial problem is whether 1–9 and 10–13 could have been part of the same letter. See W. G. Kümmel, *Introduction to the New Testament* (London: SCM, 1975), pp. 290–3. For an application of the multiple source theory with respect to 2 Corinthians, see Koester, *Introduction*, vol. 2, pp. 126–30.

54 R. F. Hock, *The Social Context of Paul's Ministry* (Philadelphia: Fortress, 1980), pp. 50–65. See also Meeks, *Urban Christians*, p. 118.

55 Meeks, *Urban Christians*, p. 118.

56 Rowland, *Christian Origins*, pp. 266–7.

57 Ibid, p. 268.
58 Meeks, *Urban Christians*, p. 81.
59 Holmberg, *Paul and Power*, p. 23; see also pp. 26−8.
60 See Meeks, *Urban Christians*, pp. 138−9.
61 Von Campenhausen, *Ecclesiastical Authority*, p. 46.
62 Ibid, p. 49.
63 Ibid, pp. 50−1.
64 Ibid, pp. 52−3.
65 Ibid, p. 53.
66 Ibid, p. 58.
67 Meeks, *Urban Christians*, p. 139.
68 Rowland, *Christian Origins*, p. 271.
69 See Theissen, 'Legitimation and Subsistence: An Essay on the Sociology of Early Christian Missionaries' in *The Social Setting*, pp. 27−67; see also conclusion of Holmberg, *Paul and Power*.
70 See Sanders, *Paul, the Law*.
71 Ibid, p. 144.
72 Ibid, p. 66.
73 Ibid, p. 147. On the lack of system in Paul's thought, see pp. 44−5, 161.
74 See C. W. Mills, *The Sociological Imagination* (New York: Oxford University Press, 1959).
75 For exposition of the insights from Berger and Luckmann's sociology of knowledge employed here, see Introduction of this book.
76 On Paul's co-workers, see Holmberg, *Paul and Power*, pp. 58−69; Meeks, *Urban Christians*, pp. 133−4.
77 On the meaning of 'apostle' here, see Meeks, *Urban Christians*, p. 133.
78 There is uncertainty as to whether ''Ιουνιᾶν' refers to a man or woman; see Meeks, *Urban Christians*, p. 57. There is some question as to the integrity of Rom 16. Some scholars have argued that it is the whole or a fragment of a letter originally addressed to Ephesus; cf. discussion in Kümmel, *Introduction to the New Testament*, pp. 317−20; Meeks, *Urban Christians*, note 41, p. 201, where he argues for the integrity of the letter; Malherbe, *Social Aspects*, pp. 64−5 with note 13, and p. 95 with note 9.
79 The connection of the role of Paul's fellow workers with a vision of universal salvation is discussed by W. Ollrog in *Paulus und seine Mitarbeiter* (Neukirchen: Erziehungsverein, 1979), pp. 96−9.
80 See P. Marris, *Loss and Change* (London: Routledge and Kegan Paul, 1974).
81 On the importance of the roles of prophet and teacher for the development of church order, see B. H. Streeter, *The Primitive Church* (London: MacMillan and Co. Ltd., 1929), pp. 69−83; H. Greeven, 'Propheten, Lehrer, Vorsteher bei Paulus' in *Das kirchliche Amt im Neuen Testament* (ed. K. Kertelge, Darmstadt: Wissenschaftliche Buchgesellschaft, 1977), pp. 305−61; Holmberg, *Paul and Power*, pp. 97−100; R. Banks, *Paul's Idea of Community* (Exeter: The Paternoster Press, 1980), pp. 148−9.

82 Holmberg, *Paul and Power*, pp. 100–3.
83 See Theissen, 'Social Stratification in the Corinthian Community' in *The Social Setting*, pp. 73–96; Holmberg, *Paul and Power*, p. 104.
84 For an excellent summary of literature on house churches, see H. J. Klauck, 'Neue Literatur zur urchristlichen Hausgemeinde', *Biblische Zeitschrift* 26 (1982), 288–94; cf. the article by F. V. Filson where he calls for more attention to be paid in New Testament scholarship to the actual physical conditions where the first Christians met and lived, 'The Significance of the Early House Churches', JBL 58 (1939), 109–12.
85 On the historical reliability of Acts 18:8 which describes Crispus as a synagogue ruler, see Theissen, 'Social Stratification in the Corinthian Community' in *The Social Setting*, pp. 73–5.
86 Holmberg, *Paul and Power*, p. 101.
87 Similarly, Paul appears to be reinforcing the authority of Epaphroditus in Phil 2:29, but this is a much less clear example; on the connection between household leadership and leadership in Paul's communities, see J. Hainz, *Ekklesia* (Regensburg: F. Pustet, 1972), pp. 345–51.
88 On Stephanas' household-related authority in the community, see Hainz, *Ekklesia*, p. 99.
89 Bultmann, *Theology*, vol. 1, pp. 313–14; see his remarks on baptism, vol. 1, pp. 311–12; Käsemann, 'The Pauline Doctrine of the Lord's Supper' in *Essays on New Testament Themes* (London: SCM, 1964), p. 116; Käsemann, 'Paul and Early Catholicism' in *New Testament Questions of Today*, p. 246. For a similar depiction of Paul as opposing the view that the sacraments were a guarantee of salvation, see R. C. Tannehill, *Dying and Rising with Christ* (Berlin: Alfred Töpelmann, 1967), pp. 11, 43; on the Lord's supper, see remarks of A. J. B. Higgins, *The Lord's Supper in the New Testament* (London: SCM, 1952), p. 67.
90 Conzelmann, *An Outline*, p. 59.
91 A more realistic approach to the contrast between worship in Paul's churches and that characteristic of later communities appears in Rowland's *Christian Origins*, pp. 237–44.
92 See M. Douglas, *Natural Symbols* (London: Barry and Rockliff, 1970), p. 6.
93 There is value in comparing the practices of Pauline Christians to the magical activities of the Greco-Roman world, as is evident in M. Smith's article, 'Pauline Worship as seen by Pagans', HTR 73 (1980), 241–9.
94 Geertz, 'Religion as a Cultural System' in *Anthropological Approaches*, (ed. Banton), p. 28.
95 Ibid, p. 25.
96 Ibid, p. 34.
97 Ibid, p. 29.
98 Meeks, *Urban Christians*, p. 142.
99 Ibid; see Rowland, *Christian Origins*, pp. 240–1.

100 See Meeks, *Urban Christians*, p. 147; on the relation between ritual in the Pauline sect and the practices of Judaism, see Meeks, pp. 147–8, 150–153; Rowland, *Christian Origins*, pp. 238–44.
101 Meeks, *Urban Christians*, p. 149.
102 Ibid.
103 See discussion in Meeks, *Urban Christians*, p. 147.
104 See Douglas, *Natural Symbols*, p. 78.
105 Geertz, 'Religion as a Cultural System' in *Anthropological Approaches* (ed. Banton), p. 34.
106 Ibid, p. 39.
107 Meeks, *Urban Christians*, p. 152.
108 See Geertz, 'Religion as a Cultural System' in *Anthropological Approaches* (ed. Banton), p. 38.
109 On this passage and its connections with the practices of Greco-Roman Society, see Smith, 'Pauline Worship as Seen by Pagans', p. 243.
110 See Meeks, *Urban Christians*, p. 151.
111 B. J. Malina, *The New Testament World* (London: SCM, 1983), p. 125. Malina draws many of his insights from another valuable book for a sociological approach to studying the New Testament by M. Douglas, *Purity and Danger* (London: Routledge and Kegan Paul, 1966); see especially 'The Abominations of Leviticus', pp. 41–57.
112 Malina, *The New Testament World*, p. 129.
113 Ibid, p. 146; Malina compares purity rules in Judaism with the boundaries that separated the Christian community from the outside world (pp. 131–43). On the relation between purity in the Pauline community and purity at Qumran, cf. B. Gärtner, *The Temple and the Community in Qumran and the New Testament* (Cambridge University Press, 1965); M. Newton, *The Concept of Purity at Qumran and in the Letters of Paul* (SNTS Monograph Series, 53; Cambridge University Press, 1985).
114 Malina, *The New Testament World*, pp. 147–150; for detailed discussion of this topic, see Newton, 'Purity and the Cult in the Letters of Paul' in *The Concept of Purity*, pp. 52–78.
115 Newton, *The Concept of Purity*, p. 99.
116 Geertz, 'Religion as a Cultural System' in *Anthropological Approaches* (ed. Banton), p. 38.
117 On the connection between baptism and the Lord's supper, see Meeks, *Urban Christians*, p. 158. On the Lord's supper in Paul, cf. Higgins, *The Lord's Supper in the New Testament*, pp. 63–73; G. Wainwright, *Eucharist and Eschatology* (London: Epworth, 1971), pp. 80–3; H. Leitzmann, *Mass and the Lord's Supper* (Leiden: E. J. Brill, 1979), pp. 182–7.
118 On the eschatological dimensions of the common meal and the connections it may have had with meals in Judaism, see Rowland, *Christian Origins*, pp. 241–2.
119 Meeks, *Urban Christians*, p. 160.
120 See Theissen, 'Social Integration and Sacramental Activity' in *The Social Setting*, pp. 145–74.

121 Ibid, p. 160.
122 Ibid, p. 164.
123 Ibid, p. 165.
124 Meeks, *Urban Christians*, p. 159.
125 Theissen, 'Social Integration and Sacramental Activity' in *The Social Setting*, p. 164.
126 On sacred symbols, see C. Geertz, 'Ethos, World View, and the Analysis of Sacred Symbols', *Antioch Review* 17 (1957), 421–37; cf. Shils, 'Ideology', IESS, vol. 7, p. 66.
127 Shils, 'Ideology', p. 68.
128 Douglas, *Natural Symbols*, p. 11.
129 See Sanders, *Paul, the Law*, p. 143.
130 On the Christocentricity of Paul's argumentation and its implications for determining membership in the body of those who will be saved, see for example, Sanders' discussion of Rom 9:30–10:13 in *Paul, the Law*, pp. 41–3.
131 Ibid, pp. 7–8.
132 Sanders notes that Paul speaks of the law in terms of how one gets 'in' in a different way than when he addresses the question of how one behaves once 'in'; see *Paul, the Law*, p. 10 and discussion, pp. 4–10.
133 On the relation between ideology and on-going culture, see Shils, 'Ideology', pp. 67–8.
134 On language of incorporation, see J. A. Fitzmyer, *Pauline Theology* (Englewood Cliffs, New Jersey: Prentice Hall Inc., 1967), pp. 67–73.
135 Cf. C. F. D. Moule, 'The Corporate Christ' in *The Origin of Christology* (Cambridge University Press, 1977), pp. 47–96; E. Käsemann, 'The Theological Problem presented by the Motif of the Body of Christ' in *Perspectives on Paul* (London: SCM, 1971), pp. 102–21; J. A. T. Robinson, *The Body* (London: SCM, 1952); E. Best, *One Body in Christ* (London: SPCK, 1955); Banks, 'The Community as Body' in *Paul's Idea of Community*, pp. 62–70.
136 Meeks, *Urban Christians*, pp. 167–8.
137 Ibid, p. 169.
138 See Rowland, 'The Gospel Before and Apart from Paul' in *Christian Origins*, pp. 198–203.
139 See remarks of Shils, 'Ideology', p. 69.
140 Geertz, 'Ethos, World View, and the Analysis of Sacred Symbols', p. 422.
141 Meeks, *Urban Christians*, p. 181.
142 Ibid, p. 182.
143 Ibid.
144 On the paradoxical nature of religious symbolism, see Geertz, 'Religion as a Cultural System' in *Anthropological Approaches* (ed. Banton), p. 23.
145 On the relation between suffering and the formulation of sacred symbols, Ibid, p. 19.
146 E. P. Sanders, *Paul and Palestinian Judaism* (London: SCM, 1977), p. 443.

147 See Meeks, *Urban Christians*, pp. 172—80. On the relation between this aspect of the Pauline belief system and Jewish eschatology, see Rowland, *Christian Origins*, pp. 207—14.
148 See Meeks, *Urban Christians*, pp. 174—5.
149 Ibid, pp. 175—7.
150 Ibid, p. 179. In order to gain greater understanding of the relation between the Pauline belief system and the social situation of adherents, Meeks appeals to the work of social scientists on 'millenarian' movements, see pp. 172—4 and notes 22 and 23, p. 240; cf. Rowland, *Christian Origins*, pp. 111—13.
151 On the relation between the problem of bafflement and the formulation of sacred symbols, see Geertz, 'Religion as a Cultural System' in *Anthropological Approaches* (ed. Banton), p. 16; cf. Meeks, *Urban Christians*, p. 174.
152 On the relation between the travel of traders and artisans and the spread of Pauline Christianity, see Meeks, *Urban Christians*, pp. 16—19.
153 Wilson, *Magic and the Millenium*, pp. 38—9.
154 See Meeks, *Urban Christians*, p. 174.
155 Sanders, *Paul and Palestinian Judaism*, p. 474.
156 Ibid, p. 484.
157 Sanders, *Paul, the Law*, pp. 70—81; *Paul and Palestinian Judaism*, pp. 474—515.
158 Meeks, *Urban Christians*, p. 184.
159 Ibid.
160 On the connection between the problem of evil and the construction of sacred symbols, see Geertz, 'Religion as a Cultural System', in *Anthropological Approaches* (ed. Banton), p. 21.
161 Meeks, *Urban Christians*, p. 189.

PART 2

1 In favour of deutero-Pauline authorship, see E. Lohse, *Colossians and Philemon* (Philadelphia: Fortress, 1971), pp. 177—83; E. Schweizer, *The Letter to the Colossians* (London: SPCK, 1982), pp. 13—26; E. P. Sanders, 'Literary Dependence in Colossians', JBL 85 (1966), 28—45; Meeks, *Urban Christians*, p. 125. In favour of Pauline authorship, see R. Martin, *Colossians and Philemon* (London: Oliphants, 1974), pp. 32—40; F. F. Bruce, *The Epistles to the Colossians, to Philemon, and to the Ephesians* (Grand Rapids, Michigan: Wm. B. Eerdmans Publishing Co., 1984), pp. 28—33; Kümmel, *Introduction to the New Testament*, pp. 340—6.
2 See for example Schweizer, *The Letter to the Colossians*, pp. 15—26; Meeks, *Urban Christians*, p. 125.
3 See E. J. Goodspeed, *The Meaning of Ephesians* (Chicago: Chicago University Press, 1933); C. L. Mitton, *The Epistle to the Ephesians* (Oxford: Clarendon Press, 1951); C. L. Mitton, *Ephesians* (London: Marshall, Morgan and Scott, 1973), pp. 2—18; Kümmel, *Introduction to the New Testament*, pp. 357—63. In favour of Pauline

authorship, see N. A. Dahl, 'Adresse und Proömium des Epheser-briefs', *TZ* 7 (1951), 241–64; Bruce, *The Epistles to the Colossians, to Philemon and to the Ephesians*, pp. 229–46.

4 On the connections between Ephesians and Pauline writings, see Mitton, *Ephesians*, pp. 13–17.

5 Ibid, p. 15.

6 Ibid, pp. 13–14; for more detailed exposition, see Mitton, *The Epistle to the Ephesians*, p. 155.

7 See discussion in Kümmel, *Introduction to the New Testament*, pp. 352–6; Meeks, *Urban Christians*, p. 126.

8 Kümmel, p. 254.

9 For discussion of the relation between Colossians and Ephesians, see especially Mitton, *The Epistle to the Ephesians*, pp. 98–157; Mitton, *Ephesians*, pp. 11–13; Kümmel, *Introduction to the New Testament*, pp. 358–60.

10 On pseudonymity in the ancient world, see Schweizer, *The Letter to the Colossians*, p. 19 and note 16 for bibliography; N. Brox, *Falsche Verfasserangaben* (Stuttgart: Katholisches Bibelwerk, 1975); N. Brox (ed.), *Pseudepigraphie in der heidnischen und jüdisch-christlichen Antike* (Darmstadt: Wissenschaftliche Buchgesellschaft, 1977); D. Guthrie, 'Epistolary Pseudepigraphy' in *New Testament Introduction* (London: The Tyndale Press, 1970), pp. 671–83.

11 E. Käsemann, 'Ephesians and Acts' in Keck and Martyn (ed.), *Studies in Luke Acts* (London: SPCK, 1968), pp. 288–97.

12 Ibid, pp. 288–9.

13 Ibid, p. 290.

14 On the relation between Acts and Ephesians, see Mitton, *Ephesians*, pp. 15–17; on the relation between Ephesians and 1 Peter, ibid, pp. 17–18 and Elliott, *A Home*, p. 85.

15 Mitton, *The Epistle to the Ephesians*, p. 264. Mitton's theory is a reworking of the earlier one put forward by Goodspeed in *The Meaning of Ephesians*.

16 See the similar discussion with respect to 1 Peter in Elliott, *A Home*, p. 85.

17 See K. Rudolph, *Gnosis* (Edinburgh: T&T Clark Ltd., 1983), p. 302.

18 Berger and Luckmann, *The Social Construction*, pp. 85–9.

19 See for example, Kümmel, *Introduction to the New Testament*, pp. 338–40 and the bibliography given by him. Note that M. Hooker has questioned the validity of the generally held theory about the problem of false teachers in Colossians. However, her analysis makes too little of what appears to be a real conflict involving a specific group in the community; see Hooker, 'Were there False Teachers in Colossae?' in *Christ and Spirit in the New Testament* (Lindars and Smalley ed., Cambridge University Press, 1973), pp. 316–29.

20 See Meeks, *Urban Christians*, p. 138.

21 The meaning of Col 2:18 is ambiguous. See Schweizer, *The Letter of the Colossians*, pp. 158–62. The nature of the Colossians philosophy will be discussed in more detail in later sections. See W. Meeks and F. O. Francis (ed.), *Conflict of Colossae* (Montana: Scholars, 1975).

22 See N. A. Dahl, 'Anamnesis: Memory and Commemoration in the Early Church' in *Jesus in the Memory of the Early Church* (Minneapolis: Augsburg, 1976), pp. 11–29.

23 See discussion of the literary problem in Kümmel, *Introduction to the New Testament*, pp. 352–6.

24 See Goodspeed, *The Meaning of Ephesians*. Goodspeed's theory won the approval of J. Knox in *Philemon among the Letters of Paul* (Chicago: Chicago University Press, 1935), p. 37.

25 Mitton, *Ephesians*, p. 29.

26 Dahl, 'Adresse und Proömium des Epheserbriefs', pp. 241–64.

27 J. C. Kirby, *Ephesians: Baptism and Pentecost* (London: SPCK, 1968); on the influence of liturgical and catechetical traditions in Eph 5:21–33, see J. P. Sampley, *And the Two Shall Become One Flesh* (Cambridge University Press, 1971).

28 Käsemann, 'Ephesians and Acts', p. 291 (cf. note 11); cf. Kümmel, *Introduction to the New Testament* for similar conclusions, p. 364.

29 Sampley, *And the Two Shall Become One Flesh*, pp. 158–63.

30 See the discussion in Mitton, *Ephesians*, pp. 57–8.

31 For arguments in favour of the author of Ephesians being a Jewish Christian, see Kirby, *Ephesians: Baptism and Pentecost*, p. 165; Kümmel, *Introduction to the New Testament*, p. 365; on the relation between Ephesians and the writings from Qumran, see Koester, *Introduction*, vol. 2, pp. 268–9.

32 See discussion in Koester, *Introduction*, vol. 2, pp. 269–70.

33 See Sanders, *Paul, the Law*, p. 172.

34 See discussion of Gal 6:16 in Sanders, *Paul, the Law*, pp. 173–4.

35 Ibid, p. 174.

36 Ibid, p. 175.

37 See discussion in Mitton, *Ephesians*, pp. 105–6. See discussion on 'the wall' in M. Barth, *Ephesians* (2 vols., Garden City, New York: Doubleday and Company Inc., 1974), vol. 1, pp. 283–91.

38 On the relation between Acts and Ephesians, see Mitton, *Ephesians*, pp. 15–17.

39 P. Esler, *Community and Gospel in Luke-Acts*, Cambridge University Press, 1987.

40 Ibid, see 'Table-Fellowship between Jews and Gentiles in Luke-Acts'; on the composition of Luke's community, see J. C. O'Neill, *The Theology of Acts in its Historical Setting* (London: SPCK, 1961), pp. 94–116; D. L. Tiede, *Prophecy and History in Luke-Acts* (Philadelphia: Fortress, 1980), pp. 127–32; R. Maddox, *The Purpose of Luke Acts* (Edinburgh: T & T Clark Ltd., 1982), pp. 31–65.

41 On the relation between Ephesians and 1 Peter, see Mitton, *Ephesians*, pp. 17–18 where he argues that the author of 1 Peter knew Ephesians.

42 Elliott, *A Home*, p. 45. Elliott argues that information about the mixed population of Asia Minor lends further support to the internal evidence. On the use of scripture in 1 Peter, see note 77, p. 55.

43 Ibid, p. 85.

44 Meeks, *Urban Christians*, p. 90.
45 The use of the term 'οἰκονομία' here and in Eph 1:10 is different from that in Paul's own letters and in Colossians. It refers not to an assignment given to Paul but specifically to God's own plan. The sense of 'οἰκονομία' in Eph 3:2 corresponds to that found in the authentic letters and in Colossians (cf. Col 1:25; 1 Cor 9:17). See discussion in Mitton, *Ephesians*, pp. 125–6.
46 On language of belonging, see Meeks, *Urban Christians*, pp. 87ff; on language to speak of the members of the Pauline groups as if they were part of a family, see D. von Allmen, *La Famille de Dieu* (Göttingen: Vandenhoeck & Ruprecht, 1981).
47 Language of incorporation will be treated in more detail in subsequent sections.
48 See Part 1 of this book, section 1.1.
49 On the developing emphasis on the settled community in early Christianity, see Theissen, *The First Followers of Jesus*, pp. 114–99.
50 The list of greetings in Colossians bears a strong resemblance to that found in Paul's letter to Philemon. The relationship will be considered in the section on ministry.
51 It cannot be determined with absolute certainty whether 'Νύμφαν' here refers to a man or a woman. That the name refers to a woman is likely however. The presence of the word his, 'αὐτοῦ', in some manuscripts rather than her, 'αὐτῆς', can easily be explained by the action of an interpolator who was uncomfortable with this role being assigned to a woman. See discussion in Lohse, *Colossians and Philemon*, p. 174. The church in Nympha's house is probably located in Laodicea. It is impossible to determine whether it is the only house church there, or one of many.
52 See W. Meeks, 'In One Body', in *God's Christ and His People* (Meeks and Jervell ed., Oslo, Bergen and Tromsö: Universitetsforlaget, 1977), p. 212.
53 See for example Schweizer, *The Letter to the Colossians*, pp. 233–4; Lohse, *Colossians and Philemon*, pp. 167–9; Bruce, *The Epistles to the Colossians, to Philemon, and to the Ephesians*, pp. 174–5.
54 'Seasoned with salt' is an idiomatic expression that was current at the time; see discussion in Lohse, *Colossians and Philemon*, pp. 168–9.
55 2 Thess may be dependent on 1 Thess and this is often held up as evidence for the inauthenticity of the letter; see discussion in Kümmel, *Introduction to the New Testament*, pp. 264–9.
56 This is against Kirby who argues for strong introversionist tendencies in Ephesians; see Kirby, *Ephesians: Baptism and Pentecost*, p. 142.
57 On Col 3:10–11, see Schweizer, *The Letter to the Colossians*, pp. 196–201; Lohse, *Colossians and Philemon*, pp. 142–6.
58 Lohse, *Colossians and Philemon*, p. 144.
59 Schweizer, *The Letter to the Colossians*, p. 199.
60 The fact that the members of the community are influenced by a kind of teaching that exhibits contacts with the requirements of the Jewish law will be discussed subsequently.

61 On the more conservative ethos of Colossians and Ephesians, see Meeks, *Urban Christians*, p. 167.

62 Malina believes that the household codes reflect the development of Christian custom into law, see 'Kinship and Marriage', in *The New Testament World*, pp. 114–15.

63 The history of the investigation of the origin of the household codes is complex. For a complete discussion of the background to the investigation of the Haustafeln, see D. L. Balch, *Let Wives Be Submissive* (Chico, Calif.: Scholars, 1981), pp. 1–20; D. C. Verner, *The Household of God* (Chico, Calif.: Scholars, 1983), pp. 16–23.

64 As well as Balch and Verner noted above, other scholars interested in pursuing the relationship between the topos 'concerning household management' and the household codes include, Elliott, *A Home*, pp. 208–20; D. Lührmann, 'Neutestamentliche Haustafeln und Antike Ökonomie', NTS 27 (1980–1), 83–97.

65 Aristotle, *The Politics* (Loeb Classical Library), pp. 12–15; Balch, *Let Wives be Submissive*, pp. 33–4.

66 Aristotle, *The Politics*, pp. 62–3; Balch, *Let Wives be Submissive*, pp. 34–5.

67 See Balch, 'The Topos "Concerning Household Management" in Eclectic Stoics, Hellenistic Jews, and Neopythagoreans' in *Let Wives be Submissive*, pp. 51–9; see especially his section on Philo and Josephus, pp. 52–6.

68 See Verner, *The Household of God*, p. 85.

69 Ibid, pp. 91–2.

70 Balch, 'Greco-Roman Criticism of Eastern Religions' in *Let Wives be Submissive*, pp. 65–76.

71 Ibid, p. 83.

72 Ibid, pp. 52–6; p. 73.

73 Ibid, p. 54; see *Philo*, vol. IX (Loeb Classical Library), p. 425.

74 Ibid; see *Josephus*, vol. I (Loeb Classical Library), pp. 372–3. On Philo and Josephus, see J. E. Crouch, *The Origin and Intention of the Colossian Haustafel* (Göttingen: Vandenhoeck & Ruprecht, 1972), pp. 77–83.

75 Balch, *Let Wives be Submissive*, pp. 54–5; pp. 74–5.

76 Ibid, p. 119; Balch believes that the exhortation to slaves (1 Pet 2:18) points to the same problem in community life as the exhortation to women. The conversion of subordinate members of the household is causing the community to come under pressure from outsiders. On the apologetic function of the household code in 1 Peter, see pp. 81–116, and his final summary and conclusions pp. 117–21.

77 See Elliott, *A Home*, p. 102.

78 See D. W. Riddle, 'Environment as a Factor in the Achievement of Self-Consciousness in Early Christianity', JR 7 (1927), 146–63.

79 See detailed criticism of Balch's work in Elliott, *A Home*, pp. 215–18.

80 Elliott argues in favour of a bifocal internal and external social perspective in 1 Peter, cf. ibid, pp. 219–20.

81 Verner, *The Household of God*, p. 86. Verner argues, however, that partial parallels are present in several Jewish sources. He recognizes the possibility that the schema was taken over by the church from the synagogue. However, he argues that the important point here is not the schema's origin, but its presence and development in early Christianity; see note 10, p. 90. Verner's conclusions are different from those of Balch who believes that the similarities in the various Haustafeln can be accounted for by the theory that they represent independent applications of the household management topos to similar problems; see Balch, *Let Wives be Submissive*, p. 120.

82 Verner, *The Household of God*, p. 87.

83 Ibid; see discussion, pp. 87–9.

84 Ibid; p. 91. On the influence of tradition in paraenesis, see pp. 112–25.

85 Crouch, *The Origin and Intention of the Colossian Haustafel*, p. 126; see Schweizer, *The Letter to the Colossians*, p. 215.

86 Crouch, *The Origin and Intention of the Colossian Haustafel*, p. 123, 139.

87 Ibid, p. 129, 150.

88 S. Bartchy, *Mallon Chresai: First-Century Slavery and the Interpretation of 1 Corinthians 7:21* (Missoula, Mont.: Scholars, 1973).

89 Ibid, pp. 114–20; on the question of slavery in the early church, see Balch, *Let Wives be Submissive*, pp. 106–7.

90 Ibid, p. 120.

91 Ibid, p. 132.

92 Ibid.

93 Ibid, p. 131.

94 There is uncertainty as to who exactly is being addressed in Col 3:25; see discussion in Schweizer, *The Letter to the Colossians*, pp. 226–7.

95 Balch, *Let Wives be Submissive*, pp. 106–7.

96 Crouch, *The Origin and Intention of the Colossian Haustafel*, p. 150.

97 See Sampley, *And the Two Shall Become One Flesh*, p. 148. The exhortation to children–parents is somewhat longer than in Colossians, including the commandment to honour parents from Ex 20:12 (Eph 6:2) and the promise of long life found in Deut 5:16 (Eph 6:3). The exhortation to slaves–masters in Ephesians follows Colossians very closely.

98 The meaning of 'ἐν ῥήματι' is ambiguous, see discussion in Sampley, *And the Two Shall Become One Flesh*, pp. 131–3. Sampley notes the connection between Eph 5:25–7 and the marriage of Yahweh and Israel as depicted in Ezekiel 16; see pp. 39–42, pp. 126–39.

99 See discussion in Newton, *The Concept of Purity*, pp. 105–6.

100 On the legal status of women in the Greco-Roman world, see discussion in Verner, *The Household of God*, pp. 39–44; Balch, 'The Political, Legal, and Economic Status of Women in the Roman World', in *Let Wives Be Submissive*, pp. 139–41.

101 See Newton, *The Concept of Purity*, pp. 106–7; cf. 1QM 7.4–6 and 1QSa 2.3–11.

102 Ibid, p. 107.

103 Ibid, pp. 107–8. Some argue that the issue of head covering does not involve veils, but rather the wearing of hair tied up, see note 40, p. 146.

104 Ibid, pp. 108–9.

105 Ibid, p. 109.

106 See Malina, 'Honour and Shame: Pivotal Values of the First-Century Mediterranean World', in *The New Testament World*, pp. 25–50 and 'Kinship and Marriage', pp. 94–121, in the same volume.

107 On the significance of the quotation of Gen 2:24 in Ephesians, see Sampley, *And the Two shall Become One Flesh*, pp. 51–61, 110–14, 146.

108 See the discussion in Sampley, pp. 86–96; Mitton, *Ephesians*, pp. 206–8; on the possible gnostic influences on the exhortation concerning marriage, see H. Schlier, *Der Brief an die Epheser* (Düsseldorf: Patmos, 1957), pp. 264–76.

109 Sampley believes that Eph 5:33a bears a close relationship to Lev. 19:18b; see discussion in *And the Two Shall Become One Flesh*, pp. 30–4.

110 Ibid, p. 162.

111 A similar neglect is made by Mitton, *Ephesians*, pp. 197–9. The following statement made by him contains no references to support his contention about the psychological welfare of women. One wonders whether such potentially offensive personal opinions should be expressed in New Testament commentaries: '... until recent times it was almost universally expected that a Christian bride would promise obedience to her husband, and indeed many still feel this is appropriate. Apart from Christian considerations, there are among psychologists those who believe that many women are happier within a marriage where ultimate responsibility for decision-making is not shirked by the husband, and that children are less likely to be emotionally stable if they come from a home where the mother dominates over the father. Today we should not wish to continue to use the word 'subordination' or 'subjection' within marriage, and within a truly Christian marriage there is real equality between partners, consultation with each other and consideration for each other. It is, however, possible that the idea that the husband is the rightful head of the home is based on more than old-fashioned custom.' (p. 198) Similar sexist remarks characterize the discussion of husband and wife in Barth's commentary on Ephesians: 'The women of Paul's time (especially in Corinth) who used the message of Christ for nothing better than a liberation movement and the enhancement of their own independence by a revolution for its own sake, fall out of that grace and freedom by and for which they were liberated. Neither a bride nor a wife can be glorious (or 'resplendent') in her own light and right. What legitimate glory she receives has come from God and is shared with him who loves her.' (*Ephesians*, vol. 2, p. 711) What evidence is there in the New Testament texts that women were beginning revolutions for their own sake?

112 A more thorough study of the role of women in the Pauline movement will be conducted in the following section on the Pastorals.
113 M. C. De Boer, 'Images of Paul in the Paul-Apostolic Period', CBQ 42 (1980), 359–80.
114 Ibid, p. 360.
115 Note, however, that outside the New Testament, the Acts of Paul point to the fact that strikingly different legends about Paul than those that were canonized circulated in the early church. The Acts of Paul will be considered in Part 3 of this book.
116 De Boer, 'Images of Paul in the Post-Apostolic Period', p. 361; he refers to H. M. Schenke, 'Das Weiterwirken des Paulus und die Pflege seines Erbes durch die Paulus-Schule', NTS 21 (1974–5), 505–18.
117 De Boer, 'Images of Paul in the Post-Apostolic Period', p. 370.
118 H. Conzelmann, 'Die Schule des Paulus' in *Theologia Crucis – Signum Crucis* (Andresen and Klein ed., Tübingen: J. C. B. Mohr [Paul Siebeck], 1979), p. 89; see discussion in Koester, *Introduction*, vol. 2, pp. 262–3.
119 Conzelmann, 'Die Schule des Paulus', p. 90; on the Pauline school, see A. Lindemann, *Paulus im ältesten Christentum* (Tübingen: J. C. B. Mohr [Paul Siebeck], 1979), pp. 36–8.
120 See Guthrie, 'Epistolary Pseudepigraphy' in *New Testament Introduction*, p. 680.
121 On this difficult passage, see Schweizer, *The Letter to the Colossians*, pp. 99–106; Lohse, *Colossians and Philemon*, pp. 68–72; F. Zeilinger, *Der Erstgeborene der Schöpfung* (Wien: Herder & Co., 1974), pp. 82–94.
122 See Introduction of this book; the situation in the churches after the death of the earliest authorities is the subject of R. E. Brown's book, *The Churches the Apostles Left Behind* (London: Geoffrey Chapman, 1984).
123 On the significance of the address, see Schweizer, *The Letter to the Colossians*, p. 115.
124 See Lohse, *Colossians and Philemon*, p. 80.
125 Ibid.
126 For a comparison of 1 Cor 5:3 with Col 2:5, see discussion in Schweizer, *The Letter to the Colossians*, pp. 119–20.
127 On this verse, see discussion in Lohse, *Colossians and Philemon*, pp. 83–4.
128 Ibid, p. 23.
129 Ibid, pp. 22–3.
130 The mention of Onesimus here raises questions about the relationship between Colossians and Philemon; see discussion in Schweizer, *The Letter to the Colossians*, pp. 24–6.
131 See Lohse, *Colossians and Philemon*, pp. 173–4.
132 Ibid, p. 176.
133 Ibid, pp. 176–7, for a detailed comparison including chart illustrating parallels.
134 Ibid, p. 176.

135 Ibid.
136 Ibid, p. 177.
137 The relationship between these two verses points to the literary dependence of Ephesians on Colossians. Thirty-two consecutive words in Ephesians are identical to those found in Colossians; see Mitton, *Ephesians*, p. 230.
138 On the identity of Silvanus, see Elliott, *A Home*, pp. 277–80.
139 See Mitton, *Ephesians*, p. 111.
140 Some believe that it is Old Testament prophets which are being referred to here. However the sense of Eph 3:5 makes it clear that they are early church leaders; see discussion in P. Bony, 'L'Épître aux Éphésiens' in *Le ministère et les ministères selon le Nouveau Testament* (Paris: Éditions du Seuil, 1974), p. 77.
141 With the exception of Acts 14:4, 14, Luke reserves the title 'apostle' for the twelve. In giving the title 'apostle' to Paul and Barnabas here, Luke may be appealing to an Antiochean tradition; see A. George, 'L'œuvre de Luc: Actes et Évangile' in *Le ministère*, p. 221.
142 Ibid, pp. 217–18, for information on 'prophets' in Acts.
143 The reference to Ps 68:18 and accompanying interpretations cause various difficulties for the interpreter. The most striking of these is the mention of the giving of gifts when the psalm itself refers to God receiving gifts; see discussion in Bony, 'L'Épître aux Éphésiens', pp. 85–6.
144 Ibid, p. 89.
145 On binding and loosing, see von Campenhausen, *Ecclesiastical Authority*, pp. 126–7; Schweizer, *Church Order*, p. 59.
146 See G. Bornkamm, 'The Authority to "Bind" and "Loose" in the Church in Matthew's Gospel' in *The Interpretation of Matthew* (Stanton ed., London: SPCK, 1973), pp. 85–97.
147 See R. E. Brown and J. P. Meier, *Antioch and Rome* (London: Geoffrey Chapman, 1983), p. 69.
148 On Matt 28:18–20, see O. Michel, 'The Conclusion of Matthew's Gospel' in *The Interpretation of Matthew* (Stanton ed.), pp. 30–40.
149 See Brown and Meier, *Antioch and Rome*, pp. 70–1.
150 On the organization of Matthew's community, see E. Schweizer, 'Matthew's Church' in *The Interpretation of Matthew* (Stanton ed.), pp. 129–55.
151 On institutionalization in Matthew's community, see G. Strecker, 'The Concept of History in Matthew' in *The Interpretation of Matthew* (Stanton ed.), pp. 67–84; see especially, pp. 77–9.
152 See Brown and Meier, *Antioch and Rome*, p. 72.
153 I have chosen not to employ the concept of 'third generation' in this book because of the ambiguity that surrounds its usage. I have found the three artificial divisions of 'community-building institutionalization', 'community-stabilizing institutionalization' and 'community-protecting institutionalization' more useful for this analysis of development in the Pauline tradition.
154 It is possible that Matthew's gospel was written in Antioch as little as ten to twenty years prior to Ignatius. On the relation between

the two writings, see Brown and Meier, *Antioch and Rome*, pp. 73–81; on the relation of the Didache to these writings, see pp. 81–4.

155 The leadership position denoted by 'elders' will be discussed in more detail in the section on the Pastoral Epistles. On 'elders' in 1 Peter, see Elliott, *A Home*, pp. 190–1.

156 E. von Dobschütz, *Christian Life in the Primitive Church* (London: Williams and Norgate, 1904), p. 175.

157 On the relation between the household codes and leadership structures, see D. Lührmann, 'Neutestamentliche Haustafeln und Antike Ökonomie', NTS 27 (1980–1), 83–97.

158 See Sampley, *And the Two Shall Become One Flesh*, pp. 150–1.

159 See discussion in Part 1 of this book, section 3.1.

160 See Lohse, *Colossians and Philemon*, p. 151; Meeks, *Urban Christians*, p. 144.

161 On the relation between ritual in the early church and Jewish worship traditions, see especially, Kirby, *Ephesians: Baptism and Pentecost*.

162 See Lohse, *Colossians and Philemon*, p. 151; Meeks, *Urban Christians*, p. 144.

163 See Schweizer, *The Letter to the Colossians*, p. 210.

164 On hymns in Colossians and Ephesians, see C. Burger, *Schöpfung und Versöhnung* (Neukirchen-Vluyn: Neukirchener, 1975); R. Deichgräber, *Gotteshymnus und Christushymnus in der frühen Christenheit* (Göttingen: Vandenhoeck & Ruprecht, 1976); J.N. Aletti, *Colossiens, 1, 15–20* (Rome: Biblical Institute Press, 1981); J.T. Sanders, *The New Testament Christological Hymns* (Cambridge University Press, 1971).

165 Kirby, for example, argues that this passage and much of Eph 1–3 show the influence of Jewish prayer; see *Ephesians: Baptism and Pentecost*, pp. 131–3.

166 See Mitton, *Ephesians*, pp. 43–5, 63–6. Mitton responds in particular to Kirby's argument that Ephesians is an example of the liturgy becoming a letter.

167 See Kirby, *Ephesians: Baptism and Pentecost*, pp. 169–70.

168 See N.A. Dahl, 'Adresse und Proömium des Epheserbriefs', TZ 7 (1951), 241–64; Dahl's thesis is that Ephesians was written to give further instruction to new converts on the meaning of their baptism.

169 On the importance of studying Ephesians in terms of a worshipping community, see Kirby, *Ephesians: Baptism and Pentecost*, pp. 59–60.

170 See discussion in Schweizer, *The Letter to the Colossians*, pp. 55–6; Lohse, *Colossians and Philemon*, pp. 41–2. One of the main reasons for understanding the hymn to be an independent construction is that it contains many words not found elsewhere in the Pauline corpus.

171 See discussion in Lohse, *Colossians and Philemon*, pp. 42–3 and Schweizer, *The Letter to the Colossians*, pp. 56–60. Beyond these rather obvious additions, it is difficult to arrive at the precise form of the hymn; for a summary of the various suggestions that have

been made, see Lohse, pp. 43–5; Schweizer, pp. 60–3. On the origin of the hymn, see Lohse, pp. 45–6.

172 See Lohse, *Colossians and Philemon*, p. 43.

173 See Schweizer, *The Letter to the Colossians*, pp. 96–8.

174 On the recalling function of liturgical influences, see Dahl, 'Anamnesis: Memory and Commemoration in Early Christianity' in *Jesus in the Memory of the Early Church*, pp. 11–29.

175 See Sanders, 'The New Testament Christological Hymns as Language' in *The New Testament Christological Hymns*, pp. 140–4.

176 See Meeks, *Urban Christians*, p. 145.

177 See Part 1 of this book, section 3.2.

178 On the cosmological symbolism of Colossians and Ephesians, see especially Meeks, 'In One Body' in *God's Christ and His People* (Jervell and Meeks ed.), pp. 209–21.

179 Ibid, p. 211.

180 On this passage, see Schweizer, *The Letter to the Colossians*, pp. 171–80.

181 On this passage, see Mitton, *Ephesians*, pp. 88–91.

182 On this topic, see Lohse's discussion of the relation between Paul's concept of baptism in Rom 6 and that which is found in Colossians; see *Colossians and Philemon*, pp. 103–5.

183 See Meeks, 'In One Body', p. 211; on the relation between baptism and the conflict with the false teachers in Colossians, see Käsemann, 'A Primitive Christian Baptismal Liturgy' in *Essays on New Testament Themes*, pp. 149–68.

184 Meeks, 'In One Body', p. 211.

185 See Part 1 of this book, section 3.2.

186 See Lohse, *Colossians and Philemon*, p. 130.

187 Meeks, 'In One Body', pp. 216–17.

188 See for example, Bultmann on Colossians and Ephesians, *Theology*, vol. 2, p. 180; Käsemann on Ephesians and the transition from the Pauline tradition to 'early catholicism', 'Paul and Early Catholicism', in *New Testament Questions of Today*, pp. 242–5. Conzelmann has a more balanced attitude toward development after Paul, see *Outline*, p. 311.

189 L. E. Keck, 'On the Ethos of Early Christians', JAAR 42 (1974), 435–52.

190 Ibid, p. 442; see his remarks on the transformation of the Pauline symbol system, p. 451.

191 An exception to this generalization is the work by Meeks. As well as relevant observations in his *Urban Christians*, see 'In One Body' and 'The Image of Androgyne', HR 13 (1974), 165–208. In addition, the introduction to the series of essays edited by Meeks and Francis on Colossians points to the limitations of the history of ideas principle; see *Conflict at Colossae*.

192 Koester, *Introduction*, vol. 2, pp. 261–72.

193 Ibid, p. 265.

194 On traditional material and how it should be interpreted, see discussion by Verner, *The Household of God*, pp. 112–25.

195 See for example, Koester, *Introduction*, vol. 2, p. 265, pp. 269–71; Lohse, *Colossians and Philemon*, pp. 129–30; G. Bornkamm, 'The Heresy of Colossians' in *Conflict at Colossae* (Francis and Meeks ed.), pp. 123–45; Mitton, *Ephesians*, pp. 20–1; F. Mussner, *Christus das All und die Kirche* (Trier: Paulinus, 1968), pp. 160–73; K. M. Fischer, *Tendenz und Absicht des Epheserbriefes* (Göttingen: Vandenhoeck & Ruprecht, 1973), pp. 173–200; Schlier, *Der Brief an die Epheser*, pp. 264–76.

196 See Lohse, *Colossians and Philemon*, pp. 127–31; Schweizer, *The Letter to the Colossians*, pp. 125–34; Francis and Meeks (ed.), *Conflict at Colossae*.

197 Francis and Meeks (ed.), *Conflict at Colossae*, p. 216.

198 On the elements of the universe, see Lohse, *Colossians and Philemon*, pp. 96–8.

199 Ibid, pp. 127–8.

200 On the meaning of 'πλήρωμα', see Lohse, pp. 99–101.

201 Ibid, p. 128.

202 Ibid, p. 130.

203 The background and significance of Col 2:18 is heavily debated. The relation between this passage and mystery rites has been considered. In his very important essay, Dibelius investigates the background of the hapax legomenon 'ἐμβατεύω'; see M. Dibelius, 'The Isis Initiation in Apuleius and Related Initiatory Rites' in *Conflict at Colossae* (Francis and Meeks ed.), pp. 61–121. For criticism of Dibelius, see Francis and Meeks, pp. 210–11; see Francis, 'Humility and Angelic Worship in Col 3:18' in *Conflict at Colossae*, pp. 171–6 and 'The Background of Embateuein (Col 2:18) in Legal Papyri and Oracle Inscriptions', pp. 197–207 of the same volume. The expression angel('s) worship (θρησκεία τῶν ἀγγέλων) in Col 2:18 is also significant. Although it is usually translated as the objective genitive to mean the worship directed to angels, Francis argues that literary evidence strongly supports a translation as the subjective genitive, to mean angelic worship (the participation in some type of angelic liturgy; see 'Humility and Angelic Worship', pp. 176–81).

204 See Francis, 'Humility and Angelic Worship', p. 180.

205 On the meaning of 'would-be-worship', Ibid, pp. 181–2.

206 Lohse, *Colossians and Philemon*, pp. 130–1.

207 In this context, it is valuable to consider the social and political implications of gnostic teaching. See especially E. H. Pagels, *The Gnostic Gospels* (London: Weidenfeld and Nicholson, 1979).

208 See Francis, 'Humility and Angelic Worship', pp. 183–4.

209 See for example, Lohse, *Colossians and Philemon*, p. 34; Conzelmann, *Outline*, p. 310.

210 See Lohse, p. 18.

211 See Part 1 of this book, section 4.3.

212 This is against Käsemann who appears to advocate such an eschatological measuring; see 'Paul and Early Catholicism' in *New Testament Questions of Today*, pp. 236–7.

213 Berger's description of the process of 'cosmetization' is suggestive for understanding the symbolism in Colossians and Ephesians, see *The Sacred Canopy*, pp. 36–7.

Part 3

1 The M. Dibelius/H. Conzelmann commentary, *The Pastoral Epistles* (Philadelphia: Fortress, 1972), provides an excellent example of this; it cites numerous parallels with the literature of the day without making any major attempt to locate the Pastorals within Greco-Roman society.

2 P. C. Spicq, *Les Épîtres Pastorales* (Paris: Librairie Lecoffre, 1947), p. i.

3 Ibid, p. xxiii.

4 Ibid, p. xxviii.

5 E. F. Scott, *The Pastoral Epistles* (London: Hodder and Stoughton, 1936), p. xxxii.

6 Dibelius/Conzelmann, *The Pastoral Epistles*, p. 51.

7 Dibelius/Conzelmann do consider v. 7 to be added to the traditional schema, but do not deal with this question.

8 Ibid, pp. 39, 41.

9 See von Campenhausen, *Ecclesiastical Authority*, p. 118; Käsemann, 'Ministry and Community in the New Testament' in *Essays on New Testament Themes*, pp. 87–8; Bultmann, *Theology*, vol. 2, pp. 115–16.

10 See E. Troeltsch, *The Social Teaching of the Christian Churches* (2 vols., New York: The MacMillan Co., 1931), vol. 1, pp. 331–72; for Wilson's seven part typology of sects and criticism of Troeltsch's understanding of sects, see *Magic and the Millenium*.

11 Troeltsch, *The Social Teaching of the Christian Churches*, p. 331.

12 Ibid, pp. 338–9.

13 See Wilson, 'An Analysis of Sect Development', in *Patterns*, pp. 22–45.

14 Note, however, that Troeltsch himself did not describe such a process; for him, the sect represented a reaction against the Church.

15 See C. K. Barrett, *The Pastoral Epistles* (Oxford: At the Clarendon Press, 1963), pp. 130–3.

16 Dibelius/Conzelmann, *The Pastoral Epistles*, p. 54.

17 Verner, *The Household of God*, p. 153.

18 Dibelius/Conzelmann, *The Pastoral Epistles*, p. 76.

19 Barrett, *The Pastoral Epistles*, p. 77.

20 Ibid, p. 82.

21 Verner, *The Household of God*, p. 140.

22 Ibid, p. 145.

23 See Spicq, *Les Épîtres Pastorales*, for examples from the inscriptions, pp. 250–2. Drunkenness among women was particularly abhored by the Roman tradition; see Verner, *The Household of God*, p. 172.

24 Both Dibelius/Conzelmann, *The Pastoral Epistles*, p. 147 and

Barrett, *The Pastoral Epistles*, p. 139 point to the traditional nature of this exhortation.
25 Barrett, *The Pastoral Epistles*, p. 134.
26 See R. MacMullen, *Christianizing the Roman Empire (A.D. 100–400)* (New Haven and London: Yale University Press, 1984), pp. 27–34.
27 See A. Malherbe, 'In Season and Out of Season: 2 Timothy 4:2', JBL 103/2 (1984), 235–43.
28 Ibid, p. 236.
29 Ibid, p. 237.
30 Ibid.
31 Ibid, p. 235.
32 Ibid, p. 240.
33 Ibid, p. 241.
34 Ibid, p. 242.
35 Ibid.
36 Dibelius/Conzelmann, *The Pastoral Epistles*, pp. 24–5.
37 J. N. D. Kelly, *A Commentary on the Pastoral Epistles* (New York: Harper, 1963), pp. 50–1.
38 Dibelius/Conzelmann, *The Pastoral Epistles*, p. 25.
39 See Spicq, 'La Psychologie de L'auteur des Pastorales' in *Les Épîtres Pastorales*, pp. lxxxix–xciv.
40 Berger and Luckmann, *The Social Construction*, p. 125.
41 Malherbe, 'In Season and Out of Season', p. 242.
42 Dibelius/Conzelmann, *The Pastoral Epistles*, p. 128.
43 Barrett, *The Pastoral Epistles*, p. 52.
44 MacMullen, *Christianizing the Roman Empire*, pp. 33–4.
45 Ibid, pp. 36–42; for a study of the workshop as a place of conversion, see Hock, *The Social Context of Paul's Ministry*.
46 MacMullen, *Christianizing the Roman Empire*, p. 40.
47 Malherbe, 'In Season and Out of Season', pp. 240–1.
48 Ibid, p. 242.
49 See especially Verner, *The Household of God*, pp. 27–81.
50 R. MacMullen, 'Women in Public in the Roman Empire' in *Historia* 29 (1980), p. 216.
51 Ibid, p. 209; see Meeks, *Urban Christians*, p. 24.
52 S. B. Pomeroy, *Goddesses, Whores, Wives, and Slaves* (New York: Schocken, 1975), pp. 198–9.
53 Ibid, p. 199.
54 Ibid, p. 200.
55 See Part 2 of this book, section 1.5. Note, however, that the Isis cult was considered revolutionary because the Goddess Isis was proclaimed as making men and women equal; on the Isis cult, see E. S. Fiorenza, *In Memory of Her* (London: SCM, 1983), p. 264; Pomeroy, *Goddesses*, p. 223; Meeks, *Urban Christians*, p. 25.
56 See Fiorenza, *In Memory of Her*, p. 259.
57 Ibid, pp. 263–4.
58 Verner, *The Household of God*, p. 176.
59 Barrett, *The Pastoral Epistles*, p. 12.

60 Dibelius/Conzelmann, *The Pastoral Epistles*, p. 65; Barrett, *The Pastoral Epistles*, p. 13; Rudolph, *Gnosis*, pp. 302–3.

61 Rudolph, *Gnosis*, pp. 302–3.

62 Some scholars connect the word 'contradictions' in 1 Tim 6:20 with the work of the same name by Marcion. Barrett argues convincingly against this interpretation: 'It has been suggested that "contradictions" refers to a work under this title by the gnostic heretic Marcion; this is unlikely, not only because it would make the Pastorals impossibly late (it would be not impossible to regard 6:20f as a late interpolation), but because the heresy combated in the Pastorals is a Jewish gnosticism, whereas Marcion's was an anti-Jewish gnosticism (Jeremias). The word may be a technical term in rhetoric, suggesting clever but empty verbiage, or may simply describe the opposition of heretics to the truth.' (Barrett, *The Pastoral Epistles*, p. 89).

63 Rudolph has indicated that the equal standing of women in gnostic communities appears to have been relatively widespread. He understands 1 Tim 2:12 as a polemical reference to this; see *Gnosis*, pp. 271–2.

64 Verner, *The Household of God*, p. 178.

65 Ibid, p. 177.

66 Dibelius/Conzelmann, *The Pastoral Epistles*, p. 116; Verner, *The Household of God*, p. 177.

67 Pomeroy has argued that remaining single was most likely related to emancipated behaviour on the part of women in Greco-Roman society. She notes that the lives of the virgin priestesses known as the Vestals were severely regulated, but in some ways they were the most emancipated women in Rome. Females who were not bound to males in a permanent relationship possessed considerable freedom; see her discussion on the privileges of virginity in *Goddesses*, pp. 210–14.

68 See E. H. Pagels, 'Adam and Eve, Christ and the Church' in *The New Testament and Gnosis* (Logan and Wedderburn ed., Edinburgh: T & T Clark, 1983), p. 150.

69 On the origin and date of the Acts of Paul, see D. R. MacDonald, *The Legend and the Apostle* (Philadelphia: The Westminster Press, 1983), pp. 17–53; see E. Hennecke, *The New Testament Apocrypha* (London: SCM, 1974), vol. 2, pp. 322–51.

70 See Hennecke, p. 323.

71 The relationship between the Pastoral Epistles and the Acts of Paul is the subject of MacDonald's book cited above. See also his article, 'Virgins, Widows and Paul in Second Century Asia Minor' in *SBL Seminar Papers* (Achtemeier ed., Missoula, Montana: Scholars, 1979), pp. 169–84.

72 Onesiphorus is also depicted as offering hospitality to Paul in the Pastorals (cf. 2 Tim 1:16; 4:19). Several of the prominent characters in the Acts of Paul and Thecla also appear as prominent names in the Pastorals. The positive and negative depiction of their characters is also consistent with the picture in the Pastorals: Demas and

Hermogenes (Paul's travelling companions in the Acts of Paul and Thecla 3:1f; cf. 2 Tim 1:15; 4:10); Alexander (the one responsible for bringing Thecla before the governor 3:26f; cf. 1 Tim 1:20; 2 Tim 4:14).

73 MacDonald, 'The Oral Legends Behind the Acts of Paul' in *The Legend and the Apostle*, pp. 17—33.

74 MacDonald, 'The Storytellers behind the Legends' in *The Legend and the Apostle*, pp. 34—53.

75 See C. K. Barrett, 'Pauline Controversies in the Post-Pauline Period', NTS 20 (1973—4), 229—45.

76 MacDonald, 'The Victory of the Pastoral Epistles', pp. 78—89, and 'The Victory of the Legends', pp. 90—6, in *The Legend and the Apostle*.

77 MacDonald, 'The Pastoral Epistles Against "Old-Wives Tales"' in *The Legend and the Apostle*, pp. 54—77. The Greek for 'old-womanish' (γραώδεις) is often translated simply as 'silly'; but this hides the force of a description found frequently in philosophical polemic (Dibelius/Conzelmann, *The Pastoral Epistles*, p. 68).

78 Fiorenza, *In Memory of Her*, p. 265.

79 Verner, *The Household of God*, p. 161.

80 Dibelius/Conzelmann, *The Pastoral Epistles*, p. 75. There is ambiguity in the Greek here. There is no subject given for 'μανθανέτωσαν', but most scholars assume that the subjects are 'τέκνα' and 'ἔκγονα'. If the subject were 'χῆραι', the author would be urging the widows to care for their households. Neither interpretation is certain, but in light of v. 8 and v. 16, the first solution appears to be the best. Whatever interpretation is preferred, however, it is clear that the author seeks to ensure that as many widows as possible will be connected to households.

81 Verner, *The Pastoral Epistles*, p. 137.

82 Some authorities have 'πιστὸς ἢ πιστή' rather than simply 'πιστή'; Verner understands this to be an attempt to improve the text; see note 40, p. 139.

83 Barrett, *The Pastoral Epistles*, p. 174.

84 Verner, *The Household of God*, p. 138; he describes the social situation of these 'real widows' in terms of the realities of Greco-Roman society.

85 Ibid, p. 139.

86 Pomeroy, *Goddesses*, pp. 149—150; on the situation of widows and divorcees in Greco-Roman society, see 'The Letter of the Law and Reality', pp. 150—76.

87 Verner, *The Household of God*, p. 163.

88 Ibid.

89 Ibid.

90 Ibid, pp. 163—4.

91 Ibid, p. 165.

92 Ibid.

93 Ibid, p. 164, including notes 125 and 126.

94 Ibid, p. 165.

95 Ibid, p. 164.
96 Ibid, p. 136.
97 Fiorenza, p. 262.
98 Orig., C. Cels. 352; see MacMullen, *Christianizing the Roman Empire*, p. 37.
99 See Malina, 'The Perception of Limited Good' in *The New Testament World*, pp. 73–4.
100 See Malherbe's essay 'Social Level and Literary Culture' in *Social Aspects*, pp. 42–3.
101 Dibelius/Conzelmann, *The Pastoral Epistles*, p. 85, with note 18 for numerous examples.
102 Malherbe, 'Social Level and Literary Culture', pp. 43–4.
103 Ibid, pp. 44–5.
104 Malina, 'The Perception of Limited Good' in *The New Testament World*, pp. 74–5.
105 Ibid, p. 75; on attitudes to wealth in the ancient world, see A. R. Hands, *Charities and Social Aid in Greece and Rome* (London: Thames and Hudson, 1968).
106 Ibid, pp. 76, 83–4.
107 The translation of the Shepherd of Hermas employed here is by Kirsopp Lake, *Apostolic Fathers* II (Loeb Classical Library). On the problems of dating, of composite authorship and sources in the Shepherd of Hermas, see discussion in C. Osiek, *Rich and Poor in the Shepherd of Hermas* (Washington, D.C.: The Catholic Biblical Association of America, 1983), pp. 6–14.
108 D. W. Riddle, 'The Message of the Shepherd of Hermas: A Study in Social Control', JR 7 (1927), 561–77.
109 Ibid, pp. 561–2.
110 Ibid, p. 564; on the relation between this condition and the problems associated with the accumulation of wealth, see Osiek, *Rich and Poor*, p. 50.
111 Riddle, 'The Message of the Shepherd of Hermas', p. 564.
112 Ibid, p. 565.
113 Ibid, p. 566.
114 Osiek, *Rich and Poor*, p. 3; on the problems of wealth and entanglement in business affairs, see pp. 47–9.
115 Riddle, 'The Message of the Shepherd of Hermas', pp. 568–9.
116 See Meeks, *Urban Christians*, pp. 19–23.
117 Riddle, 'The Message of the Shepherd of Hermas', p. 570.
118 On the dating of the writing, see Kümmel, *Introduction to the New Testament*, p. 414.
119 James is the only New Testament writing where the word 'δίψυχος' occurs. This word and its cognates appear frequently in the Shepherd of Hermas and in 1 and 2 Clement.
120 Riddle, 'The Message of the Shepherd of Hermas', pp. 571–2.
121 Ibid, p. 572.
122 Ibid, p. 567.
123 R. J. Karris, 'The Background and Significance of the Polemic in

the Pastoral Epistles', JBL 92 (1973), 549—64; see p. 552, including note 12 for numerous examples.

124 Dibelius/Conzelmann, *The Pastoral Epistles*, p. 84; see note 6 for numerous examples.

125 See discussion by M. Hengel, 'The Ideal of "Self-Sufficiency" in Popular Philosophy' in *Property and Riches in the Early Church* (Philadelphia: Fortress, 1974), pp. 54—9.

126 Dibelius/Conzelmann, *The Pastoral Epistles*, pp. 84—5; Barrett, *The Pastoral Epistles*, p. 84.

127 Verner, *The Household of God*, p. 174.

128 Ibid.

129 Ibid, p. 175; cf. 1 Clem 38:1—2.

130 Bultmann, *Theology*, vol. 2, p. 116.

131 Note, however, that some believe that the Pastorals contain some authentic fragments. The classical work on this subject is P. N. Harrison, *The Problem of the Pastoral Epistles* (London: Oxford University Press, 1921). See discussion in Barrett, *The Pastoral Epistles*, pp. 10—12.

132 Barrett, *The Pastoral Epistles*, p. 43.

133 Ibid.

134 Ibid, pp. 44—5.

135 Another possible variant instead of 'what he has put in my charge' is 'what I have put into his charge', but this is unlikely; see discussion in Barrett, *The Pastoral Epistles*, p. 96.

136 Ibid.

137 See discussion in Verner, *The Household of God*, pp. 157—8.

138 Ibid, pp. 107—11.

139 Ibid, p. 92.

140 Ibid, pp. 95, 101.

141 Ibid, pp. 99—100. The list of requirements for office-holders discloses the problem of determining the extent to which the author of the Pastorals simply reproduced wholesale fixed traditions. Verner has argued that the author produced a final written product where his own concerns gave shape to traditional and non-traditional elements. On this subject, see especially Verner's comparison of two sets of parallel passages (1 Tim 6:1—2 and Tit 2:9—10; 1 Tim 3:1ff and Tit 1:6ff), p. 102 with chart on p. 103 and pp. 104—6 with chart on p. 103. Some scholars give more weight to traditional influences shaping the exhortations concerning church offices than does Verner, see H. W. Bartsch, *Die Anfänge urchristlicher Rechtsbildungen* (Hamburg: Herbert Reich, 1965).

142 Scholars debate whether the introductory formula 'πιστὸς ὁ λόγος' in fact introduces the section on bishops or belongs with the previous section on the role of women. It seems, however, that it fits better with the exhortation concerning bishops which resembles a proverbial saying; see Dibelius/Conzelmann, *The Pastoral Epistles*, p. 51.

143 See Barrett, *The Pastoral Epistles*, p. 57; Spicq, *Les Épîtres Pastorales*, p. 77; Verner, *The Household of God*, p. 151.

144 See Kelly, *A Commentary on the Pastoral Epistles*, p. 75.
145 In addition to appearing as a desirable trait for the bishop in 1 Tim 3:2, the term 'ἀνεπίλημπτος' also appears in a more general sense in 1 Tim 5:7 concerning the nature of 'real widows' and in 1 Tim 6:14 in the demand for appropriate behaviour in the community as a whole.
146 For consideration of other possibilities, see Verner, *The Household of God*, pp. 129–131; Barrett, *The Pastoral Epistles*, p. 59; Dibelius/Conzelmann, *The Pastoral Epistles*, p. 52.
147 Verner, *The Household of God*, p. 133.
148 Ibid, p. 132.
149 Consider the activity of Diotrephes recorded in 3 John 9–10; see comments in R. E. Brown, *The Epistles of John* (Garden City, New York: Doubleday Inc., 1982); R. E. Brown, *The Community of the Beloved Disciple* (New York: Paulist, 1979); Malherbe, 'Hospitality and Inhospitality in the Church' in *Social Aspects*, pp. 92–112.
150 Verner, *The Household of God*, p. 153.
151 Kelly, *A Commentary on the Pastoral Epistles*, p. 82.
152 Verner, *The Household of God*, p. 155.
153 Barrett, *The Pastoral Epistles*, p. 61.
154 Barrett, *The Pastoral Epistles*, p. 62; Kelly, *A Commentary on the Pastoral Epistles*, pp. 84–5; Verner, *The Household of God*, p. 155; all are in agreement here.
155 Von Campenhausen, *Ecclesiastical Authority*, pp. 77–8.
156 Ibid, p. 107.
157 Ibid, p. 108.
158 Ibid, p. 77.
159 E. Schürer, *The History of the Jewish People in the Age of Jesus Christ (175 B.C.–A.D. 135)* (3 vols., Vermes, Millar, Black and Goodman rev. and ed., Edinburgh: T & T Clark, 1973f), vol. 2, pp. 427–39.
160 Ibid, pp. 427–429.
161 This is argued in detail by A. E. Harvey; 'Elders', JTS 25 (1974), 318–32.
162 See G. Bornkamm, 'πρεσβύτερος', TDNT 6, pp. 652–4.
163 Verner, *The Household of God*, p. 148.
164 Dibelius/Conzelmann, *The Pastoral Epistles*, p. 56.
165 Ibid; for similar thesis, see Barrett, *The Pastoral Epistles*, p. 129.
166 See Kelly, *A Commentary on the Pastoral Epistles*, p. 125.
167 Verner, *The Household of God*, p. 149.
168 On the relation between 'elder' and 'bishop' in the Apostolic Fathers see E. Jay, 'From Presbyter-Bishops to Bishops and Presbyters', *The Second Century* 1 (1981), 125–62.
169 See W. R. Schoedel, *Ignatius of Antioch* (Philadelphia: Fortress, 1985), p. 22.
170 See Kelly, *A Commentary on the Pastoral Epistles*, p. 108; Barrett, *The Pastoral Epistles*, p. 70; Dibelius/Conzelmann, *The Pastoral Epistles*, pp. 70–1.
171 See for example Kelly, *A Commentary on the Pastoral Epistles*,

pp. 127–8; Verner, *The Household of God*, p. 157; Dibelius/ Conzelmann, *The Pastoral Epistles*, p. 80; Barrett, *The Pastoral Epistles*, pp. 81–2.

172 See Barrett for discussion, p. 86; note that 1 Tim 6:11–16 may be an ordination address; see E. Käsemann, 'Das Formular einer neutestamentlichen Ordinationsparänese' in *Exegetische Versuche und Besinnungen* (Göttingen: Vandenhoeck & Ruprecht, 1964), pp. 101–8; A. T. Hanson, *The Pastoral Epistles* (London: Marshall, Morgan & Scott, 1982), pp. 109–13; on ordination in general, see H. von Lips, *Glaube – Gemeinde – Amt* (Göttingen: Vandenhoeck & Ruprecht, 1964).

173 Barrett, *The Pastoral Epistles*, pp. 113–14.

174 See Verner, *The Household of God*, p. 169.

175 On the background to this passage, see A. T. Hanson, 'Eve's Transgression: 1 Tim 2:13–15' in *Studies in the Pastoral Epistles* (London: SPCK, 1968), pp. 64–77.

176 W. Bauer, *Orthodoxy and Heresy* (London: SCM, 1972); see Gager, *Kingdom and Community*, p. 77.

177 Ibid, p. 175.

178 Ibid, p. 90.

179 Kelly, *A Commentary on the Pastoral Epistles*, p. 185.

180 Gager, *Kingdom and Community*, p. 76.

181 See Introduction of this book, section 2.3.

182 On the role of conflict in social development, see G. Simmel, *Conflict* (New York: Free Press, 1955); L. Coser, *The Function of Social Conflict* (London: Routledge & Kegan Paul Ltd., 1956).

183 See for example Käsemann, 'Ministry and Community in the New Testament' in *Essays on New Testament Themes*, pp. 85–7; see von Campenhausen, *Ecclesiastical Authority*, pp. 111–12.

184 See Schweizer, *Church Order*, p. 77; see similar remarks by Conzelmann, *Outline*, p. 310.

185 R. Schwartz, *Bürgerliches Christentum im Neuen Testament* (Klosterneuburg: Österreichisches Katholishes Bibelwerk, 1983).

186 See for example, Schwartz, p. 96.

187 Barrett, *The Pastoral Epistles*, p. 66.

188 Ibid.

BIBLIOGRAPHY

Aland, Kurt. 'The Problem of Anonymity and Pseudonymity in Christian Literature of the First Two Centuries.' In *The Authorship and Integrity of the New Testament*, SPCK Theological Collections 4, pp. 1–13. London: SPCK, 1965.

Alletti, J. N. *Colossiens 1, 15–20.* Rome: Biblical Institute Press, 1981.

Allmen, Daniel von. *La Famille de Dieu: La Symbolique Familiale dans le Paulinisme.* Göttingen: Vandenhoeck & Ruprecht, 1981.

Balch, David L. *Let Wives be Submissive: The Domestic Code in 1 Peter.* Society of Biblical Literature Monograph Series 26. Chico, Calif.: Scholars Press, 1981.

Banks, R. *Paul's Idea of Community: The Early House Churches in Their Historical Setting.* Exeter: The Paternoster Press, 1980.

Barrett, C. K. *The Pastoral Epistles.* Oxford: At the Clarendon Press, 1963.

'The Acts of Paul.' In *New Testament Essays*, pp. 86–100. London: SPCK, 1972.

'Pauline Controversies in the Post-Pauline Period'. NTS 20, 1973–4: 229–45.

Bartchy, S. Scott. *Mallon Chresai: First-Century Slavery and the Interpretation of 1 Corinthians 7:21.* Society of Biblical Literature Dissertation Series 11. Missoula, Mont.: Scholars Press, 1973.

Barth, Markus. *Ephesians.* 2 vols. Garden City, New York: Doubleday and Company Inc., 1974.

Bartsch, H. W. *Die Anfänge urchristlicher Rechtsbildungen.* Hamburg: Herbert Reich, 1965.

Bauer, Walter, *Orthodoxy and Heresy in Earliest Christianity.* London: SCM Press Ltd., 1972 (Ger. ed. 1934) [= *Orthodoxy and Heresy*].

Berger, Peter L. and Luckmann, Thomas. *The Social Construction of Reality.* Garden City, New York: Doubleday and Company Inc., 1966 (references here are to reprint by Penguin books, 1981) [= *The Social Construction*].

Berger, Peter L. *The Sacred Canopy.* Garden City, New York: Doubleday and Company Inc., 1967.

Best, E. *One Body in Christ: A Study in the Relationship of the Church to Christ in the Epistles of the Apostle Paul.* London: SPCK, 1955.

Bony, Paul. 'L'Épître aux Éphésiens'. In *Le ministère et les ministères selon le Nouveau Testament*, pp. 74–92. Paris: Éditions du Seuil, 1974.

Bornkamm, G. 'Elders'. In TDNT, vol. VI, ed. Gerhard Friedrich, pp. 651–83. Grand Rapids, Michigan: Wm. B. Eerdmans Publishing Co. 1968.

'The Heresy of Colossians'. In *Conflict at Colossae*, ed. Wayne Meeks and Fred O. Francis, pp. 123–45. Missoula, Montana: Scholars Press, 1975.

'The Authority to "Bind" and "Loose" in the Church in Matthew's Gospel: The Problem of Sources in Matthew's Gospel'. In *The Interpretation of Matthew*, Issues in Religion and Theology 3, ed. Graham Stanton, pp. 85–97. London: SPCK, 1983.

Brown, Peter. 'Sorcery, Demons, and the Rise of Christianity: From Late Antiquity into the Middle Ages'. In *Religion and Society in the Age of Saint Augustine*, pp. 119–46. London: Faber and Faber, 1972 [= *Religion and Society*].

Brown, Raymond E. and Meier, John P. *Antioch and Rome*. London: Geoffrey Chapman, 1983.

Brown, Raymond E. *The Community of the Beloved Disciple*. New York: Paulist Press, 1979.

The Epistles of John. Garden City, New York: Doubleday Inc., 1982.

The Churches the Apostles Left Behind. London: Geoffrey Chapman, 1984.

Brox, Norbert, *Falsche Verfasserangaben: Zur Erklärung der frühchristlichen Pseudepigraphie*. Stuttgart: Katholisches Bibelwerk, 1975 [= *Falsche Verfasserangaben*].

(ed.). *Pseudepigraphie in der heidnischen und jüdisch-christlichen Antike*. Darmstadt: Wissenschaftliche Buchgesellschaft, 1977 [= *Pseudepigraphie*].

Bruce, F. F. *The Epistles to the Colossians, to Philemon, and to the Ephesians*. Grand Rapids, Michigan: Wm. B. Eerdmans Publishing Co., 1984.

Bultmann, Rudolf, *Theology of the New Testament*. 2 vols. London: SCM Press Ltd., 1965 (Ger. ed. 1948–53) [= *Theology*].

The History of the Synoptic Tradition. Oxford: Basil Blackwell, 1972 [= *History*].

Burger, Christoph. *Schöpfung und Versöhnung: Studien zum liturgischen Gut im Kolosser-und Epheserbrief*. Neukirchen-Vluyn: Neukirchener, 1975 [= *Schöpfung und Versöhnung*].

Campenhausen, Hans von. *Ecclesiastical Authority and Spiritual Power in the Church of the First Three Centuries*. London: Adam and Charles Black, 1969 (Ger. ed. 1963) [= *Ecclesiastical Authority*].

Cannon, George E. *The Use of Traditional Materials in Colossians*. Marcon, Georgia: Mercer University Press, 1983.

Carney, T. F. *The Shape of the Past: Models and Antiquity*. Lawrence, Kansas: Coronado Press, 1975.

Case, Shirley Jackson. *The Social Triumph of the Ancient Church*. London: George Allen & Unwin Ltd., 1934.

Conzelmann, Hans and Dibelius, Martin. *The Pastoral Epistles*. Philadelphia: Fortress Press, 1972 (trans. from Ger. *Die Pastoralbriefe* by Dibelius (1966); 4th revised edition by Conzelmann).

Conzelman, Hans. *An Outline of the Theology of the New Testament*. London: SCM Press Ltd., 1969 (Ger. ed. 1968) [= *Outline*].

'Die Schule des Paulus.' In *Theologia Crucis — Signum Crucis*, Festschrift fur Erich Dinkler zum 70., ed. Carl Andresen and Gunter Klein. Tübingen: J. C. B. Mohr (Paul Siebeck), 1979.

Coser, Lewis. *The Functions of Social Conflict*. London: Routledge & Kegan Paul Ltd., 1956.

Crouch, James E. *The Origin and Intention of the Colossian Haustafel*. Göttingen: Vandenhoeck & Ruprecht, 1972.

Cullmann, Oscar. 'Les récentes études sur la formation de la tradition évangélique.' *Revue d'Histoire et de Philosophie religieuses* 5, 1925: 564–79.

Dagron, Gilbert. *Vie et miracles de Sainte Thècle*. Subsidia Hagiographica 62. Brussels: Société des Bollandistes, 1978.

Dahl, N. A. 'Adresse und Proömium des Epheserbriefes.' TZ 7, 1951: 251–64.

'Anamnesis: Memory and Commemoration in the Early Church'. In *Jesus in the Memory of the Early Church*, pp. 11–29. Minneapolis: Augsburg, 1976.

Davies, W. D. 'Paul and the People of Israel'. NTS 24, 1977: 4–39.

De Boer, Martinus C. 'Images of Paul in the Post-Apostolic Period'. CBQ 42, 1980: 359–80.

Deichgräber, R. *Gotteshymnus und Christushymnus in der frühen Christenheit*. Göttingen: Vandenhoeck & Ruprecht, 1967.

Delorme, Jean (ed.). *Le ministère et les ministères selon le Nouveau Testament*. Paris: Éditions du Seuil, 1974 [= *Le ministère*].

Deutch, Morton. 'Group Behavior'. In IESS, vol. 6, 1968: 265–75.

Dibelius, Martin. 'The Isis Initiation in Apuleius and Related Initiatory Rites'. In *Conflict at Colossae*, ed. Wayne Meeks and Fred O. Francis, pp. 61–121. Missoula, Montana: Scholars Press, 1975.

Dobschütz, E. von. *Christian Life in the Primitive Church*. London: Williams and Norgate, 1904.

Douglas, Mary. *Purity and Danger: An Analysis of the Concepts of Pollution and Taboo*. London: Routledge and Kegan Paul, 1966.

Natural Symbols: Explorations in Cosmology. London: Barry and Rockliff, 1970.

Ecks, James A. 'The Changing Church: Contributions from Sociology'. *The American Benedictine Review* 23,3, 1972: 385–96.

Einsenstadt, S. N. (ed.). *Max Weber on Charisma and Institution Building*. Chicago and London: The University of Chicago Press, 1968 [= *Max Weber on Charisma*].

Elliott, John H. 'A Catholic Gospel: Reflections on "Early Catholicism" in the New Testament.' CBQ 31, 1969: 213–23.

A Home for the Homeless. London: SCM Press Ltd., 1982 [= *A Home*].

'Social-Scientific Criticism of the New Testament and its Social World: More on Method and Models'. *Semeia* 35, 1986: 1–26.

Esler, Philip. *Community and Gospel in Luke–Acts*. Cambridge University Press, 1987.

Festinger, L. and others, *When Prophecy Fails: A Social and Psychological Study of a Modern Group that Predicted the Destruction of the World*. New York: Harper & Row, 1964 (1st ed. 1956).

Festinger, L. *A Theory of Cognitive Dissonance.* Evanston, Illinois/White Plains, New York: Row, Peterson and Company, 1957.

Filson, Floyd V. 'The Significance of Early House Churches'. JBL 58, 1939: 109–12.

Fiorenza, Elizabeth Schüssler. *In Memory of Her: A Feminist Theological Reconstruction of Christian Origins.* London: SCM Press Ltd., 1983.

Fischer, K. M. *Tendenz und Absicht des Epheserbriefes.* Göttingen: Vandenhoeck & Ruprecht, 1973.

Fitzmyer, J. A. *Pauline Theology: A Brief Sketch.* Englewood Cliffs, New Jersey: Prentice Hall, Inc., 1967.

Francis, Fred O. 'Humility and Angelic Worship in Col 2:18'. In *Conflict at Colossae*, ed. Wayne Meeks and Fred O. Francis, pp. 163–95. Missoula, Montana: Scholars Press, 1975.

'The Background of Embateuein (Col 2:18) in Legal Papyri and Oracle Inscriptions'. In *Conflict at Colossae*, ed. Wayne Meeks and Fred O. Francis, pp. 197–207. Missoula, Montana: Scholars Press, 1975.

Funk, Robert W. 'The Watershed of American Biblical Tradition: The Chicago School, First Phase 1892–1920'. JBL 95, 1976: 4–22.

Furnish, V. P. *Theology and Ethics in Paul.* Nashville and New York: Abingdon Press, 1968.

Gager, John G. *Kingdom and Community.* Englewood Cliffs, New Jersey: Prentice Hall, Inc., 1975.

'Shall We Marry Our Enemies: Sociology and the New Testament'. Int. 36,3, July 1982: 256–65.

Gärtner, B. *The Temple and the Community in Qumran and the New Testament.* Cambridge University Press, 1965.

Geertz, Clifford. 'Ethos, World View, and the Analysis of Sacred Symbols'. *Antioch Review* 17, 1957; 421–37.

'Religion as a Cultural System'. In *Anthropological Approaches to the Study of Religion*, Association of Social Anthropologists Monographs 3, ed. Michael Banton, pp. 1–46. London: Tavistock, 1966 [= *Anthropological Approaches*].

George, Augustin. 'L'Œuvre de Luc: Actes et Évangile'. In *Le ministère et les ministères selon le Nouveau Testament*, pp. 207–40. Paris: Éditions du Seuil, 1974.

Gill, Robin. *Theology and Social Structure.* London and Oxford: Mowbrays, 1977.

Gnilka, Joachin. *Der Philemonbrief.* Freiburg: Herder, 1982.

Goodspeed, E. J. *The Meaning of Ephesians.* Chicago: Chicago University Press, 1933.

Greeven, Heinrich. 'Propheten, Lehrer, Vorsteher bei Paulus'. ZNW 44, 1952–3: 1–43 (reprint in Kertelge, 1977).

Guthrie, Donald. 'The Development of the Idea of Canonical Pseudepigraphy in New Testament Criticism'. In *The Authorship and Integrity of the New Testament*, SPCK Theological Collections 4, pp. 14–39. London: SPCK, 1965.

'Epistolary Pseudepigraphy'. In *New Testament Introduction*, pp. 671–3. London: The Tyndale Press, 1970 (3rd rev. ed; 1st ed. 3 vols., 1961–5).

Hainz, J. *Ekklesia: Strukturen paulinischer Gemeinde-Theologie und Gemeinde-Ordnung*. Regensburg: F. Pustet, 1972 [= *Ekklesia*].

Hands, A. R. *Charities and Social Aid in Greece and Rome*. London: Thames and Hudson, 1968.

Hanson, A. T. *Studies in the Pastoral Epistles*. London: SPCK, 1968.

The Pastoral Epistles. London: Marshall, Morgan & Scott Publ. Ltd., 1982.

Harrington, D. J. 'E. Käsemann on the Church in the New Testament'. *Heythrop Journal* 12, 1971: 246–57.

'The Early Catholic Writings of the New Testament: The Church Adjusting to World-History'. In *The Word in the World* ed. Richard J. Clifford S. J. and George MacRae S. J., pp. 97–113. Cambridge, Massachusetts: Weston College Press, 1973.

'Sociological Concepts and the Early Church: A Decade of Research'. TS 41, 1980: 181–90.

Harrison, P. N. *The Problem of the Pastoral Epistles*. London: Oxford University Press, 1921.

Harvey, A. E. 'Elders'. JTS 25, 1974: 318–32.

Hengel, Martin. *Property and Riches in the Early Church*. Philadelphia: Fortress Press, 1974.

Hennecke, E. *New Testament Apocrypha*. Vol. 2. London: SCM Press Ltd., 1974 (Ger. ed. 1964).

Higgins, A. J. B. *The Lord's Supper in the New Testament*. London: SCM Press Ltd., 1952.

Hock, Ronald F. *The Social Context of Paul's Ministry: Tentmaking and Apostleship*. Philadelphia: Fortress Press, 1980.

Holmberg, Bengt. *Paul and Power: The Structure of Authority in the Primitive Church as Reflected in the Pauline Epistles*. Philadelphia: Fortress Press, 1980 (1st ed. 1978).

'Sociological versus Theological Analysis of the Question concerning a Pauline Church Order'. In *Die Paulinische Literatur und Theologie*, ed. Sigfred Pedersen, pp. 187–200. Göttingen: Vandenhoeck & Ruprecht, 1980.

Hooker, Morna D. 'Were There False Teachers in Colossae?'. In *Christ and Spirit in the New Testament: Studies in Honour of C. F. D. Moule*, ed. Barnabas Lindars and Stephen S. Smalley, pp. 316–29. Cambridge University Press, 1973 [= *Christ and Spirit*].

Jay, Eric. 'From Presbyter-Bishops to Bishops and Presbyters'. *The Second Century* 1, 1981: 125–62.

Judge, E. A. *The Social Pattern of Christian Groups in the First Century*. London: Tyndale, 1960 [= *The Social Pattern*].

'The Social Identity of the First Christians: A Question of Method in Religious History'. *The Journal of Religious History* 11,2, 1980: 201–17.

Karris, R. J. 'The Background and Significance of the Polemic of the Pastoral Epistles.' JBL 92, 1973: 549–64.

Käsemann, Ernst. 'A Primitive Christian Baptismal Liturgy'. In ENTT, pp. 149–68. London: SCM Press Ltd., 1964.

'Das Formular einer neutestamentlichen Ordinationsparänese'. In

Exegetische Versuche und Besinnungen, pp.101–108. Göttingen: Vandenhoeck & Ruprecht, 1964.
'Is the Gospel Objective?'. In ENTT, pp.48–62. London: SCM Press Ltd., 1964.
'Ministry and Community in the New Testament'. In ENTT, pp.63–94. London: SCM Press Ltd., 1964.
'The Pauline Doctrine of the Lord's Supper'. In ENTT, pp.108–35. London: SCM Press Ltd., 1964.
'Ephesians and Acts'. In *Studies in Luke–Acts*, ed. L.E. Keck and J.L. Martin, pp.288–97. London: SPCK, 1968.
Jesus Means Freedom. London: SCM Press Ltd., 1969.
'New Testament Questions of Today'. In NTQT, pp.1–22. London: SCM Press Ltd., 1969.
'Paul and Early Catholicism'. In NTQT, pp.236–51. London: SCM Press Ltd., 1969.
Perspectives on Paul. London: SCM Press Ltd., 1971 (Ger. ed. 1969).
Keck, L.E. 'On the Ethos of Early Christians'. JAAR 42, 1974: 435–52.
Kelly, J.N.D. *A Commentary on the Pastoral Epistles*. New York: Harper, 1963.
Kertelge, Karl. *Gemeinde und Amt im Neuen Testament*. München: Kosel, 1972 [= *Gemeinde und Amt*]
(ed.). *Das kirchliche Amt im Neuen Testament*. Darmstadt: Wissenschaftliche Buchgesellschaft, 1977.
Kirby, J.C. *Ephesians: Baptism and Pentecost*. London: SPCK, 1968.
Klaiber, Walter. *Rechtfertigung und Gemeinde: Eine Untersuchung zum paulinischen Kirchenverständnis*. Göttingen: Vandenhoeck & Ruprecht, 1982.
Klauck, H.J. 'Neue Literatur zur urchristlichen Hausgemeinde'. *Biblische Zeitschrift* 26, 1982: 288–94.
Knox, John. *Philemon among the Letters of Paul*. Chicago: The University of Chicago Press, 1935.
Koester, H. *Introduction to the New Testament*. 2 vols. Philadelphia: Fortress Press, 1982 (Ger. ed. 1980) [= *Introduction*].
Kraeling, Carl H. *The Synagogue. The Excavations at Dura-Europos: Final Reports*. Vol.8, part 1. New Haven and London: Yale University Press, 1967.
The Christian Building. The Excavations at Dura-Europos: Final Reports. Vol.8, part 2. New Haven and London: Yale University Press, 1967.
Kümmel, W.G. *Introduction to the New Testament*. London: SCM Press Ltd., 1975 (Ger. ed. 1973).
Légasse, Simon. 'L'Évangile selon Matthieu'. In *Le ministère et les ministères selon le Nouveau Testament*, pp.182–206. Paris: Éditions du Seuil, 1974.
Lietzmann, Hans. *Mass and the Lord's Supper: A Study in the History of Liturgy*. Leiden: E.J. Brill, 1979.
Lindemann, Andreas. *Die Aufhebung der Zeit*. Gütersloh: Gütersloher Verlagshaus, Gerd Mohn, 1975.
Paulus im ältesten Christentum. Tübingen: J.C.B. Mohr (Paul Siebeck), 1979.

Linton, Olof. *Das Problem der Urkirche in der neueren Forschung*. Uppsala Universitets Årsskrift. Uppsala: 1932 [= *Das Problem der Urkirche*].

Lips, H. von. *Glaube – Gemeinde – Amt: Zum Verständnis der Ordination in den Pastoralbriefen*. Göttingen: Vandenhoeck & Ruprecht, 1979 [= *Glaube – Gemeinde – Amt*].

Lock, W. *A Critical and Exegetical Commentary on the Pastoral Epistles*, New York: Scribner, 1924.

Lohse, E. *Colossians and Philemon*. Philadelphia: Fortress Press, 1971 (Ger. ed. 1968).

Lührmann, Dieter. 'Neutestamentliche Haustafeln und antike Ökonomie'. NTS 27, 1980–1: 83–97.

Luz, U. 'Erwägungen zur Entstehung des "Frühkatholizismus"'. Eine Skizze'. ZNW 65, 1974: 88–111.

MacDonald, Dennis Ronald. 'Virgins, Widows, and Paul in Second-Century Asia Minor'. In *Society of Biblical Liturature 1979 Seminar Papers*, ed. Paul J. Achtemeier, pp. 169–84. Missoula, Montana: Scholars Press, 1979.

   The Legend and the Apostle: The Battle for Paul in Story and Canon. Philadelphia: The Westminster Press, 1983.

MacMullen, Ramsay. 'Women in Public in the Roman Empire'. *Historia* (Baden-Baden) 29, 1980: 208–18.

   Christianizing the Roman Empire (A.D. 100–400). New Haven and London: Yale University Press, 1984.

Maddox, R. *The Purpose of Luke-Acts*. Studies in the New Testament and its World, ed. J. Riches. Edinburgh: T & T Clark Ltd., 1982.

Malherbe, Abraham J. *Social Aspects of Early Christianity*. Philadelphia: Fortress Press, 1983 (1st ed. 1977) [= *Social Aspects*].

   'Hospitality and Inhospitality in the Church'. In *Social Aspects*, pp. 92–112. Philadelphia: Fortress Press, 1983.

   'House Churches and their Problems'. In *Social Aspects*, pp. 60–91. Philadelphia: Fortress Press, 1983.

   'Social Level and Literary Culture'. In *Social Aspects*, pp. 29–59. Philadelphia: Fortress Press, 1983.

   'In Season and Out of Season: 2 Tim 4:2'. JBL 103,2, 1984: 235–43.

Malina, Bruce J. 'The Social Sciences and Biblical Interpretation'. Int. 36,3, July 1982: 229–42.

   The New Testament World: Insights From Cultural Anthropology. London: SCM Press Ltd., 1983 (1st ed. 1981).

   'Normative Dissonance and Christian Origins'. *Semeia* 35, 1986: 35–55.

   'The Reviewed View and What it Cannot Do: III John and Hospitality'. *Semeia* 35, 1986: 171–89.

Marris, Peter. *Loss and Change*. London: Routledge and Kegan Paul, 1974.

Markus, R. 'The Problem of Self-Definition: From Sect to Church'. In *Jewish and Christian Self-Definition*, vol. 1, ed. E. P. Sanders, pp. 1–15. London: SCM Press Ltd., 1980.

Martin, Ralph. *Colossians and Philemon*. London: Oliphant, 1974.

Meeks, Wayne and Francis, Fred. O. (ed.) *Conflict at Colossae: A Problem in the Interpretation of Early Christianity*. Sources for Biblical Study 4. Missoula, Montana: Scholars Press, 1975.

Meeks, Wayne. 'The Man from Heaven in Johannine Sectarianism'. JBL 91, 1972: 44–72.

'The Image of Androgyne: Some Uses of a Symbol in Earliest Christianity'. HR 13, 1974: 165–208 [= 'The Image of Androgyne ...'].

'In One Body: The Unity of Humankind in Colossians and Ephesians'. In *God's Christ and His People: Studies in Honour of Nils Alstrup Dahl*, ed. Wayne Meeks and Jacob Jervell, pp. 209–21. Oslo, Bergen and Tromsö: Universitetsforlaget, 1977 [= 'In One Body ...'].

'Social Functions of Apocalyptic Language in Pauline Christianity'. In *Apocalypticism in the Mediterranean World and the Near East: Proceedings of the International Colloquium on Apocalypticism, Uppsala, August 12–17, 1979*, ed. David Hellholm. Tübingen: Mohr (Siebeck), 1982.

'The Social Context of Pauline Theology'. Int. 36,3, July 1982: 266–77.

The First Urban Christians. New Haven and London: Yale University Press, 1983 [= *Urban Christians*].

Michel, Otto. 'The Conclusion of Matthew's Gospel'. In *The Interpretation of Matthew*, Issues In Religion and Theology 3, ed. Graham Stanton, pp. 30–41. London: SPCK, 1983.

Mills, C. Wright. *The Sociological Imagination*. New York: Oxford University Press, 1959.

Mitton, C. L. *The Epistle to the Ephesians: Its Authorship, Origin and Purpose*. Oxford, Clarendon Press, 1951.

Ephesians. London: Marshall, Morgan and Scott, 1973.

Morgan, Robert. 'La communion des églises dans le Nouveau Testament'. *Concilium* 164, 1981: 47–57.

Moule, C. F. D. *The Origin of Christology*. Cambridge University Press, 1977.

Mussner, Franz. *Christus, das All und die Kirche*. Trier: Paulinus, 1968.

Murphy-O'Connor, J. 'The Non-Pauline Character of 1 Corinthians 11:2–16?'. JBL 95,4, 1976: 615–21.

Newton, Michael. *The Concept of Purity at Qumran and in the Letters of Paul*. Society for New Testament Studies Monograph Series 53. Cambridge University Press, 1985 [= *The Concept of Purity*].

Neyrey, Jerome H. 'Body Language in 1 Corinthians: The Use of Anthropological Models for Understanding Paul and his Opponents'. *Semeia* 35, 1986: 129–64.

O'Neill, J. C. *The Theology of Acts in its Historical Setting*. London: SPCK, 1961.

Ollrog, Wolf-Henning. *Paulus und seine Mitarbeiter: Untersuchungen zu Theorie und Praxis der paulinischen Mission*. Neukirchen: Erziehungsverein, 1979.

Osiek, Carolyn, *The Rich and Poor in the Shepherd of Hermas: An Exegetical-Social Investigation*. The Catholic Biblical Quarterly Monograph Series 15. Washington, D.C.: The Catholic Biblical Association of America, 1983 [= *The Rich and Poor*].

Pagels, Elaine H. *The Gnostic Gospels*. London: Weidenfeld and Nicholson, 1979.

Pagels, Elaine H. 'Adam, Eve, Christ and the Church'. In *The New*

Testament and Gnosis, ed. A. H. B. Logan and A. J. M. Wedderburn, pp. 146–75. Edinburgh: T & T Clark Ltd., 1983.

Petersen, Norman. *Rediscovering Paul: Philemon and the Sociology of Paul's Narrative World*. Philadelphia: Fortress Press, 1985.

Pomeroy, Sarah B. *Goddesses, Whores, Wives, and Slaves: Women in Classical Antiquity*. New York: Schocken, 1975 [= *Goddesses*].

Riddle, Donald W. 'Environment as a Factor in the Achievement of Self-Consciousness in Early Christianity.' JR 7, 1927: 146–63.

'The Message of the Shepherd of Hermas: A Study in Social Control'. JR 7, 1927: 561–77.

Robinson, J. A. T. *The Body: A Study in Pauline Theology*. London: SCM Press Ltd., 1952.

Rodd, C. S. 'On Applying a Sociological Theory to Biblical Studies'. JSOT 19, 1981: 95–106.

Rowland, Christopher. *Christian Origins: An Account of the Setting and Character of the most Important Messianic Sect of Judaism*. London: SPCK, 1985.

Rudolph, Kurt. *Gnosis*. Edinburgh: T & T Clark Ltd., 1983.

Sampley, J. P. *And the Two Shall Become One Flesh*. Cambridge University Press, 1971.

Sanders, E. P. 'Literary Dependence in Colossians.' JBL 85, 1966: 28–45.

Paul and Palestinian Judaism: A Comparison of Patterns of Religion. London: SCM Press Ltd., 1977.

Paul, the Law, and the Jewish People. Philadelphia: Fortress Press, 1983 [= *Paul, the Law*].

Sanders, J. T. *The New Testament Christological Hymns: Their Historical Religious Background*. Cambridge University Press, 1971.

Schlier, Heinrich. *Der Brief an die Epheser*. Dusseldorf: Patmos, 1957.

Schenke, H. M. 'Das Weiterwirken des Paulus und die Pflege seines Erbes durch die Paulus-Schule'. NTS 21, 1974–5: 505–18.

Schoedel, William R. *Ignatius of Antioch*. Philadelphia: Fortress Press, 1985.

Schürer, Emil. *The History of the Jewish People in the Age of Jesus Christ (175 B.C.–A.D. 135)*. 3 vols., rev. and ed. Geza Vermes, Fergus Miller, Matthew Black and Martin Goodman. Edinburgh: T & T Clark Ltd., 1973f.

Schütz, J. H. *Paul and the Anatomy of Apostolic Authority*. Cambridge University Press, 1975.

Schwartz, Roland. *Bürgerliches Christentum im Neuen Testament: Eine Studie zu Ethic, Amt und Recht in den Pastoralbriefen*. Österreichische Biblische Studien 4. Klosterneuburg: Österreichisches Katholisches Bibelwerk, 1983.

Schweizer, E. *Church Order in the New Testament*. London: SCM Press Ltd., 1961 (Ger. ed. 1959) [= *Church Order*].

The Letter to the Colossians. London: SPCK, 1982 (Ger. ed. 1976).

'Matthew's Church'. In *The Interpretation of Matthew*, Issues in Religion and Theology 3, ed. Graham Stanton, pp. 129–55. London: SPCK, 1983.

Scott, E. F. *The Pastoral Epistles*. London: Hodder and Stoughton, 1936.

Scroggs, Robin. 'The Earliest Christian Communities as a Sectarian movement.' In *Christianity, Judaism and Other Greco-Roman Cults*, part 2, ed. J. Neusner, pp. 1–23. Leiden: E. J. Brill, 1975.

'The Sociological Interpretation of the New Testament: The Present State of Research.' NTS 26, 1979–80: 164–79.

Shils, E. 'The Concept and Function of Ideology.' In IESS, vol. 7, 1968: 68–75.

Simmel, George. *Conflict*. New York: Free Press, 1955.

Smith, Jonathan Z. 'The Social Description of Early Christianity'. *Religious Studies Review* 1, 1975: 19–25.

Smith, Morton. 'Pauline Worship as Seen by Pagans'. HTR 73, 1980: 241–49.

'Perils of the Paulines'. In *The Washington Post Book World*, XIII, 10 April 1983: 15.

Spicq, P. C. *Les Épîtres Pastorales*. Paris: Librairie Lecoffre, 1947.

Stanton, Graham (ed.). *The Interpretation of Matthew*. Issues in Religion and Theology 3. London: SPCK, 1983.

Stendahl, Krister. *Paul Among Jews and Gentiles and Other Essays*. Philadelphia: Fortress Press, 1976.

Strecker, Georg. 'The Concept of History in Matthew'. In *The Interpretation of Matthew*, Issues in Religion and Theology 3, ed. Graham Stanton, pp. 67–84. London: SPCK, 1983.

Streeter, B. H. *The Primitive Church*. London: MacMillan and Co. Ltd., 1929.

Stuhlmacher, Peter. *Der Brief an Philemon*. Zurich: Einsiedeln; Cologne: Benziger; Neukirchen: Erziehungsverein, 1975.

Tannehill, Robert C. *Dying and Rising with Christ: A Study in Pauline Theology*. Beihefte zur ZNW 32. Berlin: Alfred Töpelmann, 1967.

Theissen, Gerd. *The First Followers of Jesus*. London: SCM Press Ltd., 1978 (Ger. ed. 1977).

The Social Setting of Pauline Christianity: Essays on Corinth. Philadelphia: Fortress Press, 1982 (trans. and ed. John H. Schütz) [= *The Social Setting*].

'Social Integration and Sacramental Activity: An Analysis of 1 Cor 11:17–34'. (Trans. from Ger. art. NovT 16, 1974: 179–206.) In *The Social Setting*, pp. 145–74. Philadelphia: Fortress Press, 1982.

'Social Stratification in the Corinthian Community: A Contribution to the Sociology of Early Hellenistic Christianity'. (Trans. from Ger. art. ZNW 65, 1974: 232–72.) In *The Social Setting*, pp. 69–119. Philadelphia: Fortress Press, 1982.

'Legitimation and Subsistence: An Essay On the Sociology of Early Christian Missionaries'. (Trans. from Ger. art. NTS 21, 1975: 192–221.) In *The Social Setting*, pp. 27–67. Philadelphia: Fortress Press, 1982.

'The Sociological Interpretation of Religious Traditions: Its Methodological Problems as Exemplified in Early Christianity'. (Trans. from Ger. art. *Kairos* 17, 1975, pp. 74–99.) In *The Social Setting*, pp. 175–200. Philadelphia: Fortress Press, 1982.

'The Strong and the Weak in Corinth: A Sociological Analysis of a Theological Quarrel'. (Trans. from Ger. art. EvT 35, 1975, pp. 155–72.)

In *The Social Setting*, pp. 121–43. Philadelphia: Fortress Press, 1982.

Tiede, David L. *Prophecy and History in Luke-Acts*. Philadelphia: Fortress Press, 1980.

Troeltsch, E. *The Social Teaching of the Christian Churches*. 2 vols. New York: The MacMillan Company, 1931 (Ger. ed. 1911).

Verner, David C. *The Household of God*. Chico, California: Scholars Press, 1983.

Vielhauer, Philipp. 'On the "Paulinism" of Acts.' In *Studies in Luke-Acts*, ed. L. E. Keck and J. L. Martin, pp. 33–49. Philadelphia: Fortress Press, 1980.

Wainright, G. *Eucharist and Eschatology*. London: Epworth Press, 1971.

Walker, William O., Jr. '1 Corinthians and Paul's Views Regarding Women'. JBL 94, 1975: 94–110.

Weber, Max. *Economy and Society*. 3 vols., ed. Guenther Roth and Claus Wittich. New York: Bedminster Press, 1968.

Wilson, Bryan. *Sects and Society*. London: William Heinemann Ltd., 1961.

(ed.). *Patterns of Sectarianism*. London: Morrison and Gibb Ltd., 1967 [= *Patterns*].

Religious Sects. London: Weidenfield and Nicholson, 1970.

Magic and the Millenium. London: Morrison and Gibb Ltd., 1973.

Religion in a Sociological Perspective. Oxford: At the University Press, 1982 [= *Religion*].

Zeilinger, Franz. *Der Erstgeborene der Schöpfung: Untersuchungen zur Formalstruktur und Theologie des Kolosserbriefes*. Wien: Herder & Co., 1974 [= *Der Erstgeborene der Schöpfung*].

INDEX OF BIBLICAL PASSAGES DISCUSSED

SUBJECT INDEX